Location, location, ~~location~~ *currency*

Fluctuating exchange rates could put your dream property out of reach.

To minimise the risk of paying more when buying abroad,
call us now and speak to one of our expert advisors, or visit our website.

"For efficiency and delivery, HIFX are one of the most impressive companies I have ever encountered"
Susan Reader, private client buying property in Spain.

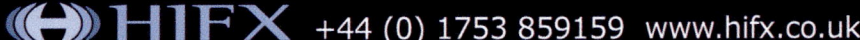 HIFX +44 (0) 1753 859159 www.hifx.co.uk

Portuguese Property

buying guide 2004

guide

Independent Legal Advice

"The **ONLY** firm of Lawyers that does **NOTHING BUT** work in France, Spain, Portugal & Italy."
Send for our **FREE** information pack

John Howell & Co

Solicitors & International Lawyers

The Old Glass Works, 22 Endell Street,
Covent Garden, London, WC2H 9AD

Tel: 020 7420 0400   Fax: 020 7836 3626
Email: info@europelaw.com
Internet: **www.europelaw.com**
Regulated by the Law Society of England and Wales

We run a series of seminars throughout the country, please call for details.

TYPICAL PROGRAMME

10.30	Buying a home in France
11.30	Tax & financial issues when buying or retiring abroad
12.30	How to make money out of property abroad
13.30	Tax & financial issues when buying or retiring abroad
14.30	Buying a home in Spain, Portugal or Italy
15.30	Buying a home in the USA & "emerging markets"
16.30 - 17.00	Question & Answer Session

Please phone for confirmation of dates and times

These seminars are presented as a part of the Homes Overseas property shows.
There is normally an admission charge to the show.

The ultimate guide to buying a Portuguese property

Portuguese Property

buying guide 2004

EDITOR
JUSTIN POSTLETHWAITE

Portuguese Property buying guide 2004

Compiled, edited and designed by
Merricks Media Ltd
Charlotte House
12 Charlotte Street
Bath BA1 2NE
Tel: 01225 786800
m.guides@merricksmedia.co.uk

Managing Director **Lisa Doerr**
Editor **Justin Postlethwaite**
Production Editors **Emma Gypps, Leaonne Hall**
Art Director **Jon Billington**
Art Editor **David Eachus**
Advertisement Design **Maya Crowe, Becky Hamblin, Steve Mallinson**
Sales Director **Keith Burnell**
Sales Executive **Greg Martin**

All rights reserved. No part of this work may be reproduced or used in any form or by any means, electronic or mechanical, including photocopying, recording or any information storage and retrieval system, without the prior written permission of the publishers.

While every care has been exercised in the compilation of this guide, neither the authors, editors nor publishers accept any liability for any factual inaccuracies or for any financial or other loss incurred by reliance placed on the information contained in *Portuguese Property Buying Guide 2004*.

The exchange rate used when the sterling price equivalent was calculated was 1.5 euros to the pound, and has been rounded to the nearest five pounds.

m guide is a trademark of Merricks Media Ltd

Cover image © Simply Travel
Many thanks to the following who have provided the majority of the images for this guide, as well as the various individuals who have been credited throughout where applicable:
Simply Travel, David Headland Associates, www.strawberryworld.com, The Portuguese Tourist Board, www.leitmotif.com and World Pictures
Map of Portugal © Michelin Tyre PLC 2003
Reproduced by permission of Michelin Travel Publications
Map of the regions © Merricks Media Ltd

Printed and bound in Croatia by Zrinski d.d
First published in the United Kingdom in 2003 by Merricks Media Ltd

Copyright © 2003 Merricks Media Ltd

ISBN 0-9543-5232-7
British Library Cataloguing in Publication Data
A catalogue record for this book is available from the British Library

THE ALGARVE

For the ultimate property in Portugal, you need the Ultimate Property Guide.

For the Algarve's ULTIMATE property guide call 01933 353333
www.headlands.co.uk

If you're seriously considering buying a property in Portugal, you simply must request your copy of the Ultimate Property Guide from David Headland Associates.

It has over 100 pages of glorious new and resale properties in all areas of the Algarve. Luxury apartments and houses on some of the finest developments, elegant quintas and country villas both on the coast and set in wonderful countryside.

With over 30 years' experience, we're now one of the UK's longest established overseas property companies. We have more knowledge of Portugal and its property market, and the experience to make your purchase go as smoothly as possible.

Having been voted the **'Best Portuguese Estate Agent'** for the third year running, you're assured of the highest standard of service and personal attention at all times. We also have our own fully staffed office and display centre in the Algarve, where our multi-lingual property experts can help you find the perfect property for you.

So for more information and to see a selection of Portuguese properties, please call us on **01933 353333** or visit our website at **www.headlands.co.uk**.

Portugal

01933 353333
www.headlands.co.uk

david headland associates
international property consultants

EDITOR'S ACKNOWLEDGEMENTS

ALL PICTURES: DAVID HEADLAND ASSOCIATES

This first edition of **Portuguese Property Buying Guide** owes a great deal to the dedication and hard work of Emma Gypps and Leaonne Hall. Thanks also to David Eachus for his design work, to Lisa McGee for her subbing and writing skills, and to Lola Dali-Kemmery for her invaluable research.

Many thanks, too, to the experts who gave their time and knowledge to ensure that the finer points of Portuguese property, law and finance detailed in the book are thorough, accurate and current. Particular mention must go to:

Manuel Caldeira of **Caldeira Stevenson**
Dr Josué Coelho of **Advogados International Law Office**
Simon Conn of **Conti Financial Services**
Lita Gale of **Lita Gale Solicitors**
Chris Gilby of **Prime Properties**
Chris Johnstone-Smith of **David Headland Associates**
Tim Lewer of **Finespo**
Sue Mackenzie of **Mackenzie Estate Agents**
Adrian Medd and Mark Rosser of **European Villa Solutions**
Ricardo Silva of **John Howell & Co Solicitors**
Dennis Swing-Greene of **FINESCO Financial International**
Simon Thorne of **Premier Properties**
Central Portugal Property Finders
Quinta Properties
SONI & Co Notaries
Sotheby's International
The Property Search
Villa Solutions

Thanks also to officials from the following authorities, who were extremely kind and helpful in providing information on living and working in Portugal:
British Embassy, Lisbon (Consular Section)
Portuguese Chamber of Commerce
Portuguese Embassy, London
The Department for Work and Pensions
Lennie Mortlock of Private Health Associates

Buying Guide

Contents

CONTENTS

Introduction	15
Buying Guide	42
Living/Working	58
The Regions	82
Price Guide	192
Directory	300

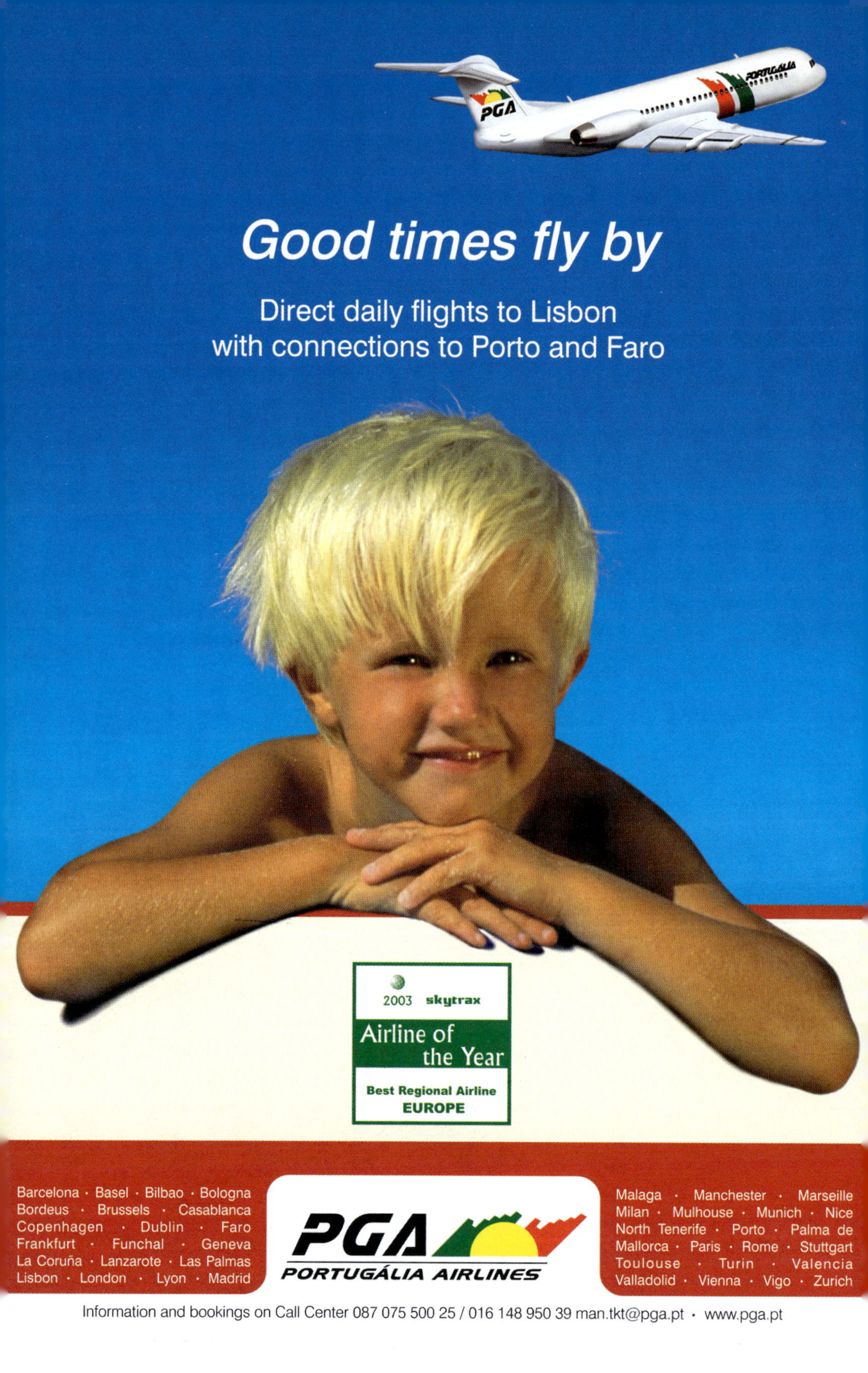

Good times fly by

Direct daily flights to Lisbon
with connections to Porto and Faro

2003 skytrax
Airline of the Year
Best Regional Airline
EUROPE

Barcelona · Basel · Bilbao · Bologna
Bordeus · Brussels · Casablanca
Copenhagen · Dublin · Faro
Frankfurt · Funchal · Geneva
La Coruña · Lanzarote · Las Palmas
Lisbon · London · Lyon · Madrid
Malaga · Manchester · Marseille
Milan · Mulhouse · Munich · Nice
North Tenerife · Porto · Palma de Mallorca · Paris · Rome · Stuttgart
Toulouse · Turin · Valencia
Valladolid · Vienna · Vigo · Zurich

Information and bookings on Call Center 087 075 500 25 / 016 148 950 39 man.tkt@pga.pt · www.pga.pt

EDITOR'S INTRODUCTION

'With its fabulously warm and sunny climate, gorgeous white sandy beaches and a sleepy ambience reminiscent of a different era, this idyll tops many people's wish-list when it comes to such a life-changing property purchase'

Buying a property abroad, either as a holiday home, a permanent family base or simply as a buy-to-let investment, has never been so appealing to British buyers. Fed up with vastly inflated UK house prices, fearful of the future value of pensions and tired of battling against frenetic daily routines, freezing, wet winters and unpredictable summers, more and more of us, it seems, are heading for foreign shores in search of better value for money and a more relaxed lifestyle.

Step forward Portugal, a country on Europe's western flank that offers a perfect blend of modernism and tradition. With its fabulously warm and sunny climate, gorgeous white sandy beaches and a sleepy ambience reminiscent of a different era, this idyll tops many people's wish-list when it comes to such a life-changing property purchase. Add to the mix its rich cultural and architectural history, fine food and wine, and improved access (thanks to budget airlines and EU-financed road networks), and you have a multi-faceted country that is quicker, easier and, crucially, much cheaper to get to than ever before.

The great thing about looking to buy in Portugal is the huge choice of affordable homes available. There is something to suit all tastes and budgets in every part of the country: sun worshippers and golfers will prefer the Algarve, while those in search of rustic peace and a slow pace of life can look for a country home further north. Vibrant city living in either Lisbon, the capital, or Porto, the historic second city, is another option for those seeking lively night-life and refined culture. Whichever area you choose, though, one thing is guaranteed: a great new lifestyle under the sun in one of Europe's most pleasant and friendly countries.

In spite of the apparent complexity of the Portuguese legal system, snapping up a dream villa or stylish apartment in Portugal is today a more transparent process than ever. And because many thousands have already taken the plunge and bought a home there, the infrastructure of lawyers and estate agents (many of whom work in English) to help guide British buyers through the purchase is both extensive and well regulated. Although such a life-changing procedure requires plenty of forethought and planning, expert advice is always at hand. Anyone keen to start up or take on a business in Portugal will also find that much bureaucratic red tape has been cut since Portugal became a member of the European Union.

In short, Portugal is a country with something for everyone, no matter what their financial constraints or reasons for buying. Great value, fabulous weather and a relaxed lifestyle…what are you waiting for?

Justin Postlethwaite

Justin Postlethwaite
m guides Editor

How to Use the Guide

USING THE PORTUGUESE PROPERTY BUYING GUIDE

For the convenience of the reader, *The Portuguese Property Buying Guide 2004* has been split into four easily distinguished sections: Introduction, Buying Guide, Region Guides and Price Guides.

The first of these begins with an overview of the economic, historical and social factors that make Portugal the country it is today. There is a look at the current property scene, with expert analysis from agents on each of the regions. For a personal perspective on living the dream, our three Case Studies are indispensable, while a handy glossary of key business and legal terms lends some factual back-up.

Next follows a detailed guide to the buying process itself, including tips on how to avoid legal and financial pitfalls associated with purchasing a property in Portugal. This section also provides extensive information on living and working there, with advice on everything from starting a business to getting electricity supplied.

The third section provides in-depth profiles of the diverse Portuguese regions, to help the potential buyer decide which part of Portugal best suits their needs. Bearing in mind important historical and geographical factors, we have divided the country

How to Use the Guide

into six regions: Algarve; Alentejo; Lisbon & Estremadura; Coimbra & the Beiras; Costa Verde & the North; and Madeira. We have omitted the Azores, due to their distance from mainland Europe. Each of the Region sections is colour-coded with a small square at the top of the page, and this can be used to cross-reference sample properties from the same region in the Price Guide section later in the book. As well as maps, information on climate, travel, local festivals and traditions, not forgetting food and drink specialities, these region guides contain handy contacts for finding work, plus information on typical local property styles and 'for sale' prices.

When you have read about a certain region and you want to find out what properties are available there, simply flip to the fourth section of the book – the Price Guides – and look for the relevant colour code. The regions are laid out in the same order as in the Regions section, with each of them containing a cross-section of homes to suit all tastes and budgets.

Finally, towards the end of the book, you will find details of estate agents, employers and service providers – from tradesmen to travel operators – that are on hand in both the UK and Portugal to make your move and new life as smooth as possible.

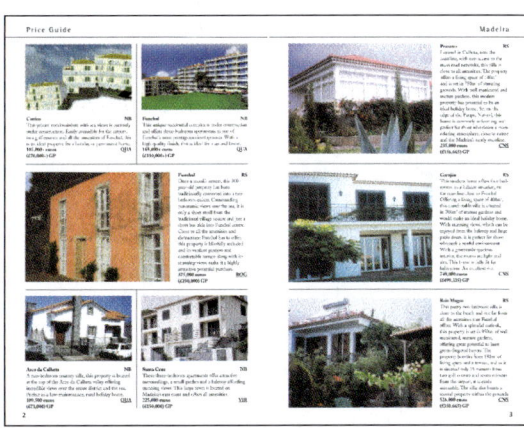

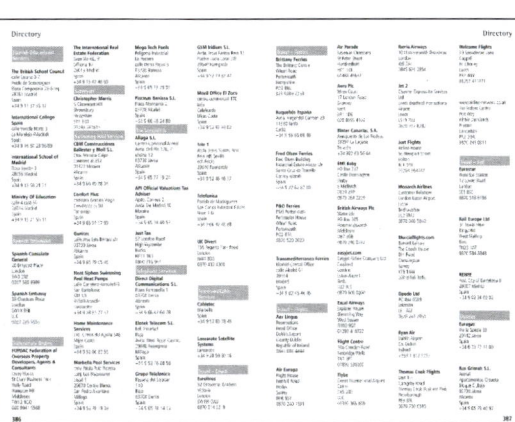

Why buy in Portugal?

WHY BUY IN PORTUGAL?

The British appetite for owning a place in a country like Portugal has been steadily growing for decades, with the desire to move abroad reaching fever pitch in the last few years. Television programmes about relocating have stirred up massive interest in life-changing house moves. Yet while many people know they want to buy abroad, many are unable to pinpoint their reasons. Here are just a few of the reasons why Portugal could be the perfect place for you…

■ A LIFESTYLE CHANGE
The most obvious benefit of such a change of location is an improved lifestyle, something that comes from a sunnier climate, a slower, more peaceful way of life, traditional values, good food and wine, and pleasant surroundings (beaches, mountains and golf courses). Although some parts of Portugal are modernising more quickly than others, buyers will always find a pace of life to suit them, often just a budget flight and short drive away. The presence of an extensive expat community also offers security to some prospective buyers, especially in the Algarve and Lisbon areas.

■ A LONG-TERM INVESTMENT FOR THE FUTURE
In an era when stock market volatility can wipe out a share portfolio in a single day, and when government pension forecasts are bleak to say the least, for many younger or middle-aged buyers, a property abroad can serve as the ultimate guaranteed income provider for the future. For those thinking about retirement, Portugal offers a great deal of stability. Prices in the Algarve, for example, are solid, and have not slipped in over a decade, making it the ideal place to invest in a haven for the autumn years of one's life.

■ BUYING TO LET
Buying to let is another popular option, with many choosing to spend just a few summer months in their new home, leaving it available for the often lucrative rental market for the rest of the year. In this case, year-round good weather will ensure year-round rentals, although thought must be given to management of the property in your absence.

■ A SHORT-TERM INVESTMENT
In recent years, previously under-developed investment markets, such as Alentejo and Madeira, have begun opening up to foreign buyers, as the Algarve gets saturated with investors. As such, short-term financial gain can be had from investments made now with the quick-fix concept of buying a property, investing in and renovating it, then selling it on – offering a rapid return on your outlay.

■ BUSINESS
Portugal's blossoming tourism and property selling industries are sure to provide more and more business opportunities as the years go on. And with legal and financial advice available in abundance to British buyers, there is no need to feel overawed by bureaucracy.

Whatever your reasons for buying in Portugal, *Portuguese Property Buying Guide 2004* provides all the information you need to make an informed decision about how, where and when to make the move.

Above: Some of the people who have chosen to live or work in Portugal. Read their stories in our Case Studies, starting on page 72

When you need global health insurance, get in touch with a specialist.

Morgan Price International Healthcare does one thing – it provides global healthcare plans for expatriates worldwide. And we believe we do it better than anyone else.

Whether it's medical, life, travel, accident or a tailor-made policy, we can give you a truly personal service.

For £2.50 per day* we can cover your GP and specialist costs, hospital treatment, routine maternity and even dental treatment costs. It's all in a day's work for us.

To find out more about us, or for a quotation, email **info@morgan-price.com**, ring **+44(0)1953 458042**, fax **+44(0)1953 458090** or visit our website.

www.morgan-price.com

MORGAN PRICE
International Healthcare

evel 3/Worldwide excl USA & Canada, 42 year old.

Introduction to Portugal

A LAND OF CONTRASTS

Portugal enjoys many splendid sandy beaches

With one foot rooted in ancient traditions, and the other striding headlong into a modern European Union of which it has been a member since 1986, Portugal is a country blessed with the most extraordinary geographical and climatic diversity and historical background.

CHILDREN OF THE REVOLUTION

Apart from periods of Spanish occupation in the late 15th and early 16th centuries, Portugal has been independent since early in the 12th century. It became a republic in 1910 after the monarchy was overthrown. The 20th century, however, witnessed radical changes in its political development. In 1974, a revolution, boosted by support from wealthy landowners in the south of the country, saw a 48-year dictatorship ended. Today, in spite of an initially unstable post-Revolution period, the country enjoys a parliamentary democracy, and is split into 18 regions and two autonomous island groups (Madeira and the Azores). For the purposes of tourism statistics, however, the country has been split into five larger areas.

THE NORTH-SOUTH DIVIDE

If you draw an imaginary line across Portugal's central heartland, what you get is a country split in

PORTUGAL AT A GLANCE

POPULATION
- Including Madeira and the Azores, Portugal has a total population of approximately 10,335,000.
- The population of mainland Portugal stands at 9,800,000.
- The population density of Portugal is 109 people per km².
- Boasting a very young population, 25 percent of Portugal's citizens are under the age of 15.
- The birth rate has fallen in recent years, and stands now at only one percent per annum.
- Portugal has a population growth rate of only 0.18 percent per annum.
- Portugal has an increasing number of foreign residents, due to investment and economic opportunities.
- The most densely populated areas of Portugal are the coastal regions.

Lisbon's population totals 2.1 million

- One-third of the population lives in rural areas, a large percentage compared to other western European countries.
- The capital of Portugal is Lisbon, with a population of 2.1 million

GEOGRAPHY
- Located in southwest Europe, bordered by the North Atlantic and western Spain, Portugal enjoys geographical diversity.
- Portugal has a total area of 92,391 km² (including Madeira and the Azores)
- Portugal boasts over 800km of coastline.
- The country is 560km long and 220km wide
- Portugal's geography varies from rugged mountains to olive groves and sandy beaches.

Portugal's coastline stretches over 800km

- The largest mountain range is the Serra da Estrela in the northeast, the highest peak of which is 1,993m above sea level.
- The main rivers are the Tagus, which divides the country from north to south, the Douro and the Minho.

ECONOMY
- Economically, Portugal still relies heavily upon agriculture, with three of the country's main natural resources being the sea, forests and arable land.
- Despite employing about one-fifth of the country's workforce, agriculture only accounts for a fraction of Portugal's overall wealth.

Facts and Figures

Agriculture employs a fifth of the workforce

- Portugal joined the EU in 1986, and is a fully fledged member of the European Monetary Union, with the euro being the country's standard currency.
- Up until 1990, Portugal was the fastest growing country in the EU, but subsequent years have seen a moderation in this expansion.
- Tourism is the country's largest industry, employing 66 percent of the workforce.
- Portugal also boasts the lowest unemployment rate in the EU, standing at only 6.7 percent.

CLIMATE
Due to Portugal's diverse topography, there is a huge variation in the weather. With a mild and sunny climate, the weather is kept temperate due to the movement of cool air off the Atlantic. Winters tend to be cooler and damp, with rainfall being at its heaviest in the North. Algarve winters are the driest and mildest.

	January	April	July	October
Lisbon	14°C	19°C	28°C	22°C
Faro	15°C	20°C	29°C	23°C
Porto	13°C	18°C	25°C	21°C

RAINFALL (mm)

	Jan	March	July	Nov
Lisbon	111	109	3	93
Faro	70	72	1	65
Porto	159	147	20	148

RELIGION
- Roman Catholicism is the dominant religion of Portugal, with 97 percent of the population practising Roman Catholics.
- Two percent of the population are Protestant, while one percent practices another religion.

The Portuguese are devoutly catholic

- Following the Church's disestablishment in 1911, it was re-established and recognised as a lawful body in 1940.

LANGUAGE
Portuguese is a Romance language combined with Arabic, and similar to Spanish except in pronunciation. Businesses and industries are increasingly speaking English, although it is recommended that basic Portuguese phrases are learnt prior to a stay in Portugal. In large cities and tourist areas, English is regularly spoken, although off the beaten track you may struggle.
- Portuguese is the fifth most widely-spoken language in the world, being the vernacular in Brazil, various African colonies, parts of India, China, Indonesia, Macau and Timor.
- A total of 200 million people speak Portuguese.
- French is the official second language of Portugal, but the younger generation are increasingly learning and using English.

CURRENCY
- Formerly the escudo. Portugal joined the Monetary Union in 1999 and now uses euros.
- One euro is worth 200.482 Portuguese escudos.
- Banknotes come in denominations of five, 10, 20, 50, 100, 200 and 500 euros.
- Coins come in denominations of one, two, five, 10, 20 or 50 cents, and there are 100 cents to one euro.

EDUCATION
- The Portuguese education system is notoriously poor, with just 25 percent of the population possessing a higher education qualification (compared to that of 82 percent in Germany).

From the age of 15, schooling is optional

- Education in Portugal is compulsory between the age of seven and 15, and is subsidised by the state.
- Once over the age of 15, secondary school becomes voluntary and fees are charged for attendance.
- Only 35 percent of 25 to 29 year olds have actually completed their secondary education.
- Portugal has 18 universities, but only 20 percent of students in Portugal go on to higher education.
- Portugal currently has 22 international primary and secondary schools.
- Most expatriate parents choose to send their children to international schools, which offer a curriculum identical to that of their mother country.
- If you choose to send your child to a Portuguese state school, permission must be obtained from the Ministry of Education:
Ministry of Education
Av. 5 de Outubro
107-13° Andar
1069-018 Lisbon
Tel: +351 217 950330
Fax: +351 217 933618

HEALTHCARE
It is strongly recommended that expatriates look into private medical care, as although there is a comprehensive state healthcare service, Portuguese hospitals are often overcrowded and standards are variable.
- No vaccinations are required to enter Portugal.
- As a member of the EU, you are entitled to free or reduced cost emergency medical treatment.
- Visitors with UK passports are generally allowed free healthcare.
- To reclaim any payment for healthcare costs, an E111 has to be filled in before you travel.
- Every sizable Portuguese town has its own *centro de saúde* (state-administered medical centre). Open 24 hours a day, it deals with minor injuries.

Introduction to Portugal

Portugal has an abundance of superb golf courses

two in more ways than one. North of the river Tagus, with the exception of the fertile Minho area, the land is mountainous and harsh, given to growing simple crops like corn and potatoes. In the south, though, fruit and olives flourish alongside fig and cork trees. Meadows and beautiful beaches are the norm here, compared to the north's ruggedness.

In terms of the population and customs, too, the north and south have broad differences. People from the north have northern European and Celtic origins, while in the south, the influence of Moorish and Roman ancestry can be seen in the darker-skinned locals. Many immigrants from Portugal's former colonies, such as Angola and Mozambique, arrived in the country in the 1970s and they have integrated well. Portugal is said to be one of the least racist countries in Europe.

A EUROPEAN PEOPLE

Portugal became a member of the EU in 1986, and enjoyed considerable growth as a result. Investment brought improved roads, communications and financial services. Alas overspending, particularly on an inefficient agriculture system (10 percent of the country's workforce here produces just four percent of its GDP) means the country is in a poor economic state. However, with tourism on the rise (it represents about 10 percent of the GDP), and the economy and facilities boosted by Lisbon's hosting Expo '98 and major cities hosting 2004's European Football Championships, Portugal is expecting growth in both its economic fortunes and its confidence.

HOSPITALS AND PHARMACIES

- For more serious injuries you should go to Accident and Emergency, *Serviços de Urgência*.
- For English-speaking doctors, go to the British Hospital in Lisbon (+351 213 955067).
- Pharmacies in Portugal (*farmácia*) can diagnose simple health problems and dispense a range of drugs that would be prescription-only in the U.K.
- Pharmacies are normally open from 9am to 1pm, and each displays a card showing the location of the all-night or late-closing pharmacies.
- **Ministry of Health** Direcçao-General da Saúde, avenida Dom Alfonso Henriques 45, 1049-005 Lisbon Tel: +351 218 430500

USEFUL NUMBERS

Emergency services: 112
Directory enquiries: 118
International directory enquiries: 179
Operator: 099
Tourist enquiries freephone: 0800 296 296
Speaking clock: 151
Dialling codes: to the UK 00 44 (minus the initial 0); to Portugal 00 351

GOVERNMENT

- Portugal is a parliamentary democracy, split into 18 districts or administrative regions: Beja, Braga, Bragança, Castelo Branco, Coimbra, Évora, Faro, Guarda, Leiria, Lisbon, Madeira, Portalegre, Porto, Santarém, Setúbal, Viana do Castelo, Vila Real and Viseu.
- The present day government was established in 1978 as a modern representative democracy.
- Portugal's President until 2006 is Jorge Fernando Branco de Sampaio, and the Prime Minister is José Manuel Durão Barroso.
- General elections are held every five years.

PUBLIC HOLIDAYS

- **Jan 1:** New Year's Day
- **Good Friday**
April 25: Liberty day (*O Dia da Liberdade*) commemorating the 1974 Revolution against the Old Regime
- **May 1:** May Day/Labour Day
- **Early July:** Corpus Christi
- **June 10:** *Dia de Camões e das Comunidades*, honouring Luis de Camões, author of *Os Lusiadas*, which was written in praise of the Portuguese explorers
- **August 15:** Feast of the Assumption
- **October 5:** Republic Day, commemorating the founding of the first Republican Government in 1910
- **November 1:** All Saints' Day.
- **December 1:** Celebration of Portugal's independence from Spain in 1640
- **December 8:** Immaculate Conception
- **December 25:** Christmas Day, known in Portugal as *O Natal*

Fireworks form part of Christmas celebrations

Facts and Figures

PUBLIC UTILITIES
Good heating is essential in Portugal, due to the damp winter months. Portugal's reliance on imported fuels also means that heating is expensive.

Electricity
- The electricity voltage in Portugal is 220/380 volts at a frequency of 50 hertz.
- Plugs have two round pins, and all lamp fittings are screw-type.
- All sockets follow European standards, therefore adapters will be required for all British electrical equipment.

Gas
- Only a small area of Lisbon is served by a natural gas network, although this is set to change.
- Most Portuguese residents buy bottled butane gas for cooking and heating, and these can be bought through private companies and in general stores.
- One bottle lasts an average family one week.
- Most modern apartment complexes have a central reserve of gas bottles, which are piped into individual homes.
- Gas bills are still delivered by hand, and payment can be made on the spot or at a supplier's office.

Water
- Tap water in Portugal is considered safe to drink.
- Water is metered and each household is billed according to usage.
- During the summer there are shortages and water cuts, which can last up to a few hours.
- Water bills are delivered by hand, and failure to pay can lead to you being cut off without warning.

BUSINESS HOURS
- Most businesses shut between 12.30pm to 2.30/3.00pm.
- Normal opening times are from 9am till lunchtime, and then from reopening after lunch until 6pm.
- Banks are the exception, opening at 8.30am and shutting at 3pm.
- Most shops tend to close for the weekend on Saturday lunchtime, although in larger cities and shopping centres, shops are open seven days a week.
- Unless specifically stated, tourist attractions are shut on Sundays and on public holidays.

NO TIME DIFFERENCE
Portugal and Madeira follow the UK in adopting GMT (Greenwich Mean Time) in the winter, and moving the clocks forward one hour from March to September (as in British Summer Time).

DRIVING IN PORTUGAL
Portugal has an expanding motorway system, but many of the smaller roads are crowded and in a poor state of repair.
- The motorways all have two lanes and tolls are paid for motorway usage.

Continental driving rules apply in Portugal

- Traffic drives on the right-hand side of the road, following continental rules. Road signs conform to the international system.
- Traffic from the right has priority at crossroads and junctions, and on a roundabout cars drive in an anti-clockwise direction.
- It is illegal to drive without a seatbelt; the limit for alcohol is 5ml per litre.
- Speed limits are 60kph in towns and 90kph on other roads (37mph and 55mph) and 120kph (74mph) on the motorway.

BANKS AND CREDIT CARDS
Portugal has *multibancos* (ATMs) in every major town and city from which tourists can withdraw cash.

It is easy to access your cash in Portugal

Travellers' cheques are expensive to cash in Portugal and, although the safest option, it is best to shop around, as rates of commission do vary. The best option is to use your card. Visa, American Express, Mastercard, Diners Club, Eurocard and Eurocheque are all commonly accepted, and can be used to withdraw cash from banks, but again be wary of incurred costs, as these do vary.

Credit Card SOS:
+351 213 509500

TOURISM
- 12 million people visit Portugal per year, and over half of these head for the Algarve.
- Portugal is the most inexpensive destination in Europe, and tourism is the

Tourism is Portugal's largest industry

country's biggest industry.
- **Portuguese Tourist Office**
22-25a Sackville Street
London
W1X 1DE
Tel: 09063 640610

TRAVEL

Air
- International airports in Portugal are located in Lisbon, Porto, Faro and Funchal (Madeira).
- Throughout the country there are many more smaller airports that can be used for internal flights and services.
- TAP Air Portugal is the main international carrier, also offering internal services, just like its rivals SATA and Portugália.
- Air Luxor offers regular flights between Lisbon and Madeira.
- Major European airlines fly into Lisbon, Faro and Porto on a regular basis.

Rail
- Regional trains run daily between Paris and Lisbon (Sud Express).
- Tourist tickets can be bought for train travel; these are valid for up to 21 days.

Portugal has a cheap and reliable rail network

23

Introduction to Portugal

Portugal has lots of quiet seaside resorts

HOT HEAT AND COOL WINDS

Located next to Spain on Europe's most southwestern edge, Portugal has over 800km of coastline, varying from surf-friendly Atlantic waves to calmer Mediterranean waters.

Portugal's steadily mild climate is well known throughout Europe, and can be broadly categorised into several smaller climactic zones. The southern and western coasts enjoy a Mediterranean feel, with summer temperatures that are high but not uncomfortable. Differences exist between the Algarve's eastern and western tips, with the latter experiencing more winter storms.

Rainfall differences become more noticeable the further north you go, as the Atlantic weather patterns exert their wet influence. Inland, meanwhile, micro-climates dictate that the mountainous regions of the northeast are very hot during the summer and very cold in winter.

ECOLOGICAL WAKE-UP CALL

The combined effects of mass tourism (particularly in the south), waste disposal, soil erosion, industrial pollution and the widespread growth of water-sapping eucalyptus plantations means that Portugal is facing considerable environmental headaches as it begins the new millennium. Another problem is that many of Portugal's rivers rise in Spain where they are dammed, cutting off previous water supplies. To create their own much-needed dams, Portuguese authorities have controversially destroyed millions of trees, as with the Alqueva dam in Alentejo, in 2002.

Motorways
- The main E1-E80 motorway runs from Porto in the North down to Lisbon, while from Lisbon, the A6 runs across to Évora.
- From Lisbon, the A2 runs down to the Algarve and across the Algarve from Lagos to Faro. The IP1-E1 runs on into Spain.
- A new motorway is being built, starting in the western Algarve and opening up the Alentejo region, which is leading to increased property development in the area.

Taxis
- Taxis are usually painted cream with an identifying roof light, although some keep their old colours of green and black.
- From 10pm to 6am the rate increases by 20 percent, and the normal practice is to pay an additional tip of 10 percent on top of your fare.

Car hire
- In order to hire a car, proof of identification is required, as is a valid driving license. The minimum age for car rentals is 21, and it is advisable to have extra insurance.
- There are car hire depots in all main cities and towns and at international airports.

Ferries
- If you want to enjoy the more leisurely pace of a ferry to Portugal, the quickest route is from Portsmouth to Bilbao or Santander in North Spain and then via car to Portugal.
- There are various services between the islands, with Porto Santo Ferries offering services between Madeira and Porto Santo.
- There are ferry connections between the five Azores islands, while various private companies offer services between coastal cities in Portugal.
- Lisbon has a river ferry service which operates up and down the River Tagus.
- There are no direct ferry links to Madeira or the Azores, although cruise ships arrive at Funchal harbour regularly.

USEFUL TRAVEL NUMBERS
- Tap Air Portugal: +351 808 205700
- Portugália: +351 218 425500
- Air Luxor: +351 210 026800
- SATA: 0870 606 6664
- Portuguese Railway: +351 218 884025

Porto Santo ferry links Madeira and Porto Santo

- National Bus Network: +351 213 545439

FESTIVALS
JANUARY
Epiphany: (Jan 6); During this festival, a crown shaped cake is eaten. The cake, known as a *bolo do rei*, contains a lucky charm and a bean; if your slice contains the bean you have to buy the cake next year.
FEBRUARY
Carnival: Lisbon and the Algarve offer various

Facts and Figures

carnivals due to a desire to rekindle the interest in Rio de Janeiro style processions.

MAY
Queima das Fitas: held in mid-May, this is a celebration of the end of the academic year in Coimbra.
Fátima: (May 13) Portugal's most famous pilgrimage.

JUNE
Festa da São Gonçalo: (first weekend) Young unmarried men and women in the town of Amarante swap phallus-shaped cakes as a token of love.
Santos Populares: In honour of Santo António (June 12-13), São João (24 June) and São Pedro (June 29), celebrations are held throughout the country.

JULY
Festa do Colete Encarnado: (first weekend) Held in Vila Franca de Xira, this festival consists of bullfights and the Pamplona-style running of the bulls.

AUGUST
Romaria da Nossa Senhora da Agonía: Held in the third week of August, this is a combination of a carnival and a fair, with Viana do Castelo celebrating *Our Lady of Sorrows*.

SEPTEMBER
Romaria de Nossa Senhora dos Remédios: Running throughout the end of August and the beginning of September, this pilgrimage is held in Lamego.
Feiras Novas: (second and third weekend) *New Fairs* in Ponte de Lima, is a huge fair and market with fireworks, a fairground and musicians.
Festa de Senhora da Consaolação: (throughout September) A celebration of Portugal's patron saint, with a month of parties, music, food and drink in the Assafora area.

OCTOBER
Feira de Outubro: Takes place in the first two weeks of the month in Vila Franca de Xira, with more bullfighting and bullrunning.

Fátima: (Oct 13) This is the second great pilgrimage of the year, dated on the Virgin's last appearance.

NOVEMBER
Feira Nacional do Cavalo: Held in Golegã in the first two weeks of the month, this is a time for horse enthusiasts and bullfighters to watch the horse parades and races. Included in this are celebrations for St Martin's Day (Nov 11).

DECEMBER
Christmas: Shops and churches throughout Portugal display cribs. The main service is the Midnight Mass, which is followed by a traditional meal of *bacalhau* (salted dried cod).
New Year: Individual towns organise their own events, usually with fireworks at midnight and the banging of pots and pans to welcome in the new year.

TELEVISION
- Portuguese television has four domestic stations and many subtitled American and British programmes.
- The two national stations are RTP1 and RTP2, and there are two private stations: SIC and TVI.
- Satellite television is popular in Portugal, with Sky One, Sky News, Eurosport and the Discovery Channel among the available channels.
- BBC Europe can be received with the aid of a decoder.
- Most bars and hotels offer satellite television.

RADIO
- There are four national radio stations in Portugal, as well as numerous local and pirate stations.
- Several international stations can be received, including BBC World Service on 648kHz medium wave and 15.007MHz short wave.
- Voice of America can be received on 6040 on the 49m short wave band.

NEWSPAPERS
- The two biggest Portuguese newspapers are *Diario de Noticias*, based in Lisbon, and the Porto-based *Jornal de Noticias*.
- The *Publico* offers good foreign news and listings, while the *Jornal de Letreas* offers an interesting insight into the country's culture.
- The main English papers are the *Anglo-Portuguese News* (APN) and the *International Herald Tribune*.
- International daily newspapers are also available, usually on the day after general issue in their country of publication.

One of Portugal's best-selling daily papers

DISABLED FACILITIES
- Previously Portugal lacked awareness in the provision of disabled facilities, but now Porto, Lisbon, Coimbra and Braga offer disabled bus and taxi services.
- Most public areas in Portugal now offer parking and toilet facilities for disabled people.

POST
- Post offices are open Monday to Friday, 8.00am to 10pm.
- Airmail takes three days to reach Europe and five days from Madeira.

Carnivals mirror the style of Rio de Janeiro

A traditional folk dancer in action

Portugal Property Guide

The beautiful riverfront of Tavira in eastern Algarve

A PORTUGUESE LOVE AFFAIR

With its proximity to the UK and the availability of almost year-round golf and sunshine, Portugal is still one of the key choices in Europe for discerning overseas property buyers. **Simon Conn** (left), Senior Partner of the UK's leading independent overseas mortgage brokers Conti Financial Services (CFS), offers an overview on the Portuguese property market, and what to consider when buying in the region

Over the past 20 years, interest in buying a home in Portugal has always remained buoyant. A country of rich contrasts – from the sophisticated, rugged Algarve to the superb golfing facilities in the west of the area and north of Lisbon – Portugal has long been perceived as a region catering to the higher quality end of the property market. As such, it is consistently to be found on the wish list of those UK buyers looking for a more exclusive holiday home, future retirement home or investment property.

The country offers something to suit everyone's taste and budget, however, be it a luxury villa in a cosmopolitan resort near one of its famed sandy beaches, a property on a top-class golf complex or a quiet seaside apartment on the coast near the university city of Coimbra. This diversity, combined with ease of access from UK airports, means that Portugal continues to draw overseas property buyers from the UK.

For all its exclusive reputation, it is still possible to buy a reasonably priced property in Portugal. 'In the up and coming eastern Algarve, near the picturesque fishing port of Tavira, an apartment or townhouse can cost from around £70,000 to £120,000,' says Adrian Medd, Managing Director of Cambridge-based specialists European Villa Solutions. 'With its proximity to the Spanish border, as yet undeveloped coastline and prospect of golf courses to come, the east of Portugal could prove a good investment for the future.'

For those on an even tighter budget, it is possible to buy a slice of a property in Portugal under a co-ownership arrangement, an innovation that is becoming increasingly popular. For around £25,000, it is possible to buy a one-quarter title on a villa, which enables the purchaser to enjoy the property for a three-month 'slot' each year. These arrangements are co-ordinated by the developer, such as at Parque da la Floresta in the stunning western Algarve, with time slots rotated annually and rental income shared equally to ensure fairness among the parties involved.

At the other end of the spectrum, the luxury of an exclusive golf course development, such as those at Quinta da Lagos, can cost upwards from

Expert Overview

Luxury properties in the exclusive golf course development at Quinta da Lagos can cost upwards of £2.5 million

Portugal Property Guide

Portugal caters for every taste and budget

Give yourself a 'cooling off' period before buying

£2.5 million. The average price of a more modest villa with pool, however, starts at around £150,000.

As with any financial investment, it is essential that you take the best advice before considering buying any property in Portugal. Always consult a legitimate company with an up-to-the-minute understanding of the local legal and financial requirements of such a life-changing purchase. This will save you time, additional costs and, crucially, the heartache of disappointment.

The property buying process in Portugal is constantly evolving. For example, as of June 2003, it is possible to save money when you buy in Portugal with the replacement of the old SISA tax (comparable to the UK stamp duty) by the *Imposto Municipal sobre Transmissoes* (IMT). The new IMT rate is six percent of the purchase price on a property over 500,000 euros – a reduction of four percent – with properties under 80,000 euros free. However, it is important to note that the local tax departments, who will co-ordinate the IMT, have stated that it will levy a hefty penalty on anyone found to deliberately undervalue a purchase price, so buyer beware!

HINTS AND TIPS
Simon Conn offers some top advice for buying a property in Portugal

- Always ensure you seek specialist advice from independent solicitors, architects and surveyors before considering a purchase in Portugal. They should be proficient in local laws and processes, and know the specifics involved in buying a property there.

- Where possible, try to arrange your mortgage in the currency that you earn in, unless you are going to receive rental income from the property in euros, in which case this may be a possible alternative option, depending upon the lender's lending criteria.

- Using your potential Portuguese property as security, either repayment or interest-only mortgages are available.

- Based on the purchase price or valuation, loans of up to 80 percent can be arranged.

- Currently the minimum loan for Portugal is £20,000, with a term of five to 30 years.

- Try and arrange your mortgage finance 'in principle', before agreeing to purchase the property or signing any contracts and handing over a deposit.

- Choose a mortgage lender that is regulated, such as in the UK under the Consumer Credit Act and the Mortgage Code.

- When choosing an estate agent, try to ensure they belong to a recognised trade body, such as FOPDAC, the Federation of Overseas Property Developers Agents and Consultants (www.fopdac.com).

- It is advisable to open a bank account in Portugal, and ensure you get a certificate of importation for money you bring in from your home country.

- It is a good idea to set up standing orders in a local bank account to meet bills and taxes.

Expert Overview

Always take the best advice before buying in Portugal

The average cost of an Algarve villa is 250,000 euros

One of the most important things to remember when you arrive in Portugal, with your money burning a hole in your pocket, is not to be impressed by the first local, highly persuasive estate agent you meet. For peace of mind, make sure that they belong to a recognised trade body like FOPDAC, the Federation of Overseas Property Developers Agents and Consultants (www.fopdac.com), who monitor the property market in many countries, and are acknowledged in Europe as one of the leading trade associations.

Portugal has so much to offer the UK buyer – high quality properties, beautifully designed golf courses, sandy beaches and welcoming people. However, it is essential to remember to take the appropriate independent advice – as you would do when buying in the UK – only then you can enjoy your property in Portugal with confidence and security.

Conti Financial Services

204 Church Road, Hove, East Sussex, BN3 2DJ
Tel: 01273 772811
Fax: 01273 321269
e-mail: enquiries@contifs.com
website: www.mortgagesoverseas.com

Fail to pay your taxes in Portugal, and the courts could possibly seize your property.

- Never sign a contract that you do not understand. This doesn't matter whether it's because it is written in Portuguese or because it contains too much legal jargon. Get it translated and explained to you thoroughly before you add your signature.

- Always give yourself a 'cooling off' period of a few days (or even weeks) if you have seen a 'must-have property' and are tempted to put down a deposit there and then.

- If you are arranging finance on the property, ensure that this is stated in any contract, and make sure that you have an 'opt-out clause' if the loan is not agreed (which will ensure any deposit paid is refunded).

- Remember that bills do not end at the asking price. Lawyers' fees, taxes, insurance and so on must all be met in Portugal, and are often more expensive.

- Ensure that you do not inherit a debt on the property before you purchase it. A good solicitor should be able to check this out before proceeding with any completion on a sale. A typical example of this would be if the developer has borrowed money to build the development, and this amount has been allocated against each plot as additional security to the developer's bank.

- The majority of mortgages overseas require a suitable life policy assigned to the lender.

- Bank and employer's references are required if you are employed (together with relevant supporting documentation, such as the last three payslips and latest P60). If you are self-employed, however, a minimum of two years' audited accounts are required, and in some cases, the last two years' tax returns.

Portugal Property Guide

The Algarve offers plenty of options for an idyllic coastal life, with many new developments built on marinas

ALGARVE PROPERTY MARKET OVERVIEW

BUYING PROPERTY IN THE REGION

Despite the tumbles in world stock markets of late, figures have consistently shown that investing in a well researched overseas market can achieve significant gains. Despite its rise in popularity, particularly in the last few years, many investors still look to the Algarve, where the best properties in good locations can make decent profits.

Increasing numbers of buyers – serious investors and holiday home seekers alike – are purchasing developable land and building their own home or holiday developments. There are good opportunities to purchase land with planning permission for larger holiday complexes from around 1.5 million euros upwards (£1 million) and, of course, this area offers access to many English-speaking or expatriate building and development companies.

The Algarve region has always been popular with the British due to its charm, clement weather, easy lifestyle and abundance of golf courses, and it has consequently attracted many second home buyers, willing to pay a little more for their place in the sun.

Many potential homes are new-builds, and Vilamoura in particular boasts lots of new developments, mainly around the recently built Millennium courses, with a two-bedroom luxury apartment for around 250,000 euros (around £165,000). In Vale do Lobo, there are luxury one- and two-bedroom apartments for sale in Jardin do Golfe. Priced from 161,000 euros (£107,000) for one bedroom and 237,000 euros (£158,000) for two bedrooms, they are located on a site that comprises two swimming pools, tennis courts, a clubhouse, on-site security and a putting green. Vale do Lobo has experienced a consistent rise in property prices since 1982, and no decrease in property prices has ever been recorded here, not even in the challenging years of the early 90s.

In Lagos, Aquarius Properties recently launched a development of apartments overlooking the marina, with a communal pool and underground parking. These properties start at 143,620 euros (around £96,000) for a one-bedroom apartment and 174,590 euros (£116,000) for a two-bedroom property. These types of apartment developments, with the added bonuses of on-site facilities, are becoming more popular in this area of the Algarve, appealing to retirees and holiday home-seekers alike. Lagos, in particular, is a popular location, especially as the building of the new highway makes it only a one-hour drive from Faro airport. The area has much to offer, including beautiful beaches and many attractions, and is regarded by many as the cultural capital of the Algarve.

In areas like Quinta do Lago, Vale do Lobo and Vilamoura, all privately run resorts are sound buys, due to the strict nature of building regulations, which are controlled both by the local government

Algarve Market Overview

Most new-build villas come with swimming pools…

…all you have to do is decide on the size of the villa!

and by the owner. For the more discerning buyer, it would be hard to find a more luxurious villa than those available in the lovely Quinta do Mar development beside Quinta do Lago. Located on plots of various sizes, they are priced from 995,000 euros (around £660,000), and the quality of the finish is magnificent. Luxury apartments are currently being constructed on the same complex, again of various sizes and most offering a terrace or a small garden. These apartments are priced from 495,000 to 895,000 euros (£330,000 to £600,000), with nearly all affording terrific sea views.

MARKET TRENDS

Property prices have risen in the Algarve by as much as 20 percent per year in some areas of the Algarve. With the new motorway to Lagos near the western coast now completed, this area is likely to become even more popular and, as a consequence, property prices are expected to rise in this area. Although there has been a slight slump in interest from British buyers and investors here in recent months, especially in the more exclusive million-pound properties, the fact that some of the 2004 European Football Championships matches are being held in the area is likely to increase foreign demand on property in the Algarve. The boost to the property market from Euro 2004 will obviously push up prices, and discerning buyers would do well to seek out potential property before the expected rush. But with stunning new developments around the Vilamoura and Vale do Lobo area, there will be ample choice. High rental income is achievable from these properties, allowing owners to earn income as well as good capital appreciation. Appreciation for 2002 was around 20 percent in these areas, and a simliar increase in 2003 is also expected.

WHO BUYS THERE?

The Algarve market combines a real cross-section of nationalities. Predominantly a British market, many other northern Europeans and Americans buy here, while a recent drive in Madrid attracted many Spanish nationals to the Algarve. The market is dominated by those of retirement age seeking to settle in the sun. However, more recently young families have been buying in the Algarve too, spending one or two months a year in their second home, then benefiting from the rental income it generates for the rest of the year. The Algarve is a more expensive property market than elsewhere in Portugal, although resale properties can be picked up relatively cheaply, especially in comparison with other second home destinations. With a guaranteed return on your investment – thanks to the stability and ever increasing price of property – the Algarve market offers excellent investment opportunities.

With thanks to Noreen Hynes, Managing Director of **Aquarius Properties** *('Somerton', Cross Avenue, Blackrock, Co. Dublin, Ireland; +353 1 278 2900; www.aquariusproperties.com).*

> *The market is dominated by those of retirement age seeking to settle in the sun, but more recently young families have been buying here too*

Portugal Property Guide

Much of the Alentejo region consists of sprawling heathland, fields of crops and an enormous amount of space

ALENTEJO PROPERTY MARKET OVERVIEW

BUYING PROPERTY IN THE REGION

Why would you want to buy in a home in Alentejo? With Portugal's least developed property market, yet constituting a third of Portugal's land area, these sparsely populated plains are devoted mainly to farming and forestry. The terrain is harsh, with hills and forests, while to the west lies the Atlantic and, to the east, Spain. Characterised by fiery summer heat and the abrupt winter's chill, Alentejo's greatest draw for the second home-owner is the escape from civilisation… and then there are the great property prices. Homes range from old stone ruins to watermills (all under £100,000), from modern houses up to grand manor houses or *palacettes*.

Alentejo's vast plains are filled by large estates and farming properties, and property here is generally limited to those interested in making a living from farming or intent on accumulating vast tracts of land. For a typically sized farm of roughly 2,000 acres, you would expect to pay approximately 4 million euros (around £2.8 million). For a more manageable estate with 225 acres of mixed farming land, the typical cost would be around 600,000 euros (about £420,000). These kinds of prices buy you mostly grazing land for livestock or cereal crops, but for a 450-acre cork farm – 90 percent of Portugal's cork is produced in this region – you should expect to pay up to 2 million euros (£1.4 million). Smaller tracts of land, roughly two acres in size, cost approximately 60,000 euros (or around £40,000).

Alentejo's Atlantic coast is an altogether different proposition. With its high plains tumbling down through wooded valleys on to a narrow coastal plain, the land is much more difficult to work, and consequently plots of land are smaller. For example, a three-acre plot with a stream, olive trees and fertile soil, including a ruin requiring renovation, would fetch roughly 38,000 euros (£27,000).

Needless to say, the closer the property is to the coast, the more expensive it is likely to be. This is not simply due to demand from northern European sun-seekers, but also due to agricultural value. Over the centuries, the fertile topsoil has been washed down from the higher hills into the fields nearer the coast. This, combined with moderate Atlantic breezes, makes for very successful farming.

MARKET TRENDS

Recently there has been an upsurge in the property market and prices for Alentejo, thanks to foreign buyers investing in large tracts of land, pushing land prices up by 30 percent. Good agricultural land is always in demand in Portugal, and the fact that goods grown here can be easily shipped to the rest of northern Europe helps its desirability.

As with many rural areas in Europe, the hard lifestyle and low financial rewards, especially for

Alentejo Market Overview

A typical Alentejan one-storey farmhouse

It is possible to buy land and construct a new home

the young, has led to many seeking employment in larger towns, resulting in a population drop. As a result, many farmhouses have been abandoned. The majority require renovation, if not complete restoration. However, if you are willing to undertake the work, the result can be a lovely stone house in an idyllic setting.

The southern half of the Alentejan coast, running down towards the Algarve, is a protected national park, the Costa Vicentina. Old, ruined properties are abundant here, and restoration is the only real means of securing a property sale in this protected area. In the popular areas further south, scarcity of homes has led to a price rise, and the newly opened trans-Algarve motorway now brings tourists an easy 45-minute journey from Faro to Bensafrim, just 20 minutes from Alentejo's west coast. There has always been an interest in regions of Portugal beyond the Algarve, and the opening of the new highway has further added to existing demand.

The pressure on the property market in this area will undoubtedly continue, and will probably lead to a continued upward trend in prices. However, unwanted cottages and small plots of land do provide alternatives to modern villas. Foreign buyers tend to gravitate towards Odemira and Vila Nova de Milfontes on the west coast of Alentejo.

WHO BUYS THERE?

Tourism plays a big role in Alentejo's economy, and there is a continued influx of second home-seekers who choose to buy here as the Algarve becomes increasingly over-populated and over-developed. Historically, foreigners who gravitate to this area are of mixed age and nationality, seeking an alternative lifestyle geared towards relaxation, for example surfers, small B&B owners, artists and writers, and some small farm operators. However, for those thinking of moving to central Alentejo, you will need dedication and patience to cope with the climate and harsh, secluded environment.

In northern Alentejo, the climate is more temperate, and many residents have retired here from the hotter Algarve and southern coasts of Spain. Since it is easy to grow fruit, it is particularly productive as a market gardening area, with fresh produce being easily attained and available all year round. Several farms also specialise in the production of organic produce in Alentejo, many of which supply the British market. Younger foreign residents pursue similar interests, but are also adept at diversifying into handymen to cater for the demands of the older expatriates. It is also worth noting that Alentejo's seclusion, and essentially traditional environment, means there is a greater need to communicate in Portuguese compared to Algarve or other major cities.

With thanks to **Bougainvillea Properties** (Barreiras Brancas, 8100-227 Loulé, Portugal; +351 289 413199), voted Best Portuguese Estate Agent 1999, 2000, 2001, 2002.

> *Old ruined properties are abundant on the Costa Vicentina and restoration is often the only means of securing a property sale here*

Portugal Property Guide

The sprawling city of Lisbon, Portugal's capital, has properties to suit all tastes and budgets

LISBON PROPERTY MARKET OVERVIEW

BUYING PROPERTY IN THE REGION

Whether looking for a permanent residence or a holiday home, the greater Lisbon area is attractive for many reasons. A thriving metropolis, with an abundance of cultural life, good shopping facilities, many championship golf courses, several marinas and many other amenities, all within striking distance, the Lisbon area provides all the entertainment opportunities one can ask for. When this is combined with its mild and pleasant year-round climate, the well functioning infrastructure and, of course, the friendly welcome of its residents, Lisbon proves itself to be the perfect location in which to buy a property. Whether you are interested in a downtown apartment, you prefer a quieter location in Lisbon's surrounding areas or you fancy striking out and exploring the historic cities and beautiful countries of the neighbouring Estremadura and Ribatejo regions, you can be sure there is a property to suit your requirements.

The most sought after areas in the region are central Lisbon and the coastline stretching from to Estoril, Cascais and Sintra, an area that has been the preferred summer resort for the Portuguese royal family since the 13th century. These areas have provided popular luxury residences for centuries, but recently finished resort developments have lent wider variety to the property market, with something to suit most budgets and tastes. Style wise, there is diversity too. Properties range from typical historic buildings that have been modernised, usually in central parts of the city (central properties are preferred by foreign and British buyers) to villas and penthouses mostly out-of-town. Farmhouses and manor houses are also available for restoration in the more rural areas outside the city, but these come at a cost. Usually in a highly desirable location, these properties can often demand prices up around 400,000 euros (about £265,000).

Luxury residential properties of good quality and location are selling well, and at stable prices. Luxury apartments average between 2,500 and 3,500 euros (£1,650–£2,330) per square metre, while luxury villas fetch between 2,000 and 4,000 euros (£1,330–£2,660) per square metre. Thus a medium sized villa, set in a decent location will cost between 1.2 and 2 million euros (£800,000–£1.3 million). That's quite an investment!

MARKET TRENDS

Portugal builds, on average, 240 new houses a day, and half of all Portuguese families live in the

Lisbon Market Overview

In the outskirts of Lisbon you'll find a lot of beautiful villas, many of which have been built in the last 20 years

metropolitan area around Lisbon. In the last 11 years, the number of buildings in Lisbon and the suburbs increased by 20 percent per year to approximately 1,800,000. 600,000 of these buildings required repairs or restoration, costing the market approximately 40 billion euros.

Over the last 20 years, property prices have risen to varying degrees across the Lisbon, Estremadura and Ribatejo regions. Inside the city of Lisbon, prices have risen by approximately 100 percent. A newly built three-bedroom apartment in one of Lisbon's cheapest areas costing 10,000 euros (£6,660) in 1980, would now fetch between 125,000 and 150,000 euros (£83,000–£100,000).

In Cascais, prices have experienced the same price rises as in Lisbon itself.

In areas such as Sintra, Vila Franca de Xira, and areas south of the Tagus river, meanwhile, properties are 50 percent cheaper than in Lisbon itself or in Lisbon's outskirts. Prices have not risen as much in these areas over the last couple of decades; in fact, the market has experienced a decline in sales. Nevertheless this has not led to a decrease in property prices. In general, prices for residential properties have doubled over the decade from 1990 till 2000. Since then the annual growth has slowed, becoming more moderate and standing at two percent during the past 12 months.

WHO BUYS THERE?

Traditionally, the property market in greater Lisbon has been dominated by Portuguese buyers. In recent years, however, more foreign buyers have entered the market. This is only natural as, generally speaking, more and more people from Scandinavia and northern Europe are retiring at a younger age than previous generations, and more and more British and Irish buyers are choosing Lisbon. For these people, greater Lisbon is the perfect place to settle down and enjoy a relaxing lifestyle, while still having all amenities close at hand. And this trend is expected to continue.

Traditionally the property market in Lisbon has been dominated by Portuguese buyers. In recent years, however, more foreign buyers have entered the market

As well as in the capital, British purchasers particularly favour properties near the beaches of Guincho, Praia da Monte Estoril, Praia de Estoril, Tamariz, Praia de São Pedro and Carcavellos, and there are well defined expat communities in Estoril and Cascais. Many British and Americans have settled in Lisbon's surrounding areas of Estoril, Cascais and the golf resorts of Quinta da Marinha and Praia d'El Rey. But the British and Irish are found dotted throughout the capital, and often elect for apartments in the city centre.

With thanks to **Sotheby's International** (+351 289 392780) and **Premier Properties International** (01935 881199)

Portugal Property Guide

The Coimbra & Beiras region features many quaint towns packed with characterful stone-built properties

COIMBRA & THE BEIRAS PROPERTY MARKET OVERVIEW

BUYING PROPERTY IN THE REGION

The Coimbra & the Beiras region includes the area of Costa da Prata, also known as the Silver Coast. Beautiful, unappreciated and quite undiscovered, the coastline consists of sandy bays and long stretches of beach with rocky cliff faces. Inland, hills rise to forested regions containing some of Portugal's highest mountains in the Serra da Estrela national park. On the approach to Coimbra, the forests become denser, and property here can be purchased at a reasonable price. In Pombal, for instance, just 30 minutes from bustling Coimbra, a two-bedroom villa costs approximately £130,000. The Coimbra region also offers some spectacular coastal properties, overlooking miles of ocean. A coastal villa consisting of six bedrooms, a swimming pool and a well manicured garden with beach views will cost roughly £490,000.

The villages and countryside of the Serra da Estrela park offer the double advantage of spectacular scenery and pleasant weather; imagine sitting in the comfort of a sunny café garden, drinking coffee, with snow-capped mountains in the distance. The area is very beautiful, with mountains, pine forests, rivers and streams. Offering an abundance of inexpensive ruins, small cottages with a generous patch of land can be found for around £35,000, which has led to many foreigners moving to the area. However, in reality, the demand does not come close to matching the availability.

For those seeking a more dynamic environment, an urban relocation close to the resort town of Aveiro in a four-bedroom, modern property would cost approximately £145,000. Homes in the busy coastal town of Figueira da Foz, meanwhile, tend to come in slightly higher than that.

When approaching Viseu, the rugged nature of the landscape becomes apparent. The greenery of the environment and morning mists reflect the higher level of rainfall and cooler temperatures. The pace of life is gentle, with the area being highly secluded. Spectacular trout fishing is guaranteed, especially with a river-front property. For a three-bedroom property near Viseu on the river, with a guest cottage and grounds offering a natural spring, swimming pool and gardens, you should expect to pay about £295,000. The average price of a country house is £150,000; this is for a property without a river frontage and with no additional buildings.

Continuing east around the Serra da Estrela, to Guarda and onwards to Castelo Branco, there is an abundance of forests, and the landscape becomes rugged, highly reminiscent of the Scottish highlands, yet affording a comfortable climate.

Coimbra & the Beiras Market Overview

Renovation projects are popular but not too common

Coastal villas are a great option for seaside lovers

Properties in this region tend to be lower in price, due to availability of land and minimal demand from both home and foreign markets. A six-bedroom home can be bought for as little as £140,000, and a four-bedroom house in town fetches £70,000. There is a limited expat community in this area, however, so it is essential to learn Portuguese, and a high level of integration with the local community is required and should be expected.

Although Portugal is not a large country, it does provide an incredible choice of terrain in which to live. Many options will necessitate adapting to local cultural and social activity that can offer a great deal of fun, and will help guarantee new Portuguese friends. Best of all, you will participate in a lifestyle and experience traditional social values that have disappeared from much of northern Europe.

MARKET TRENDS

So how has the property market within Coimbra & the Beiras changed? The answer is hardly at all. There is a slowly growing realisation that the Coimbra coast offers a very interesting alternative to the Algarve, affording an exceedingly comfortable climate and attractive rural surroundings. However, whereas in the Algarve prices have increased sharply over recent years, prices within this region have only gone up by around 20 percent. The staggering increase in Algarve prices has led to a slight reduction of interest in Portuguese property, with a knock-on effect on other Portuguese regions.

There is a slowly growing realisation that the Coimbra coastal region offers a very interesting alternative to the Algarve, offering attractive surroundings

This decrease in interest, though, is not yet of a sufficient proportion to affect property sales and prices.

WHO BUYS THERE?

Inland there is no evidence yet of a change in demand. As foreigners choose a life of seclusion tucked away in peaceful countryside, there are always those moving back 'homeward' due to age and health. An example of this is one couple who, after 15 years in Portugal, sold their property and moved due to the lack of assurance offered by the Portuguese health service. The coastal region attracts a mixed community of various ages, while the inland sector experiences demand from retirees seeking utter peace, and from young couples opting for alternative lifestyles. Since prices in this region are generally lower than the 'known' parts of Portugal, and have only increased due to an escalation of living costs, it does signify an excellent purchasing opportunity for foreigners.

Initial moves by foreigners to the area have tended to be towards the coastal regions, and it may be many years before there is any graduation to inland areas. As a consequence, there is little likelihood of significant price change occurring in the foreseeable future.

With thanks to **Bougainvillea Properties** *(Barreiras Brancas, 8100-227 Loulé, Portugal; +351 289 413199), voted Best Portuguese Estate Agent 1999, 2000, 2001, 2002.*

Portugal Property Guide

Portugal's second city of Porto on the river Douro represents the hub of Costa Verde's property market

COSTA VERDE PROPERTY MARKET OVERVIEW

PROPERTY IN THE REGION

Consisting of the Minho, Douro and Trás-Os-Montes, Costa Verde occupies Portugal's northern border with Spain. The hinterland of Trás-Os-Montes has an abundance of hills and lakes, while all around the area of the Douro and Minho, are the vineyards which produce local wines and, of course, port.

Costa Verde's property market is characterised by a wealth of traditional-style properties. Many require renovation, while others need a complete makeover; some have already been lovingly converted, and are ready for habitation.

It goes without saying that Porto and the surrounding area represents the hub of north Portugal's property market. Here you will find your new builds and exquisite restoration projects, with the average home costing 200,000 euros (£133,000). Aside from Porto, the coastal areas of the Douro and Minho are also more expensive than the majority of northern areas. Once you head away from the coast and Porto, prices drop dramatically, with ruin and renovation properties around 10,000 to 30,000 euros (£6,000–£20,000) dominating the property market. Further east into Trás-os-Montes, the remote nature of the area means the property market is practically non-existent. Again, ruins and plots of land govern the market.

More recently there has been an increase in modern developments, including condominiums, mainly in the coastal areas. These new-build properties are generally built to very high specifications, and usually boast top-end interior design standards, quality kitchens and appliances, as well as many communal on-site facilities, such as laundry rooms and garages.

Relatively speaking, prices are low compared to other areas of Portugal, as Costa Verde has yet to be discovered by the majority of foreign buyers. This renders demand on the properties very low. For example, 60,000 euros (£40,000) will buy a rustic, fully renovated dwelling, with two bedrooms and a swimming pool, while 460,000 euros (£305,000) will secure a luxury manor-style house on the river, set in extensive grounds. Located on the Spanish border, there is a palace worth 22 million euros (£14.5 million), highlighting the characteristically diverse nature of Costa Verde's

Costa Verde Market Overview

Costa Verde represents a stable investment

The Minho offers some exquisite and palatial homes

property market. With such a broad range of prices and property, the northern market is difficult to categorise, yet promises something for all.

MARKET TRENDS

Over the last ten years, the market has experienced a marked change, due to the advances made in Costa Verde's communication network. With the introduction of budget flights to the international airport at Porto, which regularly receives services from Birmingham and Manchester, it has become much easier to reach northern Portugal. And, thanks to invested European Union money, the road network has also been upgraded in recent years, making it easier for people to explore rural areas of Trás-Os-Montes and the Minho. Remote homes in these areas were previously very difficult to view, but of late they have enjoyed a substantial boost in advertising and publicity spend, making their appeal more widely known.

Historically, Costa Verde's port and wine companies have had close ties with the area, especially Porto. As a consequence of the British love of these tipples, there are many established British firms in the area, and there is, in general, a marked affinity between the British and north Portugal. Now, with the presence of Porto's modern international airport, and with Lisbon being easily accessible by motorway, the property market is beginning to open up further to foreign investment. What's more, the broadband telephone system will soon cover the whole of Portugal, making the more remote areas more suitable for businesses.

WHO BUYS THERE?

Costa Verde is unlikely to generate a huge demand upon its property market, but it does enjoy a well developed foreign buying scene, mainly consisting of British and German buyers. This has developed rapidly in the last ten years, and although being a much smaller and less advanced than areas such as the Algarve and Lisbon, it still represents a quality, stable investment for any foreigner seeking to buy abroad. The quality of the wines and the tranquillity of the rural life, away from the heat and turmoil of the Algarve, are the key assets of the area. Furthermore, for those who want a stable investment for years to come, and a guaranteed increase in the value of their real estate, Costa Verde is an ideal area to choose.

With thanks to Katherine Spode of **Luso Properties** *(+351 263 274878; www.lusoproperties.com). Luso Properties also work closely with* **Prestige Properties** *(www.prestigeproperty.co.uk) in the UK.*

Madeira's capital Funchal offers everything from high-rise apartments to villas with lush gardens

MADEIRA PROPERTY MARKET OVERVIEW

BUYING PROPERTY IN THE REGION

Recent advances in communications infrastructure and technological developments in Madeira have made the Island one of the most desirable holiday and retirement havens in Europe. The island's traditional characteristics have been preserved, while increased numbers of flights to the island have opened Madeira up to short-term holiday-makers. The sun-kissed Portuguese island now offers long-term foreign residents an incomparable lifestyle, yet within easy reach of their home countries.

The regional government's policy of expanding and improving the island's road system has greatly contributed to the opening up of Madeira's rural areas. The new motorway system has brought once distant parts of the island, like Calheta and São Vicente, to within a mere 30 minutes' drive from the capital, Funchal. It is now perfectly viable to consider living in these areas while benefiting from the facilities Funchal has to offer. Services and commerce in these rural areas have also been greatly improved, making it unnecessary for residents to have to commute to Funchal for their shopping, banking, entertainment and medical needs.

The telecommunications boom has had a great impact on the Madeiran way of life. Mobile phone reception is available practically anywhere on the island, while the internet has further reduced the isolation factor previously associated with living in a rural part of Madeira.

How does this affect a foreign investor considering buying a property in Madeira? Obviously the availability of facilities and services makes the prospect of residing in any particular area more desirable. One does not want to feel that moving to a foreign location entails sacrificing your home comforts. There is no reason for you to feel isolated in Madeira. On the contrary: in Madeira you will find all that you need, while enjoying the unique peace and beauty that the island has to offer.

MARKET TRENDS

The aforementioned factors have had a significant effect on the Madeira property market, especially as regards the actual locations of demand for properties. There is one other factor that has been just as influential in determining the market, and this was the fairly recent introduction of bank mortgages into the Madeiran way of life.

As recently as nine years ago, mortgage rates were around 20 percent, which made buying property with bank finance practically impossible. The majority of Madeirans resorted to sharing

Madeira Market Overview

Most foreign buyers invest in upmarket villas

Demand for property in Madeira is on the increase

homes with parents or relatives. Some looked to the rental market as a solution for their housing needs. A lucky few could actually afford to buy a property outright, without resorting to bank finance.

When interest rates dropped to around 15 percent, this started having an effect on the demand for new properties. At that stage, a relatively significant section of the market could afford to buy their homes with some financing, and many did so. The market forces were still fairly well controlled as the demand was growing slowly, with more buyers gaining the confidence to explore this novel prospect.

The boom happened when rates dropped below 10 percent, and kept dropping to as low as four percent in the first quarter of the year 2000. The attractive rates, combined with the aggressive marketing on the part of banks to sell their new mortgages, caused something of a frenzy in the first-time buyer market. New developments started springing up at an unprecedented rate, but were still not sufficient to satisfy demand, which had grown exponentially as people realised that the possibility of owning their own home was now within their grasp.

At this point, buying new property from plan became the norm rather than the exception. Developments were more and more frequently sold out in their early stages of construction, and differentials of over 15 percent between the pre-construction prices and the finished prices become the norm. Buying from plan has become the new tradition.

WHO BUYS THERE?

This frenzy had little effect on the foreign buyer. Most developments were aimed at first-time Madeiran homebuyers, and had little to offer the retiree who wanted peace and quiet, rather than the atmosphere typical of a large apartment block with young couples and children.

Most foreign buyers prefer to invest in a villa or in a more upmarket apartment or townhouse development. More of these types of properties are becoming available as developers realise that good design and high quality will always have a market.

Prices in this category vary for the usual reasons of location, size and so on, but figures are around 120,000 euros (£80,000) for a two-bedroom apartment, 160,000 euros (£110,000) for a three-bedroom townhouse, and starting at 190,000 (£133,000) euros for a villa. Prices at this end of the market have grown consistently over the last 12 years, at a rate of around five percent per year. While this growth is not earth-shattering, it has been regular and is expected to continue as demand increases.

With thanks to **Caldeira & Stevenson Real Estate** (rua da Carreira 92, Funchal, Madeira; +351 291 228435; www.caldeirastevenson.com).

> New developments started springing up at an unprecedented rate, but were still not sufficient to satisfy demand, which had grown exponentially

■ Buying Guide

BUYING, LIVING AND WORKING IN PORTUGAL

Everything you need to know about finding and purchasing a property in Portugal, and exactly what you can expect once you move there

Buying, Living and Working contents

Steps to buying	44
Living and working	58
Case studies	72
Business/legal glossary	80

Buying Guide

If you are among those thinking of buying in Portugal, it is first crucial to understand the procedures involved

Steps to Buying

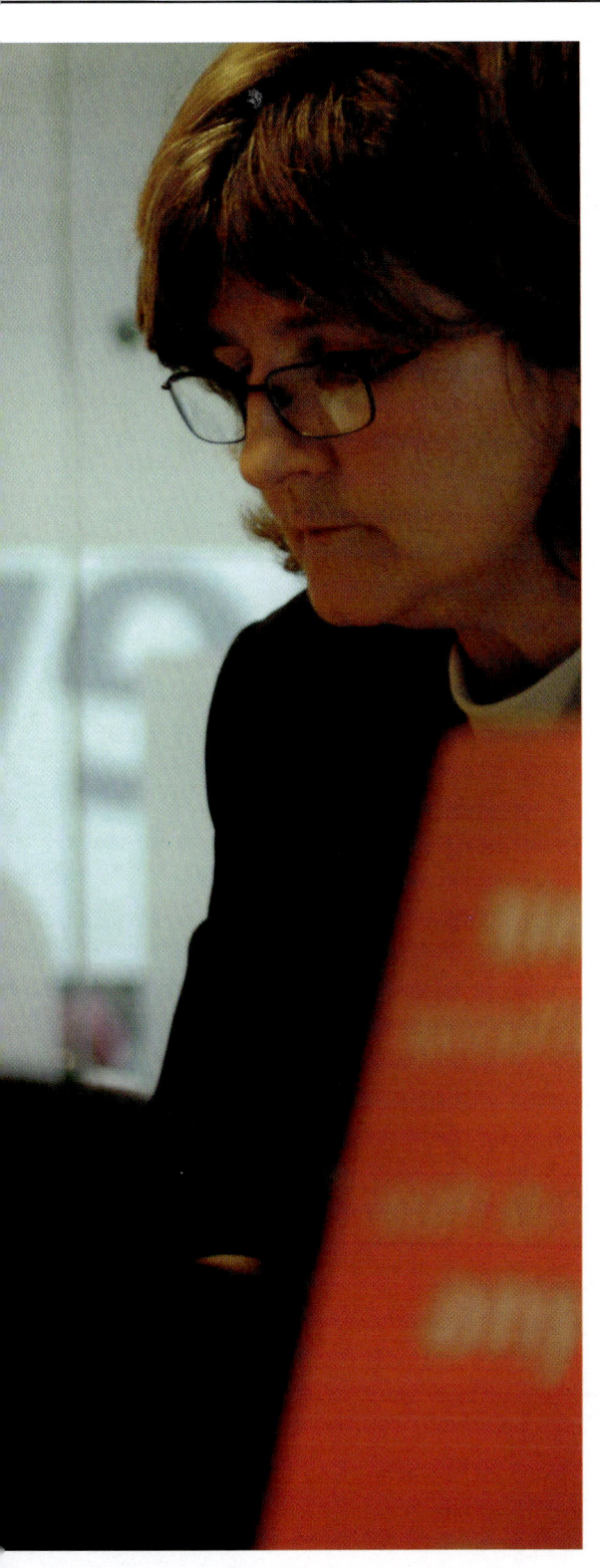

STEPS TO BUYING

Over the next 12 pages, you'll find a complete guide to the buying process from finding a property to signing the final contract

Before you even think about buying a property in Portugal, it is first crucial to understand the many procedures involved, from the idiosyncrasies of Portuguese property law to the complicated subject of finance and taxes. This chapter gives you a thorough and accurate guide to negotiating a safe and easy path through the various processes and changing laws involved in financing a home (whether it's a permanent home, a holiday home, a buy-to-let purchase or a new-build), and makes essential reading for anyone wanting to avoid the possible pitfalls and problems of entering the Portuguese property market. Follow our simple steps, and yours should be a smooth and simple experience

Finding your dream property or plot of land is just the start of the process – getting the right financial and legal advice is vital

Buying Guide

FINDING AN AGENT

- Government licenced estate agents (*imobiliarias*) are identifiable by their *mediador autorizado* number, which always starts with the letters AMI.
- There are a huge number of reputable British estate agents (as listed in our Agents Directory) dealing with Portuguese property, with offices or representatives based in various areas of Portugal, although the largest number of Portugal-based British agents is in the Algarve.
- Good agents will save you time and trouble by giving honest advice on the climate, ambience and lifestyle of your chosen area. They will also put you in touch with a surveyor and lawyer (*advogado*).
- Ensure anyone acting for you is entirely independent and not reliant upon regular recommendation.

POOC LAW

The European Union's POOC (Classification Plans of the Coast Border) law will have an impact on property development and therefore prices in the Algarve. Designed to protect the environment of coastal areas with special protected areas or *zona terrestre de protecção*, it enforces a limit of 200m distance from the coastline for new developments on the Sines/Algarve coastline. Properties already built close to the sea will have an added value as a result.

The first step is to find the right property

STEP ONE: FINDING THE RIGHT PROPERTY

Before you even begin to contemplate the financial and legal complexities of buying a house in Portugal, you have to find the right property in the first place, and while some people find this a stressful process, for many this is the most enjoyable part. Choosing between Portugal's many beautiful and interesting regions is the very first step on the ladder, and our Region Guides later in the book (starting on page 82) should help put some flesh on the bones of what you already know about the country.

Of course, most people will immediately think of the popular region of the Algarve, on the southern coast of Portugal, as a potential location for their new home, and with its regular (and affordable) transport links to the UK, its pleasant climate, its beautiful beaches, its well developed tourist infrastructure and pockets of expat communities, it is certainly an obvious choice. However, this overlooks the attractions of all the other regions of Portugal, from the peaceful rural life of the Beiras to the bustling city pace of Lisbon, Porto and Coimbra, from the amazing scenery and cheaper prices of Alentejo to the greenery and tranquillity of the Costa Verde and the flower bedecked, near-tropical island of Madeira.

The most obvious way to get acquainted with a particular region is to spend some time there, and perhaps you have already spent a holiday in your chosen area and this has influenced your choice. Although this is a great start, you should assume that your chosen region won't always be the same as it was when you were on holiday there. In many Portuguese towns, including even the busiest coastal resorts, many gift shops and restaurants will close down outside the main summer season. At the other extreme, the quiet fishing village where you spent a pleasant, warm autumn fortnight may turn into a bustling, tourist-ridden strip of bars and discos in high season!

Also consider the environs of your chosen location well: think about amenities (hospitals, shops, beaches, sports facilities, schools) that you may want within walking (or a short drive's) distance, see if there are

Steps to Buying

good schools in the area and find out how near the place is to the main road and rail routes. These can make or break a decision, depending on your reasons for moving. For instance, the expat communities and international schools found in Lisbon and the Algarve are ideal for families and retirees, while those wanting to immerse themselves in genuine Portuguese life will probably avoid these places. Meanwhile those looking to run an agricultural or wine business or simply enjoy a rural style of life will be looking at the quieter areas such as the Beiras, Ribatejo and Costa Verde.

Then, of course, there is the style of property to think about and Portugal certainly has the lot. With everything from new-build apartment complexes (many of which are constructed within the grounds of the various high quality golf courses and country clubs) and smart city townhouses to tumble-down farmhouse ruins and village cottages, as well as grand manor houses and modern villas, there's plenty of choice in the Portuguese property market. This is borne out by our overviews of each of the Portuguese regions' property markets, starting on page 26.

But where to start? As is the case wherever you look for a house, whether in the UK or abroad, there are many ways of going about finding the right house for you. You should start by deciding what style of house you are looking for. Are you prepared to put in the large amount of work and money required by a renovation project? Are you looking for a modern apartment in a serviced complex with all amenities on site? Are you seeking a period property in the countryside with a large plot of land?

Once you have a rough idea of what you want, you then need to find it. These days this can be done quite easily on an independent basis, and the many specialist magazines and websites available (and, of course, the Price Guides that you'll find later in this book, from page 192) should give a good idea as to what is available in your chosen area. There are also plenty of contacts throughout the book for agents, either UK- or Portugal-based, who have plenty of further properties on their books.

If you have the time to spare, the ideal way to find your dream property is to visit your chosen region and pop into the various estate agents (*imobiliarias*) offices to see what property is for sale at that moment. If your time in Portugal is likely to be limited to a week's or even a weekend's viewing trip, many Portugal-based agents will be happy to round up a selection of properties (based on a set of criteria that you can provide them with) to view over a few days. Most Portuguese agents have English-speaking staff who will do everything from showing you round prospective properties to explaining the buying system, but make sure you have a phrasebook handy, just in case!

You should also bear in mind that in some areas of Portugal, especially outside the main urban and tourist centres, many properties are sold privately. So if you are looking in a particular village or town, look out for For Sale (*venda se* or *para venda*) signs in windows of houses and speak directly to the owner. This is where the help of a Portuguese friend to act as interpreter may come in useful!

When you do make your trip out to Portugal for your viewings, be prepared to dismiss some properties from the agent's shortlist straight away. Once you get to the *imobiliarias* office and see the properties' specifications in detail, you might discover that, for instance, the dimensions of the rooms are too small, the house is right next to a railway or that it's not connected to the mains electricity or water (and you're not prepared to take on the extra work needed to

ARCHITECTS

- Architects can command between 8 and 10% of the entire construction figure.
- Architects should make daily site visits to resolve queries and to ensure quality control in terms of work and materials used.
- Provisional acceptance of the property by you is usually made when the civil engineer fully inspects the property and checks that corrections are made. There are specific time limits within which to inspect the constructed property and if you fail to keep them, you may lose your rights to have matters put right.
- Ensure that, prior to acceptance of the property, you prepare a 'snagging list' which is agreed by the engineer/architect and the builder and agree a time limit to have all these problems completed.
- Once the property has been provisionally and/or finally accepted, the *engenheiro civil* has to formally confirm that the property's construction is in line with planning permission, and then apply for the habitation licence (*licença de habitabilidade*) from the Land Registry. (This is vital as without this the property cannot be sold.)
- A properly drafted building contract will avoid some basic pitfalls.

Buying Guide

PROPRIEDADE HORIZONTAL

● Before an apartment block or townhouse can be sold, the building must be officially divided into individual units via the deed of *propriedade horizontal*. This should exactly describe each unit (listed alphabetically) including measurements of rooms, floor space, parking and the location of the unit within a property's structure. All shared areas will be shown.

● Until the *propriedade horizontal* deed has been drawn up, a property does not legally exist. Without it, you cannot formally buy or sell a particular apartment, register it at the Land Registry or register it for a mortgage.

● Apartments may have two sets of title deeds: one for the individual unit and one for the property or block it belongs to.

● Usually a monthly fee is paid by each unit owner for the property's upkeep, the amount depending on the allocated percentage value of their property within the building as a whole.

● While the democratic voting system allows all owners within the property to elect and dismiss administrators, in some developments (especially those sold under specific tourist legislation), it is impossible to dismiss the administrator unless there is undeniable evidence of their negligence.

Before the work begins, make sure you draw up a detailed schedule, with deadlines set for all stages of construction

connect it up). However, on the other hand, you may also find that you spot a couple of other prime candidates, which for some reason the agent didn't think you'd like, that you add to the viewing list.

The important thing to remember when viewing a number of properties over just a few days is to take notes and ask plenty of questions. Quite often you will get to the end of the day, having viewed three or four houses, and you'll find that you've already forgotten which of them had, say, the open fireplace or the nicest swimming pool. If you have a digital camera, take pictures in each property as you make notes, as this is a great help when reviewing which houses you'd like to visit for a second time.

A second visit is usually necessary to cement your first impressions of the place, but also to confirm details that may have been overlooked in the initial excitement. Check for things like damp, subsidence, access, boundaries, roof and exterior wall quality, flooding and other details. Most of these things can be seen while you're there, although some things you will have to ask the agent to confirm. And while these details will also be checked when you get a survey done, it's worth getting some impressions of overall quality and upkeep at this early stage, especially in the upcoming areas where the property market doesn't hang around!

In Portugal all properties are sold on a freehold basis. However, if the property you're looking at is in a shared building (such as an apartment block), the shared areas are sold under of the law of *propriedade horizontal* (for more information on this, see the Propriedade Horizontal box, left) This law specifies details of payments covering the common areas in a property (including things like the division of service charge payments for upkeep of, say, the stairwell, roof, intercom system and so on), stating what these common areas are and who is to manage the building. The law stipulates that a condominium association must be created with administrators (voted for by the co-owners at an annual meeting) who will be in charge of cleaning and upkeep.

STEP TWO: STARTING FROM SCRATCH

If you have looked at a wide range of properties in your chosen area and none seems right, you may consider the possibility of buying a plot of land and building your own home. Or perhaps it has always been your dream to oversee the construction of your dream villa overlooking the Atlantic, or maybe sitting on the hills of the Serra da Estrela national park. However you end up at the decision to building your own home, there are plenty of things to take into account, even before the foundations are dug.

Firstly, you will need to find a suitable plot of land. As you will see in the Price Guides later in this book (starting on page 192), there are plenty of plots of land for sale in all regions of Portugal. Some will just be plain, uncultivated land; others will be worked farmland perhaps planted with fruit or pine trees, vines or crops; while others will include some outbuildings or perhaps ruins of an ancient home or mill. Whichever of these options you decide upon, there are some basic yet important things to bear in mind. These include size (will it be large enough to accommodate the size of house and grounds you want?), access (will you have to lay a driveway to link it to the nearest road?),

Steps to Buying

If you plan to add a swimming pool to your garden, get a few estimates before deciding on a particular builder

utilities (does the plot have an electricity and water supply or will you have to arrange to have them connected?), boundaries (is it clear where your plot ends and your neighbours' plots begin?), restrictions (are you allowed to build on the land?), terrain (is the land too steep, rocky or riven with tree roots to be able to build a stable home on?) and rights of way (are there any public footpaths or neighbour's access roads that cross your land?). Most of these details will be checked by your estate agent or lawyer, but they are fundamental details that all too often get overlooked in the excitement and exhilaration of finding the right location.

You will, of course, need to find out if the legal permitted use of the land fits with your project. To find this out, you (or your representative) will need to check the municipal plans (*planos directores municipais*) and the Land Registry records (*conservatória do Registro Predial*). These dictate whether or not a construction is permitted on the land, and if there are any further restrictions on the construction (perhaps it is designated to only be used in connection with agriculture or non-tourist development).

With these details cleared up, you are ready to employ a professional architect (*arquitecto*) to draw up the plans of your dream home. Your estate agent, lawyer and new neighbours should be able to recommend one, although you can approach the Association of Portuguese Architects (AAP) as a starting point. You should also ask any *arquitecto* for his references, whom you should contact and, if possible, arrange to visit to inspect the work completed.

Once you've chosen the right *arquitecto*, you should obtain a full quotation from them for drawing up the initial sketches of your ideas, calculating costs, producing the final plans and supervising work on the build. Getting the initial design right at an early is vital as redesigns can work out as costly and time consuming, especially once planning permission has been granted. After these initial plans have been approved by you, they will be sent to the local *câmara municipal* (town hall) for inspection. An experienced *arquitecto* should be able to identify potential problems such as poor drainage, but you or your architect will also need to employ the services of a civil engineer (*engenheiro civil*) who will ensure that your planned construction is in line with planning permission.

BUILDER CHECKLIST

- Any contract between you and the builder should be checked and amended by your *advogado* to ensure it is legally binding and fair.
- Ensure that the quotation you choose has building schedules, dates of phase completions and stage payment dates.
- Watch out for hidden extras and make sure VAT (*imposto sobre o valor acrescentado* or *IVA*) has been included.
- Stick to agreed schedules.
- You may want to employ a project manager to oversee the build for you. Although they may charge a hefty fee, they can pull strings to get deadlines met and materials delivered on time, thus saving you money in over-stepping schedules.
- Under general law, broadly speaking the builder must guarantee the construction minor works for the period of one year and major works for five years. This guarantee is, however, only as good as the builder.
- Remember that in Portugal, new houses have a five-year guarantee that builders must respect.

Buying Guide

Discuss all your ideas with your architect and builder, right down to the quality of finish in your completed rooms

COMMERCIAL NEW-BUILDS

- If you are constructing a property for use as a business premises, you will need a *licença de utilização* (licence for use) from the town hall (*câmara municipal*).
- Non-residential licences must exactly show the commercial or industrial usage of a property (for more on this, see the *Starting A Business* section within the Living & Working chapter).
- The *escritura's* (title deeds) contents are perhaps even more crucial, and should include an accurate land and property description.
- On completion of a build, the local authority will inspect it and grant the *licença de habitabilidade*. *Escrituras* cannot be signed without this.

With the plans drawn up, you now need to find a builder (*construtor*) and, again, these can be recommended by your estate agent, neighbours and even by the *arquitecto* and *engenheiro*. When looking for a *construtor*, check they have a permit to build (*alvará*). If hiring a builder and architect together, be aware that while the architect's job is to monitor the work done by the builder, your builder will also need a tender to contract from you to start work. Ensure, too, that you have a contract between you and the builder, drawn up with reference to the Portuguese Civil Code. With the building contract signed, the builder will apply for a *licença de habitabilidade* (habitation licence) and *licença de construcçao* (construction licence), as these are legal requirements for the completed building to be registered with the Land Registry (*Registro Predial*).

Before the work begins, make sure you draw up a detailed schedule, with deadlines set for all stages of construction, from the digging of foundations and laying of cables through to the roof being tiled, the interior being decorated and the house being habitable. If you're not planning on staying in Portugal throughout the period of construction, you should instruct the architect to oversee the works for you, and inform you of any hitches that may occur. However, some people also consider employing a project manager, who will keep a close eye on the work and do their best to make sure deadlines are met.

Building your own home certainly isn't a project to be taken on lightly, but the satisfaction of having had a hand in designing your dream property often outweighs the problems that crop up during the construction stage.

STEP THREE: MONEY MATTERS

As already discussed, finding your dream property or plot of land in Portugal is just the start of the process. One of the most crucial aspects of securing your dream home, however, is obviously ensuring that you have sufficient funds to cover your new property. You must ensure that you have enough to cover not only the asking price of

Steps to Buying

the property, but also the cost of any legal fees, deposits, agents' fees, *notário* charges, renovations, essential works and the cost of moving itself.

Many people will opt for a mortgage (*hipoteca*), either with a Portuguese or UK bank. If the Portuguese property is to be a second or holiday home, the mortgage may well be taken out on an existing property in the UK. Or it can be taken out directly on the Portuguese house. There are also the options of buying through an offshore company (explained in more detail below) or, if you're lucky enough to have the funds, of buying with cash. This is a route that more and more people are taking these days, having cashed in on the property price increases in the UK by selling their British home and funding their new home abroad with the profits.

Whether you take out a mortgage with a Portuguese or British bank, a deposit of between 10-25 percent of the purchase price will normally be required to secure your mortgage as well as the legal fees. For all borrowers, the Portuguese legal system's rule of using the purchase property as security for the loan sets out several mortgage types, and the types of mortgage available are repayment, endowment, ISA and pension-linked.

It is often considered easier to take out a mortgage with a Portuguese bank, thus avoiding the problems of the ever-changing exchange rate between the pound and the euro. However, there are certain things that go against having a Portuguese mortgage. Firstly, overseas mortgages are not under the protection of the UK Consumer Credit Act or the UK Mortgage Code. Secondly, the Portuguese mortgage system is mainly designed for permanent residents and its limitations can be strict regarding those purchasing a property in Portugal as a second home.

If you are seeking a mortgage to fund a renovation or new-build you'll find that mortgages can usually be obtained for construction projects but probably not on the price of the plot. A lender requires a life policy and building insurance for the final property value.

If, on the other hand, you are buying a commercial property (a working farm or vineyard, perhaps, or a restaurant or shop), Portuguese lenders require a thorough business plan before agreeing to lend money to fund the purchase.

Both foreign and Portuguese resident buyers' loans are capped at a maximum of 80 percent of either the valuation or purchase price (whichever is less). A buyer's net take-home pay, pension or rental income plus existing financial burdens (such as an UK mortgage/rent, bank loans or maintenance payments) are used for assessment. No more than 40 percent of the net monthly income is allowed for Portuguese mortgage payments; so, for example, a net income of £2,000 would mean your maximum mortgage repayment is £600.

The option to buy through an offshore company is perhaps best suited to buyers at the top end of the market who want to remain anonymous, due to the costs involved in setting up an offshore company and annual costs including making the company accounts available for auditing. Buying through an offshore or so-called 'shelf company', created specifically for the purchase of property, will encounter capital gains tax (*imposto de mais valias*) in the UK. Residents are only asked for 25 percent on half the capital gained on selling.

As an offshore company never "dies", there will be no change of ownership but you will still attract inheritance tax (*imposto sobre de successões e boações*) in the UK, as the value of your shares in the

MORTGAGES

- The mortgage will not begin until you have provisionally registered your purchase and the mortgage, so your loan should be in place before looking for a property.
- The purchase of the property and the mortgage must be registered at the Land Registry before the final deed of sale, and purchase and mortgage cannot be signed before the bank releases the funds. In the case of apartments or town houses under *propriedade horizontal*, this will be impossible until the property is fully completed from a legal point of view.
- There is a minimum borrowing figure of £15,000.
- Although mortgages can run from five to 30 years they normally coincide with your retirement age.
- Your home is at risk if you do not keep repayments on a mortgage or other loan secured on it.
- The sterling equivalent of your liability under a foreign currency mortgage may be increased by exchange rate movements.

When buying offshore, rather than buying a property and registering it in your name with the Land Registry, the offshore company buys it and you own shares

Buying Guide

Expect to pay around 450 euros for a full structural survey, 350 euros for a valuation and 450 euros for a homebuyer's survey

company will be added to your worldwide estate and when you die your executors will pay 40 percent on any value over the £250,000 limit. (This figure is subject to fluctuation, and may go up or down in the Chancellor's budget.)

The key point is that, rather than buying a property and registering it in your name with the Land Registry (*Registro Predial*), the offshore company buys it and you own shares in it. This means that your company's name will be registered as owner at the Land Registry and your personal details will remain private. When you sell, instead of selling the property, you sell shares in the company. The company normally avoids paying capital gains tax and inheritance tax in the offshore country.

STEP FOUR: MANAGING YOUR EUROS

Buying in Portugal inevitably means converting your pounds sterling into euros at some point during the purchase. You will already know the price of your new home in euros, and this should not change unless, for example, you upgrade the specification of a new-build villa by adding a swimming pool. However, you will not know the ultimate cost in sterling until you have bought all the euros.

The key question, then, is when to do it. The risk-free solution, which is offered by many foreign exchange brokers – often at better rates than banking institutions – is to buy all your euros at the outset, so that fluctuating exchange rates and global currency influences do not affect the value of your money. This is called buying currency for 'spot', and it often also includes the option to fix exchange rates for the future, making savings as you do so. For example, you may save 4.25 percent if you buy six months ahead, and up to nine percent if you buy 12 months ahead.

A less risk-free option is to simply buy euros as and when you need to transfer them to Portugal. Remember, however, that the exchange rate could vary wildly between the moment when you make the initial signature on the property contract and that when you come to make payment. (The value of the euro against sterling can go up as well as down, though!). Always take some independent financial advice, perhaps from several sources, and think this option through very carefully before committing yourself.

RATES OF INTEREST IN PORTUGAL

Set by the European Central Bank, these mortgage rates were in place in July 2003:

- 3% for marginal lending facility
- 2% for main refinancing
- 1% for deposits

Borrowers normally begin by paying a low amount in the first year, the sum increasing slightly thereafter. In some instances, advances made during the construction of the property are payable at a higher rate than when the property has been built.

STEP FIVE: THE SURVEY

Obviously when buying a property in the UK, it is actually impossible to secure a mortgage from most financial institutions unless you have had a structural survey made on the property you are buying. In Portugal, having a survey (*inspeção*) is not a legal requirement for buying a property, but it is definitely worth doing, if only to put your mind at rest about potential problems the property may have.

While it is possible to discuss and check out all kinds of things like damp, cracks and boundaries at the first and second viewings, there are many things that an engineer (*engenheiro*) or valuer (*availiador*) may

Steps to Buying

In some cases, surveys can be tied into the contract as a condition of purchase to be paid for by the vendor

Even the most attractive pools may have hidden problems

pick up by doing a survey. These can include subsidence and the problems of flooding and termites that can affect properties across Portugal. There are the more immediate issues of water ingress, structural problems with swimming pools, aged electrics, badly connected gas or water facilities, corroded plumbing and leaking roofs to bear in mind.

Having a survey is a wise move to protect against paying over-inflated prices or purchasing a property that will require lots of work. This is particularly the case for renovated properties, especially those that have been done as basic DIY projects, perhaps using low quality materials. It is also important to get a survey done on 'new'-builds that are over five years old, as this is generally the limit of guarantee that builders offer on work. So even if the property seems in relatively good order, there may be hidden problems laying in wait for you that a surveyor should be able to pick up on.

If you instruct a surveyor to perform a full structural survey, they will usually check electrical wiring, sewage removal, plumbing, electricity supply, all heating, swimming pools and any other structures on the property, such as outbuildings, poolhouses and stables. Problems such as rising damp, cracked walls, levels of flooring, rusting water pipes and holes in the roof will also be picked up on, but if there are particular areas of concern, such as a particular patch of garden, for instance, or the swimming pool heating system, these can be specified when you commission the survey in the first place.

In some cases, surveys can be tied into the contract as a condition of purchase to be paid by the vendor and some lenders will want to see a survey's result before agreeing to any loan. But bear in mind that many lenders will insist on nominating a surveyor themselves. In these cases, you can also employ your own surveyor to get more in-depth picture of the fabric of the building for yourself. If you use a UK surveyor ensure they have professional indemnity insurance covering Portugal.

Expect to pay around 450 euros for a full structural survey,

OFFSHORE LENDERS

● As the buyer, you need to thoroughly research the offshore company, and have a share purchase agreement prepared, with warranties for the company and property to secure your investment's full protection.
● Pending property tax reforms, which come to fruition in January 2004, will mean a flat rate of 15% property transfer tax, regardless of the value of the property. (See box on this new IMT tax, which will replace
the old SISA tax, on page 55).
● These changes will also impact capital gains tax charged, and sellers could incur a 25% charge on the difference between the registered value of a property and the actual value it is sold for, instead of the 10% currently charged. This tax will be asked for in cash, which could hit owners whose financial gain looks good on paper but is not yet realised.

Buying Guide

No matter how good the property looks, try to get a survey before signing any contracts or parting with any cash

around 350 euros for a valuation and 450 euros for a homebuyer's survey (very similar to a structural survey) on an average size house with a swimming pool.

If purchasing a plot of land, you can pace its boundaries and check for anything that interrupts them initially. A surveyor will be needed if any boundaries need redefining. Surveyors should belong to the *Associação Portuguesa dos Chartered Surveyors*, a branch of the Royal Institution de Chartered Surveyors (RICS).

STEP SIX: THE BUYING PROCESS

Before you go ahead and buy your property, you will need a *número de indentificação fiscal* or *NIF* (fiscal identity number). Like the National Insurance number in the UK, the *NIF* will in turn allow you to gain a tax card (*cartão de contribuinte*) without which it is impossible, legally, to buy a home or open a bank account in Portugal. To obtain a temporary *NIF* number (until your final number is issued), take certified copies of your passport, plus a small fee, and attend a fiscal department or tax office (finanças). (An *advogado* can apply for your *NIF* on your behalf). You should keep hold of notification of your *NIF*, as it is crucial for for all future correspondence with the tax authorities, including the payment of property and income taxes, and registration of your property with the Land Registry.

Like the National Insurance number in the UK, the NIF will allow you to gain a tax card, without which it is impossible to buy a home or open a bank account in Portugal

Once you have your *NIF* and your *cartão de contribuinte* (and of course you have picked out your ideal property and organised your finances) you will now need to instruct your *advogado* to undertake a number of checks.

First you will also need a certified copy (usually this will be done by a *notário* at the town hall) of the vendor's *escritura* (title deeds) that proves their ownership of the property. Your *advogado* will confirm this with the Land Registry (*Registro Predial*), where the

Steps to Buying

property's legal title will be checked against a Land Registry certificate (*certidão de teor do Registro Predial*). This crucial document is proof of ownership and is vital for the final exchange of ownership. The *certidão de teor do Registro Predial* shows the property's legal owner and gives a full legal history of a property. Furthermore its thorough physical descriptions of the property and included land show any potential faults or structural problems that have been noted in the past. The *certidão* is a public record that also reveals any charges and mortgages existing on the property which should be discharged on or before the signing of the transfer deed under which you are to acquire the property.

Your *advogado* will also check the *caderneta predial* (the tax registration of a property as filed with the Land Registry). Again, key to the exchange of the property title, the *caderneta predial* from the finance department (*repartição de finanças*) is linked to the tax office notification of the property. It proves that the property is registered at the tax office and, crucially, that the vendor has an official tax number. The property's full description must match exactly the contents of the Land Registry certificate (*certidão de teor do Registro Predial*).

The *caderneta* will also detail the property's fiscal value (*valor trubutável*), which determines the rates (*contribuição autárquica*) you will be charged on the property. (Newer properties may not have a *caderneta predial*, but prior to the transfer deed's execution you will have to show that an application has been made for registration of the property at the fiscal department.)

Your *advogado* will also check with the tax office (*finanças*) for payment of community charge and municipal rates (*contribuição autárquica*) on the asset worth, split, if necessary, into rural and urban property. They will also (as long as time permits) obtain a certificate confirming that there are no debts secured against the property at the tax office.

Once these details have been confirmed and the checks completed, you will need to sign the initial promissory contract (*contracto promessa de compra e venda*). This is signed in the presence of a *notário*, usually at the *câmara municipal* (town hall) with the vendor and buyer (or their representatives) and their *advogados* present.

If you aren't able to be present, you can either assign a representative to sign on your behalf (probably your *advogado* in Portugal) or you can meet a UK-based notary who will witness your signature and pass it to the *notário* in Portugal. At this point, the deposit is payable.

Not to be confused with a lawyer, the *notário* is a government legal representative who usually works at the town hall as a witness or registrar, executing public documents. Their signature and official seal attests contracts and title deeds, and a *notário* must be present at the signing of the two main documents involved in the sale of a Portuguese property, namely the *contrato promessa de compra e venda* (initial promissory contract) and the *escritura publica de compra e venda* (the transfer of title deed).

The initial *contrato promessa* details the finer points of exactly what you are purchasing, and includes all the fundamental information about the sale. It will include the name and full description of the parties (vendor and buyer) and their legal representatives and the capacity in which they intervene. It will also include the full description of the property in terms of a physical

THE NEW IMT TAX

● The Portuguese government is introducing radical changes to the property transfer tax system, which will affect all existing and potential property owners, but are especially punitive on anyone buying through an offshore company.

● Up until now, under the SISA transfer tax system, the purchaser and vendor could agree a sale price, but then write a much lower figure into the transfer deeds on completion. This way, less tax would be payable by both parties, and the government lost out on revenue.

● Now, though, far-reaching reforms under the proposed IMT (*imposto municipal sobre as transmissões*) tax will mean that only an official valuation will count for the taxation of a property transfer. The notary will have to have a copy of the promissory contract to make sure the sale price tallies with the declared value in the *escritura*.

● IMT charge rates on property will be banded as follows:
up to 80,000 euros = 0%
80,000-110,000 euros = 2%
110,000-150,000 euros = 5%
150,000-250,000 euros = 7%
250,000-500,000 euros = 8%
over 500,000 euros = 6%
All rural properties will initially be charged at 5%.

Buying Guide

BUYING: A CHECKLIST

DO ensure you use only a fully qualified *advogado* or *solicitadores*, or international lawyer practised in Portuguese property law.

DO make sure you can understand all the professionals you deal with. If you don't, take along an interpreter.

DON'T sign any contract or agreement you don't understand.

DON'T sign a promissory contract (*contrato promesso de compra e venda*) without having a property surveyed (especially if the property is more than five years old). You stand to lose your deposit should you withdraw.

DO get a survey, even if vendors and agents try to discourage it to speed up the process.

DON'T move somewhere without researching the climate and spending time there first.

DO ensure your estate agent has an AMI number.

DON'T go ahead with a purchase without having checked the legal title (*escritura*), the habitation licence (*licença de habitabilidade*) and the licence of use (*licença de utilização*).

DON'T buy a property without checking its *certidão de teor* from the Land Registry, otherwise you may be taking responsibility for its debts.

DON'T buy a resale project without stipulating that any existing mortgage is discharged at the point of sale, to avoid taking on debts.

DO Arrange for a survey of the property and ascertain whether it is insured and see if it meets your requirements.

description, dimensions and included land as well as the title number at the Land Registry and fiscal department or tax office (*finanças*). Also spelt out in this initial *contrato* are the purchase price (including how and when it should be paid), the list of fixtures and fittings, known as the *inventário* or inventory, included with the property (or the extra price being asked for these if they are not included) and the confirmation of the completion date, which is when the property will be transferred into your name and the *escritura* signed.

In Portugal, the buyer is liable to pay for all of the purchase costs, including *notário* fees, Land Registry fees and transfer taxes. The tax currently known as SISA, which was charged on a sliding scale depending upon the property's 'declared value' is to be replaced in January 2004 by the new IMT tax (see box on page 55). The vendor is liable for all costs in connection with the property up to the completion date. In the instance of any dispute, the law and courts which govern the *contrato de promesso* will deal with it.

The signing of the *contrato* binds both buyer and vendor to the sale, and at this stage it becomes an expensive process for either side to pull out. Unless the *contrato* states otherwise, if a vendor changes his mind after having signed the *contrato*, he is liable to pay twice the amount of the deposit into the buyer's bank account. If a buyer changes his mind at this stage, they will lose their deposit.

With the demands of the *contrato promesso de compra e venda* secured, your *escritura de compra e venda* will be drafted by the *notário*. Before this *escritura* is signed, a final inspection of the property is recommended and, on a more fundamental note, it must be declared that both the buyer and vendor understand the procedure (this is often the part of the process that requires an interpreter).

Both the buyer and vendor (or their legal representatives) will need to sign the *escritura* in the presence of the *notário*, and upon payment of the remaining purchase balance to the *notário* and the *advogado*, the title of ownership will pass from the vendor to the buyer. The *notário* will check that the stamp duty (*imposto de selo*) has been paid, ask to see receipts proving tax has been paid and that the property's required habitation licence (*licença de habitabilidade*) exists before allowing the exchange of title to take place. All other legal fees will be paid outside of the meeting with the *notário*. The *escritura*, being a public document, will be kept at the public records office. You can access it whenever you choose upon payment of a small fee.

Finally, now that the property is legally in your name, you must register it with the Land Registry (*Registro Predial*) by sending a certified copy of the *escritura* to the local *Registro Predial* office. It may take some time to complete registration process, depending upon the workload of each office. However, when registration is completed, you are confirmed as the full owner. Simply put, this seals your ownership at the Land Registry office and the tax office (*repartição de finanças*).

And with that, you are now the proud owner of your very own property or plot of land in Portugal. Whether you are retiring to the country, moving there to work or simply investing in a holiday home, from page 58 you'll find a complete guide to living and working in Portugal, from finding a job to registering for a residence's permit. But first, it's worth totting up the final costs of all the key expenses, just so you have a rough idea of how heavily your dream life abroad could hit your pocket...

Steps to Buying

Before collecting the keys to your dream Portuguese property, you need to register it with the Land Registry

THE FINAL BALANCE SHEET

Based upon the purchase of a property costing 150,000 euros in Portugal, with a deposit of 20 percent, here is a summary of the typical costs involved

Bank or finance company loan	120,000 euros
Monthly repayments (rate of 3.75% over 20 years)	£514.28 / 720 euros
Arrangement fee (0.25% loan)	£215
Valuation fee 0.20% of purchase price or £1,000, whichever is lower	£215
Legal fee – in own name – if offshore	£1,400 / £1,000
Searches	approx £100
Notary fees*	approx 2,000 euros
Land Registry* * Notary fees and Land Registry costs vary from area to area	approx 1,000 euros
Stamp Duty	approx 2,600 euros

Buying Guide

LIVING AND WORKING IN PORTUGAL

Over the next 14 pages, you'll find a complete guide to what your new life in Portugal might hold, from how to renovate a property to finding the right job

What may seem like a romantic dream prospect to a British buyer can be expensive and hazardous if not tackled carefully

Once you have bought your dream property in Portugal, there are a thousand and one things to think about to ensure that the transition to a new life in the sun goes as smoothly as possible. For example, you may be thinking of carrying out some home improvements, or you may have nagging doubts about the standard of health provision there. Then there is the question of residency and all the legalities that must be adhered to. And what if you wish to let your property out for parts of the year? Who can manage it for you in your absence? And what taxes must be paid? And to whom? And when?

All these vital questions, and many more, are answered in this fact-filled, easy-to-follow chapter on the practical realities of beginning a new life in Portugal.

Living & Working in Portugal

It is essential to obtain a true costing for a renovation project, so ask various reputable builders and architects for estimates

YOUR NEW HOME

RENOVATION PROJECTS
The Portuguese home owner's preference for all things modern means that Britons shouldn't face stiff competition on the property market when seeking renovation properties. But what may seem like a romantic dream prospect to a British buyer (and indeed such dreams *do* come true, as shown in the Case Studies section, starting on page 72), can be expensive and hazardous if not tackled carefully. Consideration should be given to your budget and how you'll recoup what you spend before even thinking about getting the builders in.

Remember, too, that unless the project is a genuine labour of love, it's unlikely that the market value of your renovated home will reflect the time and effort you have put into it. Of course, this all depends on the degree of work and amount of renovation needed, but repairing fundamental parts of the building's structure, like its walls or roof, may not always reap the amount you spend on it if you're thinking of selling on sooner rather than later.

Buying Guide

RENOVATION TOP TIPS

- Roofs can be expensive to repair, so check the existing roof is sound. If it is in disrepair, get a proper estimate.
- Check that an existing structure is waterproof.
- Damp-proofing isn't essential but, if needed, can become a major budget drain.
- Look out for steel or iron pipes in older homes' plumbing, as their replacement is costly and, if unattended, they could corrode or leak.
- Check for basic utilities such as water, sewers, electricity and gas connections in rural locations; their addition can be costly.
- Ensure that your property is not at risk of flooding, and that your electricity is installed above established floodlines.
- Get hold of a building licence (*licença de obras*) from the local authority before work is undertaken.
- Adopt a precise approach to the rebuilding of an original feature. Leave it alone or hire a competent craftsman.
- Have a clause in your *escritura* stating that your purchase rests upon the granting of planning and building permissions if considering adding new windows or extensions.
- Do ensure that any timber is insulated from damp and, if timber treatment is needed, budget for it.
- Specify starting/finishing dates in your builder's contract, with financial forfeits if these are not met.

BUDGET

Depending upon the work involved in renovating your picturesque *casa de país* (country house), you can often expect to pay half the purchase price again for renovation costs. The choice of carrying out work yourself or employing a renovation team will affect this sum, and while doing it yourself will necessitate a command of Portuguese in terms of getting materials and planning, it will also curtail labour costs.

The most important first step is obtaining a *true* costing of the renovation project, and for this you will need to ask a number of reputable builders and architects for *orçamentos* (quotes) or *estimativas* (estimates). Both should cover all building, electrical and plumbing work, materials and labour but remember that the lowest quote won't always guarantee the highest quality or quickest job. Look at the estimates carefully and bear in mind that you're always likely to need a back-up pool of funds in case things go over budget.

EMPLOYING A RENOVATION TEAM

A renovation team will feature an architect, a builder and labourers, and, unless you're prepared to do it yourself, securing a project manager to keep an eye on schedules and works done should avoid nightmare scenarios of incomplete jobs and huge bills from elongated schedules and missed deadlines. Keep around 10 percent of the total costs for your manager's fees. Giving a thorough explanation of works you require will avoid disappointment and throwing good money after bad.

UTILITIES

ELECTRICITY

The question of installing your own generator will depend on whether or not your new home is off the beaten track and if electricity is already supplied. Installing electricity in a rural area currently costs around 4.50 euros per metre of cabling used. If buying an older property, ask a qualified electrician to inspect and approve the existing wiring for safety. Portuguese homes commonly have just one plug point per room, serviced by a two-round prong plug, so invest in adaptors or multi-point extension leads (unless you intend to rewire).

GAS

Gás de Portugal is the main supplier of piped gas in Portugal, largely around the Lisbon area. However, most people use butane or propane gas bottles (*garrafa de gas butano*) for cooking and heating the home, and these cost around 30 euros a bottle. A combined gas heating system for water and home heating is a relatively cheap energy source.

WATER

The presence of a water supply is not to be taken for granted. Rural homeowners with a well (*poço*) in the grounds will need to check its reliability over a number of years. An alternative is to locate a borehole (*furo*) but you will need the necessary licence from the town hall (*câmara municipal*). Alternatively, you may have a water tank (*cisterna*) that will need occasional replenishment by a water company or from the village pump.

Under the remit of the local authority or a private company, water connection charges vary and you may need to pay a standing charge whether you have used the water or not. Water can be an expensive commodity and your geographical location will affect the price you pay.

Living & Working in Portugal

In the north of the country, water is more plentiful (the Costa Verde's greenery has not appeared by accident!), while the Algarve's arid nature means householders with swimming pools can pay very high prices for their water supply.

If you are buying a more modern apartment, remember to have your water contract registered in your name with the local authority.

Most newer homes in Portugal are well insulated and should not need much heating in winter

- As with all bills, if you are a non-Portuguese resident, you should give your home address in Britain or that of your financial representative or *advogado* to the local authority.
- Check that your supply is healthy to drink; if discoloured, definitely do not drink it! Do as the Portuguese and buy bottled water for drinking.

HEATING

Even if the main reason for moving to Portugal is for the climate, you'll still need to consider heating your home in winter. Once you've resigned yourself to leaving the creature comfort of central heating back in Britain, you'll have to choose *how* to heat your house. Many homes use gas heaters, while older properties will often have an open fire or wood-burning stove that also heats water. Electricity is generally not favoured, due to its costs, although some homes use night storage heaters, but damp-proofed and well insulated homes (especially new-builds that must have double-cavity walls) balance out big bills.

On the rare occasion that you find a central heating system, check that the ventilation is adequate, as gas and carbon monoxide poisoning is a possible result if not. You may also find you need a dehumidifier.

Solar heating is viable, and this can be economical and efficient when combined with electric or gas heating and, in fact, it is possible to obtain tax allowances or grants to help install such a system.

GAS CHECKLIST

- Get gas heaters serviced, descaled and checked for carbon monoxide leaks.
- Keep a spare gas bottle in your property.
- Propane gas canisters can be stored outside, as they cope with varying temperatures better than butane gas bottles that must be kept indoors.
- Local shops deliver gas bottles to your home. Simply pay a deposit of around 17.50 euros and exchange empty bottles for new ones.
- Gas tanks can be installed under or above ground.

Buying Guide

UTILITIES AT A GLANCE

● Older *propriedade horizontal* (freehold title properties) may have a shared electricity meter with usage divided per property size.

● The electrical current in Portugal is 220 volts, so powerful appliances like washing machines and even kettles may need an earth built into their plug.

● It is essential for safety that earthed appliances incorporating a three-strand wire should not be used with a two-prong plug outside of an earthed socket.

● Ensure your vendor has paid his utility bills before you move in (see Steps To Buying), and that all bills are in your name.

● Transformers are needed for any appliance you have with a motor, such as a washing machine, so it may be worth buying these appliances when in Portugal.

● Electricity is charged by kWH and your cost rating relies upon your rate of power (*potencia*). You can pay by direct debit (*known as conta certa EDP*) but you will need a form in advance from your bank, not the supply company.

● You will receive bills (*facturas* or *recibos*) on a monthly basis and these include *IVA* and *Taxa Rs* or exploration charges. These will be estimated as meters are read at the end of each year (with adjustments made if necessary).

● Rural electricity supply is often limited to a 15A current; this may limit the number of demanding appliances you use at one time.

AIR-CONDITIONING

An air-conditioning (*ar condicionado*) system is vital in the heat of the summer, but ceiling fans are a cheap alternative, as are portable air-conditioning units. These cost from around £250 and can be bought in Portugal or in Britain then shipped over and installed. (Air conditioning companies and installers are listed in the Service Providers Directory at the back of this book.) Shopping around for a good quote is essential, however, as prices can vary widely from one supplier to the next.

HOME SECURITY

A key issue, especially if you are buying to let, is to ensure you install new locks and keep track of all copies of keys, as insurers will usually give you a cheaper premium for high levels of security. If buying a property in a rural area, be aware that a sounding alarm doesn't do much to deter a burglar who knows no one can hear the alarm and that the police are at least half an hour's drive away. The questions you are likely to be asked for your new home's insurance are as follows:

● What type of property is it?
● Is it a permanent residence or a holiday home?
● Will it be vacant for more than 60 days?
● Is it isolated?
● What security arrangements do you have?
● What is the rebuilding value of your property? (This is generally three-quarters of the price you have paid, plus the contents value)
● Do you require electrical risk cover (protection against power surges for machines including washing machines, televisions)?
● Do you want volcano cover? (Portugal is in a volcano belt)

Security alarms and good lighting are two basic measures to counter criminal activity, while newer-build apartments often also incorporate dead-bolt locks and armoured doors (*porta blindada*). Iron grilles (*grades de segurança*) and locks for shuttered windows are essential in resort areas of the Algarve. Your insurance policy may even specify that metal brackets are employed on doors entering your property, particularly if it will be left empty for periods of time. Other forms of security to consider include:

● 24-hour surveillance
● Motion-sensitive external lights
● Guard dog
● Window locks
● Toughened UPVC glass
● A spy-hole and a door chain
● A housesitter, especially if your home is isolated
● Smoke alarms
● An electric-powered gas detector

PROPERTY TAXES

As with all your taxes, your NIF number (fiscal identity number) is essential for form-filling, and identifies you as a tax-paying resident. Annual taxes range from 1.1 percent to 1.3 percent over the patrimonial value (the property's fiscal figure, dictating its rateable value; this is declared by the tax authorities and is different to market value) and are calculated every six months. From January 2004, it will be 0.8 percent for rural properties and 0.4 to 0.8 percent for urban homes.

Living & Working in Portugal

PROPERTY LETTING

If you are intending to let a holiday home, your property usually needs to be furnished. However, properties in Lisbon and Cascais – which have recently claimed the highest rents in Europe – often don't need to be furnished, as long-term tenants often bring their own.

Usually one month's rent is asked in advance by landlords, and taking an inventory of the property's contents before each new tenant moves in is wise. The landlord usually pays property taxes, while utility bills are met by the tenant, especially if long-term. Tenancy agreements are vital. If you are letting on a holiday basis, however, you will either need to give power of attorney to a third party to supervise tenancies or employ a property agent.

Although your property can be let all year round, June to August is peak season for holiday lettings and the period of guaranteed occupancy. Rental values vary from region to region, dependent, of course, upon location and size. For example, a three-bedroom villa by a golf course in the Algarve can earn £850 per week in July and £500 in winter. A two-bedroom apartment on the island of Madeira, meanwhile, can command £475 throughout the year.

PROPERTY MANAGEMENT

A good property management company will take care of your new home and deal with any problems while keeping you informed. They should alert you regarding prospective tenants' bookings and arrange for maid service, key collection and minor repairs. You can also ask a property manager to keep the property vacant at certain times of the year, freeing it up for your own stay.

Their monthly charges can work out at around 60 euros for a two-bedroom apartment and around 210 euros for a four-bedroom villa. It is possible to have fees deducted from rent payments received by them, and the same applies to rental agents. As with any professional linked with your property, get the contractual agreement between you

If you are planning to rent out your Portuguese property, it will usually need to be furnished

The landlord usually pays property taxes, while utility bills are met by the tenant, especially if long-term

RENT TYPES

In Portugal there are three forms of rental scheme available:
- Liberated rent – worked out via negotiations between the landlord and tenant.
- Conditioned rent – worked out via free negotiation, but with a maximum capped figure
- Supported rent – subsidised rent (under review and amendment).

Buying Guide

Properties with pools are always popular for holiday lettings

BEING A LANDLORD

● You don't need to register your property as a 'let' with the local authority. Tax (*IRC*) is demanded from landlord earnings. You can declare it to the UK's inland revenue and, should you pay tax in the UK for your earnings, you won't pay again in Portugal, thanks to a dual tax agreement between EU countries.

● Long-term tenants must have an NIF number and a bank account for protection; without these you could ask for up to six months' rent in advance.

and your property manager approved by an *advogado*. If you have the time and energy, you can manage your own property, sourcing tenants by advertising in publications like Merricks' *Holiday Villas* magazine or expat publications such as *The Algarve Resident*.

MOVING TO PORTUGAL

If you are embarking on the adventure of moving to Portugal to live and perhaps work, you will be pleased to know that your new EC home is one of the most co-operative in terms of accommodating foreign residents. As a member of the European Economic Area, it has signed a reciprocal agreement with the UK meaning that certain social security benefits accrued in the UK will be transferred to Portugal. And moving to your new home, while it involves some bureaucracy, is easily managed provided you follow the straightforward guidelines outlined in this section, covering everything from tax and residence permits to work visas and retiring.

RESIDENCY AND TAXES

As a member of the EU, Portugal allows residency within its borders to residents of other EU countries. However, upon moving to Portugal, you will need to apply for a residence permit (*autorização de residência*) from the *Serviço de Estrangeiros e Fronteiras* (Foreigner's Service). This five-year permit can take up to 60 days to be confirmed, and if denied, you are entitled to appeal the decision. To gain the permit, you simply need to prove you can support yourself financially in the country without relying on benefits. You don't have to be employed to gain residence, and children up to the age of 14 can be included on a parent's permit. Spouses of people with work contracts need their own independent residence permit. However, to obtain residency, you must produce evidence of your means of support, whether by employment, savings or money sent from another person in the UK.

ABOUT THE RESIDENCY PERMIT
EC regulations state that to retain the right to live in Portugal you will need a residence permit (*autorização de residência*). The first residence permit lasts five years unless it is awarded in line with a work contract, in which case it lasts one year and is renewable. Anyone dependent on you (children up to the age of 18 and elderly parents, for example) can be included on your permit. Note that non-EC members need to obtain a residence visa from the Portuguese Consulate General, in the form of a stamp on their passport. This lasts for 120 days from the issue date and allows them to live in Portugal for a maximum of 90 days. It can be extended twice by applying to the *Serviço de Estrangeiros* (Foreigners' Service) in Portugal. Those intending to stay longer than 90 days should apply for a residence permit.

TO GET YOUR *AUTORIZAÇÃO DE RESIDÊNCIA*:
● First get your UK citizenship confirmed with the British Consulate in your area of Portugal. Then visit the *Serviço de Estrangeiros* with your passport, two photographs and any employment contract. To obtain your permit, you will either need to prove you can support yourself without benefits, or that you are working and paying local taxes. It could take up to 60 days to be processed.

● Portuguese nationals have a Portuguese identity card (*bilhete d'identidade*), but EC members will need a residence permit and a *bilhete d'identidade para residentes*. (This will enable you to apply for a Portuguese driving licence, although if you have a European driving licence, this is valid throughout the EC.) The police can ask to see your *bilhete* at any time, and you are legally obliged to apply for it after six consecutive months in the country.

TO OBTAIN YOUR *BILHETE D'IDENTIDADE PARA RESIDENTES*:
● Take an application form from the British Consulate to the parish council (*Junta de Freguesia*). Once your address is confirmed and your card verified, you will receive your ID card, although this process can take up to a month.

TO OBTAIN THE RIGHT TO VOTE:
● Election cards (*cartão de eleitor*) are given when an individual presents two neighbours' signatures proving their location or a declaration from their parish council. All EC residents can vote in the local elections of the country they are staying in, and this card enables you to vote in every type of election in Portugal.

WHEN LEAVING PORTUGAL
● Upon departure from Portugal your *autorização de residência* should be returned to a police station.

INCOME TAX
Your tax number and *cartão de contribuinte* (tax card) are essential for declaring income tax (*Imposto sobre o Rendimento das pessoas Singulares* or *IRS*). Once you have lived more than 183 days in Portugal

The first residence permit lasts five years unless it is awarded in line with a work contract, in which case it lasts one year and is renewable

IMPORTING GOODS
As an EC member country, UK goods require no original documentation when imported into Portugal. A copy of your passport or identification card and an inventory of goods are all that is needed. Importing your furniture by sea is the cheapest option than by air or road. It is also wise to carry a copy of your *escritura* if moving a substantial amount of household goods across the border. But importing a UK car requires either the original receipt or a current valuation and its registration document. A car can be driven in Portugal with UK plates for up to 12 months; after this, it must be re-registered and any import tax paid. (This tax is substantial on a new vehicle, but drops off with age.) See the Directory at the back of this book for details of removals carriers.

Buying Guide

Unemployment benefit is an exportable benefit that will be honoured in Portugal; however, this is not regarded as supporting yourself and the Portuguese government do not want incomers forming a pull on public funds

in any calendar year, or have a residence definable as a permanent residence at the year end, you are considered a tax resident and liable for income tax. Portugal's *IRS* system relies on self-declarations that must meet a March 15 deadline. Payment is due within one month of receiving the bill, which is charged on all income earned in and outside of Portugal. If your dwelling can be assumed to be your long-term home on December 31 of a given year, you are seen as a tax resident.

Family members living outside Portugal with their family head based in Portugal also receive tax residence status. If your home country has a tax treaty with Portugal (as the UK does), the treaty's rules will define where their residence is recognised.

Non-residents are taxed on Portuguese-derived income only, and generally have withholding tax that symbolises a final payment and don't have to complete tax returns. But such residents earning income on property in Portugal, whether through renting or selling on, must make tax returns to the Portuguese authorities. Appointing an *advogado* to complete such returns will satisfy this legal demand.

The band of *IRS* (income tax) runs from 12 to 40 percent. Shares, royalties and bank account interest are also defined as earnings, as is money made from sale of property, unless it is reinvented.

Your marital status, the number of workers in your family and the number of family residents can be factored into how much IRS you pay. For instance, if a couple both earn, their income is divided by two before taxes are applied.

UNEMPLOYMENT/SOCIAL SECURITY BENEFITS

As an unemployed person, it is impossible to gain a resident's permit in Portugal, as to move to the country you must prove that you are actively productive (able to support yourself or employed) or a pensioner. If you are claiming benefit for at least four weeks before moving, this will be honoured by the DSS in the UK, who will ensure that a monthly payment hits your account. Unemployment benefit in the form of Jobseeker's Allowance is an exportable benefit that will be honoured in Portugal; however, this is not regarded as supporting yourself and the Portuguese government do not want incomers forming a pull on public funds. (Contributions based on benefits alone will be honoured in Portugal and this is reliant on what you have paid in while in the UK.)

The DSS Overseas Department's advice for Brits moving to an EC country is to take an E301 certificate to claim unemployment benefits and an E104 form. The E104 shows that you have been insured in the UK; the top half shows your National Insurance payments to date and the bottom half is needed to prove that you have been resident in the UK. This form details whether or not you have been getting credits in the UK's social security system. For further information contact the Department of Work and Pensions (0845 915 4811).

NB: As an EC member state, Portugal will allow you to continue drawing benefit (from the UK) for a reasonable time (up to 90 days). However, you will have to produce an E303 form to the employment service in Portugal and prove that you are looking for work.

TAX BANDS

Taxable income:
Up to 4,182.12 euros = *12%*
4,182.13–6,325.45 euros = *14%*
6,325.46–15,682.96 euros = *24%*
15,682.97–36,070.79 euros = *34%*
36,070.80–52,276.51 euros = *38%*
52,276.52+ euros = *40%*

WORKING IN PORTUGAL

It is illegal to get a job without a *número de contribuinte* (tax number), which is used for National Insurance (caixa) deductions. Having this protects you from unethical employers who could withhold pay or skimp on caixa deductions, which would in turn affect your

Living & Working in Portugal

healthcare rights. Your tax number is awarded by the tax authorities when you start work and is dealt with by your employer. Otherwise you must register yourself with the tax authority. If you intend to work for more than 30 days, you will require a residence permit (see previous section) plus a work permit, unless you are self-employed and have residence status.

Those moving because of a secure job with a Portuguese firm automatically gain residential standing. For temporary work (less than 30 days), written permission from the Ministério do Trabalho (Ministry of Labour) in the area you plan to work is necessary. The exception to this rule is seasonal work for less than eight months, but a temporary or full-time resident permit is still needed for this.

Portuguese legislation has clamped down on foreign employees from non-EU countries, and a Portuguese employer can only employ one in 10 non-EU nationals, whether they like it or not! Au pairs and Portuguese university-employed academic professionals do not need work permits, while companies can request exception for workers with special skills.

● Professionals including dentists and solicitors intending to set up in practice in Portugal must present their qualifications to the relevant Portuguese body, which will give permission or not.
● Portuguese employers will need to see your degrees or professional qualifications translated for any job; this can be completed by the Portuguese Consulate.
● The Portuguese Public Employment Services must be contacted for registration and application forms to retain benefit rights.
● Trade unions receive beneficial insurance rates with insurers in Portugal. Eurocadres (+351 223 398800) advise on trade unions.

TO START A BUSINESS

In order to set up a business in Portugal, you will simply need a residence permit, unless you are working with food, fish or property rental, in which case you will need to apply for a business licence. You will need to register your intention, and gain approval of your

Don't let the look of your dream home make you lose sight of the paperwork that needs to be carried out to turn the dream into reality

NATIONAL INSURANCE

Ensure that your employer has registered you with the government for National Insurance (*caixa*), which pays for health treatment in Portugal as in the UK. After 15 years of paying *caixa*, you earn the right to a Portuguese state pension.

● Around 11% of a monthly gross salary is taken in *caixa*.

● An employer pays around 24%.

Buying Guide

Wherever you decide to live, if you are setting up a business, you will have to keep track of your own tax returns and payments

business whether you are a sole trader (*estabelecimento individual de responsabilidade limitada* or RIRL), a general partnership (*sociedade em Nome Colectiva* or SNC), a corporation (*Sociedade Anónima* or SA) or a private limited company (*Sociedade por Quotas* or Lda). (Estate agents are often private limited companies/corporations.) As you will be liable for *caixa*, VAT (*IVA* or *Imposto sobre o Valor Acrescentado*) and corporate income tax (*IRC* or *imposto sobre o Rendimento das pessoas Colectivas*), keeping accounts for yearly auditing is crucial. Paid in three stages – by July 20, September 20 and December 20 – these instalments represent 85 percent of the previous two years' income, less any withholding tax and common deductions. Erroneous bills are rectified in the next annual *IRC* return.

As in the UK, deductions for business-related expenses, including travel and equipment, can be made. Self-employed individuals pay *IRS* and can deduct health, education, pension payouts, rent, health and life insurance policies, books and IT, while travel expenses are written off against *caixa* payments you have made. Your *IVA* can be written off against outlays for some raw materials.

Self-employed individuals pay IRS *and can deduct health, education, pension payouts, rent, health and life insurance policies, books and IT, while travel expenses are written off against* caixa *payments you have made*

BUSINESS TAXATION
- Normally 12 percent *IVA* is charged for tourist letting.
- Taxpayers whose turnover is less than 200,000 euros must enter their tax return and payment by the 15th of the second month of each quarter.
- All allowances must be backed with receipts (*facturas*).
- In 2001 a new category, B, was added to the tax return for the self-employed, encompassing previous categories C (commercial) and D (agricultural) unless their sales volume exceeded 150,000 euros and their 'services & others' reached 100,000 euros.
- Incorporated or unincorporated companies with or without a head office or management in Portugal earning income there

are charged corporate income tax (*IRC*). Any properties with tourism-based incomes are seen as permanent establishments and are treated as resident companies.
● Properties let mid- to long-term, or sold and incurring capital gains from a sale of business, can be seen as *not* permanently established and are treated differently in their tax status.
● The IRC general rate for resident entities with taxable profits, including offshore property companies and permanent establishments of non-resident entities, is 30 percent.
● Non-resident bodies not established in Portugal or deriving income pay *IRC* at 25 percent.
● Portugal is foreign investment-friendly and you should register with the *Investimentos, Comercio e Turismo* (*ICEP*) corporation within 30 days of investing in a Portuguese company.

STEPS TO SETTING UP A BUSINESS
● Apply to the Official Certificate of Admissibility for the use of your chosen name.
● Request a provisional company ID card.
● Open a bank account in your company name and deposit the legal minimum.
● Sign the company's Articles of Incorporation at a public *notariá*.
● Effect the public deed of incorporation.
● Register the start of activity (*declaração de ínicio de actividad*) at the *finanças* (tax department).
● Enrol the company with the local commercial registrar.
● Publish the deed in the *Diário da República* newspaper as well as a local paper.
● Enrol the company in the social security system.

Portugal is foreign investment-friendly and you should register with the Investimentos, Comercio e Turismo *(ICEP) corporation within 30 days of investing in a Portuguese company*

HEALTHCARE

Having a check-up in Britain before you move to Portugal is wise. For short-term medical cover and emergency medical attention, you'll need to fill out an E111 form (obtainable from the Post Office), which details the reciprocal healthcare provision scheme for EU members. For 90 days after you have registered your arrival in Portugal, treatment is free in state hospitals. Once a resident in Portugal, all your emergency and medical (including hospital) treatment is free and a nominal fee of around three euros is asked when you visit a doctor at a health centre (*centro de saúde*), provided you produce your social security number (*NIF*) and health service card (*cartão de saúde*). This should be applied for when you have your resident permit. With this card, you will receive free treatment. The *centro de saúde* is part of the national health service scheme. When your tax number comes through, you must register your details with a health centre. If you want to see a particular specialist doctor you may have to pay, unless your GP issues you with a *credencial* or confirms that you need to see a particular specialist.

People belonging to private health care insurers' policies usually pay a percentage of the cost of seeing a specialist, and these costs vary. Remember that a *centro de saúde* has an emergency department and allow you to see any doctor.

If not a resident, additional treatment after initial care will be charged and refunded via the DSS overseas arm or the *centro de saúde* (health centre). Doctor's appointments and medicines are paid on top of the *caixa* scheme, so for a first stop people usually visit the pharmacy

If you are not a resident in Portugal, and you visit a hospital (like this one in Guimarães), any costs after initial treatment will be refunded by the DSS overseas arm

Buying Guide

The availability of private clinics across Portugal is mainly concentrated in popular tourist and expat areas like the Algarve and Lisbon

for information on illnesses (as in France and Spain). Emergency chemists will have an *de serviço* or emergency sign displayed, and most local newspapers (as in the UK) will give up-to-date information on pharmacy opening hours.

As in the UK, larger hospitals' casualty departments are open 24 hours a day and you will be able to get treatment in any state-run hospital. Working residents paying into Portugal's social security system receive free treatment at any state district hospital. English-speaking GPs can be found in various hospitals (contacts are given in the Region Guide sections, starting on page 82), but wherever you seek treatment, your social security number will be needed to secure the services of a GP. Such policies cover private hospital and clinic treatment.

Dentists are expensive in Portugal and they generally charge by the hour. As with finding a dentist in the UK, simply ask around for recommendations of a reliable one.

STATE SYSTEM VS PRIVATE

Currently under modernisation, the *Ministério de Saúde* (Health Ministry) runs the system via administration centres (*administração regional de saúde*), although the Ministry has been up against it in terms of resources and has been historically under-resourced. Healthcare is free in hospitals but not *centros de saúde*, where a nominal fee is asked (as previously explained). The availability of private clinics across Portugal is mainly concentrated in popular tourist and expat areas like the Algarve and Lisbon, although the university city of Coimbra has some of the best teaching hospitals in Portugal.

Specialist, independent health insurance brokers in the UK can be used to get comprehensive cover. Health insurers incorporating an international assistance company are best, as they will arrange transportation by ambulance or air ambulance to hospital and, unlike many insurers, pay your bills direct, so you don't have to go through the process of reclaiming expenses. Such insurers also offer interpreting services. There are a plethora of international insurers specialising in or offering health insurance. If you belong to a private health insurance scheme, you will be entitled to see any doctor within its remit.

It's also worth noting that healthcare is tax deductible and whether you have used a private clinic or paid the nominal fee, if you take your receipts along to the tax office this will be written off against the income tax you pay. (Residents with a healthcare policy purchased in the UK which they move with them, will not qualify for deductions, because the Portuguese government view such a product as offshore. In practice, individuals moving to Portugal will usually move their policy with them, and then a few years later opt for a Portuguese policy, which may be cheaper.)

PROPERTY SELLING TIPS

- Find an AMI-numbered estate agent (*Associação de Mediadores Imobiliários*).
- Choose an *advogado* to represent you.
- Ensure possession of your property documents, including the *escritura*, and make sure you have paid any outstanding *contribução autarquia* (rates/community charges).
- Consult your *finanças* for information on how much IRS will be charged.

EDUCATION

If you are moving to Portugal with children, then you'll need to make provision for their education in their new country. Most children under 10 can quickly adapt to their new surroundings, and so it's often best to seek out a local school. They will normally be put in a class below their equivalent in the UK until they catch up with the language. However, if you have older children, or you want them to be taught in English, Portugal does have a plethora of international schools around the country, details of which are given in the relevant Region Guides (page 82 onwards), as are contacts for the Ministry of Education.

Living & Working in Portugal

RETIREMENT

Pension details and proof of your sustainable income (to show you won't be a burden on the Portuguese social security system) are needed for retirees to enter Portugal. This should be shown when applying in the UK or when applying for the *autorização de residência*. Pension contributions made in the UK will be honoured, as your pension rights move with you, provided you produce all UK documents relating to your pension. Registering them immediately with a social security office is important. UK tax offices will arrange for non-resident and British tax duty exemption for your pension before you move.

Portuguese pensions are awarded for more than 15 years of contributions, at around 2 percent of the 10 greatest earning years' salary. If you are still working and interested in signing up, contact the National Pensions Centre (*Caixa Nacional de Pensões*) or the social security centre (*Centro Regional de Segurança Social*) with proof of ID.

And of course, it's worth mentioning that securing private health insurance is vital for those of retirement age.

SELLING YOUR HOME

When you come to sell your first Portuguese home or business premises, it is advisable to remain in the country during the sale period. Some vendors do complete their sale from outside Portugal via a trustworthy third party, an *advogado* or a friend. But it always helps to be on hand, if only to ensure the signing of the promissory contract (as if you change your mind, you are obliged to pay twice their deposit to them). You should also investigate how much *IRS* your sale will incur.

One of the most sensible options for parents of young children moving to Portugal is to enrol them in an international school

When you come to sell your first Portuguese home or business, it is advisable to remain in the country during the sale period

Buying Guide

The river Guadiana is flanked by many pretty white-washed villages

PETER SHAND

LOCATION, LOCATION, LOCATION
ALCOUTIM IN THE ALGARVE

Retired chartered surveyor and property consultant Peter Shand looks back on his reasons for choosing Portugal as the location for his holiday development

A windmill located on the Moinhos dos Cadvais estate

'We all have our own reasons for wanting a second home or a business in Portugal,' says retired property consultant, Peter Shand. 'Mine began with short golfing visits to Portugal, followed by a family holiday near Lagos in the Algarve in 1985. Our rented villa gave us all the luxury of a five-star hotel, yet we felt we were closer to the local people.'

Following a succession of enjoyable holidays in rented accommodation, Peter decided to take the step of buying overseas, but where? He looked at Spain, France and Florida, but felt drawn to Portugal. He had found the people so friendly, the lifestyle so relaxed and the year-round warmth so appealing.

They narrowed the search for a property to the area around Lagos, but choosing the area was the easy part, as Peter explains: 'With the location decided, finding the right villa within our budget should have been easy, but it wasn't. We couldn't find a property to our liking, and all the while the cost of our numerous visits was mounting. Disappointed, we thought about buying a plot of land and building our own home but, in 1990, we found finally what we wanted: a ruined farmhouse on a south-facing ridge, with countryside and sea views.'

Looking back on his experience, Peter's biggest regret was that so much time was wasted when, with the right help and advice, so much more could have been achieved at a fraction of the cost, and without making so many trips to Portugal. At the time, there were few reliable estate agents, finding a good solicitor was tricky and legal fees seemed far too high given the relative simplicity of Portugal's conveyancing procedures.

With this in mind, in 1996 Peter set up a UK-based property location business, designed to help clients avoid the problems he had experienced. Running the business from the UK, he used a team of representatives in Portugal to carry out the actual searches. In 1998, however, his hands-on approach to finding a home for one particular client led to him discovering lesser known areas of the Algarve and finding his current Portuguese home.

Case Study 1

Peter had been asked to find a villa for a keen fisherman, and after looking at areas in northern Portugal and the Alentejo coast, he turned to the river Guadiana, on the Algarve border with Spain. 'Without my fisherman client,' says Peter, 'I doubt I would have travelled further east than Tavira.'

In this eastern stretch of coastline, he discovered the unassuming resort of Altura, the lovely beach of Praia Verde and the estuary town of Vila Real de Santo António, and Peter felt immediately drawn to the area. 'Best of all was the Guadiana itself, with mile after mile of magnificent, breathtaking scenery unfolding in the drive from Foz de Odeleite to Alcoutim, a drive only surpassed by the boat trip up river from Vila Real,' he enthuses.

Despite the beauty of the area, the client search was still proving difficult, the homes with most potential being houses in one of the tiny villages on the river or one of the few ruined farmhouses. What made things worse was the lack of a structured property market, making it hard to identify which houses were for sale, let alone locate their owners. Just as things were looking most bleak, Peter stumbled across the Moinhos dos Cadavais estate on the outskirts of Alcoutim, set among 120 acres of rolling hills with superb panoramic views. With its own little lake, pine trees and a four-bedroom villa, it seemed the perfect spot for Peter's fisherman client. The only drawback was the asking price… it was way over budget.

By this time, however, Peter was smitten, and offered to buy the land with the ruins as a renovation project, leaving the four-bedroom villa for his client. It meant the incomplete renovation venture in Lagos would have to be sold, but he

Peter was attracted by the area's scenery (top and centre) and the potential for renovation (bottom)

'Without my fisherman client, I doubt I would have travelled further east than Tavira. Best of all was the Guadiana itself'

felt that in the ten years since buying that property, things had changed in that part of the Algarve, with lovely fishing villages becoming booming, over-developed resorts. 'I hate stress, crowded beaches, traffic jams, restaurant queues, concrete and poor food,' admits Peter, 'and as I've grown older I suppose I'm less prepared to put up with second best.'

Delighted with his project, Peter couldn't wait to start planning the renovations, although illness and other setbacks prevented this until mid-2002, and now a design team is hard at work to bring this dream to reality. Peter intends to turn the estate into a holiday development offering leisure and spa facilities, swimming pools, tennis courts and a magnificent clubhouse. Taking pride of place will be the lake for fishing, but other watersports, cycling and horse riding will also be on offer. Also planned is the construction of timber lodges built into the hillsides to accommodate visitors, and the first of these will be available by summer 2004.

It's a huge project, but Peter is confident. 'The location is right,' he asserts, 'and lodge prices will be unmatched anywhere in the Algarve. There will be activities for the energetic, and ample amenities for those holidaymakers who just want to relax and do nothing.'

Hopefully the experience Peter has gained in helping so many UK clients find their dream homes will help him turn his Moinhos dos Cadavais project into a perfect business.

PETER'S RECOMMENDATIONS

- Take time over choosing location by visiting as many areas as possible. Revisit the chosen area in and out of season, as it can change.
- Think about how you and your family will use the home you buy after purchase. How long will you spend there? Will you rent it out?
- View as many properties as possible.
- Seek advice and make sure you make your requirements clear (preferably in writing) to those professionals you appoint to help you.

For those interested in Peter's developments, or for advice on relocating, contact him on 01865 883154.

Buying Guide

People who relocate to Coimbra should be prepared for a simpler, more traditional way of life

OFF THE BEATEN TRACK
RENOVATION IN COIMBRA AND THE BEIRAS

Former guidebook writer *James Lawrence* tells how his passion for the Lousã area has led him to a renovation job and helping other Brits move to the area

'Often people are overly concerned with matters such as planning permission, but the Portuguese system of buying is quite good'

'Arriving here, I had no idea of how I would support myself, merely a resolve to stay in this wonderfully laidback part of Portugal,' says writer and property finder James Lawrence of his arrival in the town of Lousã near Coimbra. 'I fell in love with the relaxed pace of life and felt the need to educate other Brits about the area,' he states.

In November 1997, James's search for a more relaxed way of life led him to the Beiras region, where he bought and renovated a property with its own separate goathouse set in its own grounds. James had to work quickly to turn the shell of his house into a cosy home for his first Portuguese winter, and he later converted the goatshed into a cottage for holiday lets. 'The main house was barely habitable when I bought it, and I wouldn't have wanted to winter in it!' he recalls. 'The sitting room floor was rotten, the walls needed painting, the one bedroom was barely big enough for a bed and the roof was so dilapidated you could see daylight through it!'

It was a labour of love that involved James having to get a new roof, floor, doors, terrace and various room conversions. 'I turned the existing kitchen area into a double bedroom,' he explains, 'and what was formerly a covered veranda – just bare cement – I had turned into a "galley" kitchen, just by tiling, painting and putting in handmade chestnut cupboards. I also had the exterior walls stripped of some fairly awful plastering and returned to the natural stone, which looks really good and lasts for ever.' The house and cottage now sit in a lovely garden with great views.

The process of buying and renovating made James realise that a host of British purchasers were unaware of the benefits of the Coimbra region. 'If few agents spoke English, then even fewer Brits were considering moving to this rural location,' begins James, 'so I offered English introductions to the agents in town. A few took me up on it, and I ended up bringing millions of pounds of investment into this otherwise sleepy region.'

He admits that the people who relocate to this region should be prepared for a simpler pace of life than that in some

Case Study 2

Peter's renovation project was a labour of love that involved a new roof, floor, doors, terrace and various room conversions

expat areas such as Lisbon and the Algarve, and accept that it rains here! 'My introductions are individuals deliberately moving away from British-style colonies,' explains James. 'Many are in their 50s taking early retirement or young couples who feel that Britain is no longer the best country in which to live. In moving to this part of Portugal, they are definitely getting the benefits of the beautiful mountain scenery and easier lifestyle. They are also not upset if only Portuguese is spoken in a shop or restaurant!'

James has spent much of the past four years explaining the actual buying process to UK buyers and soothing their fears of the unknown.

'Often people are overly concerned with matters such as planning permission, but I feel that the Portuguese system of buying is actually quite good,' James reveals. 'The system of forfeiture for pulling out of a sale, applied to vendors who must pay back double on withdrawing from a sale and the loss of a deposit for a buyer doing the same, has, in my experience, tended to cut out gazumping and chains falling down at the last minute.'

His main aim is to inform foreign buyers of the ease of buying in Portugal. 'The system is so simple that some Portuguese do not bother with solicitors, as they are invariably slow and often incompetent,' James laughs. 'I did not use one when I bought my house; it was as easy as buying a car!'

He enjoyed his renovating experience so much that now, James plans to renovate and sell further properties in the area. 'Portugal is very mountainous, so land prices are at a premium and wealthy Lisbon residents are looking to move to this region,' he says.

His final piece of advice to anyone considering a move to Coimbra is to go with the flow. 'I would say to anyone moving here to remember that this is not England with sunshine, and so, if things are done differently or take a bit longer, just relax. I have been made to feel very welcome and I am now a valued member of the community.'

JAMES'S BUYING TIPS

- Keep a close eye on Portuguese builders, as they often fail to turn up, and have been known to take shortcuts.
- English-speaking German builders can be a much safer bet.
- The Land Registry can prove problematic in rural areas, as properties in the more remote locations historically changed hands mostly on a handshake, with nothing put in writing.
- In many rural areas, there are no site plans with deeds, so boundaries are often defined by the names of the neighbours and by the number of fruit trees! As nobody ever bothers to update this, it is often the case that the neighbours named on the deeds died years ago!
- Don't fear the buying process or the Portuguese. It is safe and straightforward in my experience, and the Portuguese prove themselves to be incredibly warm hosts.

Buying Guide

The greatest demand within the market is for two-bedroom apartments

MOVING ON UP
RESALES IN THE ALGARVE

How hotelier and estate agent *Sue Mackenzie* went from helping her friends find a home to setting up a successful estate agency business

'We just find that British buyers want to deal with a British agent, who understands them and whom they can understand, and my clients feel they can trust me,' says Sue Mackenzie, figurehead of the thriving resales specialist, Sue Mackenzie Real Estate. Today her customers include celebrities such as Anita Harris and *Dad's Army* star, Clive Dunn. Indeed, the legendary Manchester United footballer, Denis Law, now helps Sue and her husband Charlie (who operates a separate business specialising in new builds) to promote developments, such as the one at Victoria Gardens in Vilamoura, where they live.

Sue explains how their collaboration came about: 'We met him in Manchester ten years ago, then later read that his son was ill with meningitis, so we offered him some accommodation at The Four Seasons hotel in which to recuperate, and he fell in love with Vilamoura.'

Sue's life in Portugal began in 1985, when she and Charlie moved from Cornwall to Vilamoura (known by some as Portugal's answer to Marbella) after the death of her parents. Sue had grown up in the hotel trade, and had run the Rosevine Hotel in Roseland before deciding it was time for a change. 'I felt Cornwall was changing,' she reveals, 'and the slower, gentler pace of life here appealed to me. My husband Charlie was working as project director at the Four Seasons hotel here, and I took a job in the marketing department.'

After working in Vilamoura for over a decade, in 1997 the couple moved to Amman in Jordan, when Charlie took a job selling holiday property ownership at the Meridian Hotel there. They enjoyed their time in the Middle East, but the pull back to Portugal proved too much, and they

Case Study 3

Left: Sue, seen here with a client, has experienced no prejudice against her as a businesswoman.
Above: Footballer Denis Law, a previous client, promotes Sue's new developments

returned to their villa in Vilamoura in 2000, which is when the idea for Sue's business venture took shape. 'I worked in several other countries, but Portugal always remained home and, when I got back, I couldn't believe how Portugal's property market had developed with the British buyers,' explains Sue. 'Then a friend asked me to help them find a property in the Vilamoura location and it just took off for me.'

By this time, Sue had gained a promotion licence, allowing her to promote Vilamoura and the surrounding area to visitors, tourists and prospective investors, but she wanted to set up a business properly, selling property to British buyers. It took a little while for the idea to come to fruition, but during this time, Sue spoke with plenty of friends and professionals to get as much background about setting up a business and selling property as she possibly could. 'Because I lived and worked in Portugal,

> *One of the most important things to remember is the necessity to secure a 'trespass' and check the property's background*

my many friends, including accountants and lawyers, offered excellent advice,' she says.

Out of all the advice she received, Sue realised that one of the most essential things to do first was to sign up with a good solicitor (*advogado*), and this would help her become aware of the many ins and outs of running a business and selling property in Portugal.

One of the most important things she found out was the necessity for what is known as a 'trespass'. As well as buying the existing business, you have to purchase its tenure separately,

and, as Sue found out, this can eat up a lot of your capital when you're first starting out. 'Trespasses can cost as much as 200,000 euros,' explains Sue, 'and the value depreciates from the point of purchase. So after this huge outlay, if you sell the business on without many years left on the trespass, the owner will not be able to ask the same price, and get their money back.'

And these aren't the only charges that have to be taken into account. Sue relates how prospective entrepreneurs must remember that they need a licence to carry out any task that requires the use of machinery, and that's not all: 'Factors such as heavy ground rents also have to be factored into the running costs,' advises Sue.

The business was soon up and running, having taken all the legalities into account, and Sue's first sale was to her and Charlie's old bank manager from Amman in Jordan. He bought a

Buying Guide

Golfing brings business to the Algarve throughout the year, and consequently, there is a continuous demand upon the property market

retirement home on a swish golf complex and Sue is rightly proud of this first success. As well as it signalling the start of things to come, Sue can see the irony in the fact she's given her old bank manager a financial leg-up. 'The good thing about his purchase,' she explains with a smile, 'is that if he wants to sell, it will give him a better investment than any bank could offer. Property returns have beaten the stock market in recent years!'

Despite doing the groundwork and getting off to a flying start, Sue admits it hasn't all been plain sailing, and as time has gone on, she has encountered various hiccups and problems. Many of these complications are related to land and title ownership, and Sue admits that this simply adds to the importance of being signed up with a decent *advogado* who can carry out the proper legal checks. There is also another

Sue recommends autumn as the best time of year in which to look for a business, as property prices tend to remain lower

benefit of having good legal advice: 'You can sign over power of attorney to a lawyer if you're not around,' she adds.

Other nightmare scenarios experienced by Sue in the last three years include a few that unfortunately involved dishonest vendors. 'In one case,' she relates, 'a man was selling his property because of divorce and my client was the purchaser. At the last minute, it came out that it was the man's father who was in fact paying the mortgage. The father then made a claim on the title deeds from his son and consequently sold the property to someone else! But that's why ensuring thorough legal checks are completed is so important when purchasing.'

Sue has also found that complications arise when more than one party have claims on the title deeds. 'Cases exist where, for instance, three or more brothers own the same plot, it having been handed down through the family,' explains Sue. 'The trouble is that all must agree to sell for it to be legally acceptable.'

Unrealistic expectations from vendors have also been a pitfall experienced by Sue. 'Vendors tend not to ask you for a valuation, but rather tell you what they think it should sell for, because "so-and-so-down-the-road's property sold for that", which can cause problems,' she admits. 'I have also had experiences where purchasers have pulled out because there was a palm tree in the garden… now, I would have thought that this would benefit the property by giving shade, but not everyone would agree! Having said that, these occasions are few and far between, thankfully.'

Now with four staff and a client list of around 50, Sue says that the business has snowballed. And despite the fact that the past 12 months have been a quieter year for business in the Algarve, she says there is still interest in the property market, with the greatest demand being for two-bedroom

Case Study 3

SUE'S HOT BUSINESS TIPS

- When investing in a property for business purposes, always go for location. Golf and beaches together boost the potential for rental income.
- Employ a good lawyer. Conveyancing fees range from one to 2.5 percent.
- Ensure that your estate agent is reputable.
- Always check your facts. The Portuguese are very friendly and helpful and tend to say 'yes' to everything you ask... even if it's not always correct!
- Time is very flexible here, and the attitude can be 'why rush to do things today, when there is always tomorrow'. I'm used to this *mañana* attitude, but it can be frustrating for clients who are in a hurry to see their purchase through.
- Autumn is the best time to look for a business in Portugal, as prices tend to be lower. The nearer the peak season, the higher the prices.
- If you are planning to buy a bar or a restaurant, try to rent one first.
- Remember that many bar, hotel and restaurant businesses are sold as a 'trespass', which can be expensive.
- A 'trespass' gives less rights, and usually incurs a higher ground rent.
- If you take on a 'trespass', get good legal advice and ensure that you have enough finances to tide you over for the first few months of expenses.
- For those starting a business in Portugal, the first place for advice would be the British Chamber of Commerce.
- When arriving in Portugal, the AFPOP (Association of Foreign Property Owners in Portugal) offers a wealth of information and assistance.

apartments, particularly near the marina in Vilamoura. 'This year's good weather in Britain has meant that people have not wanted to come here in force, in the early part of the summer,' she reflects, 'but the golfers come throughout the year, and this area is also popular with footballers.' Indeed, Portuguese footballer Luis Figo has a club named *Sete* (seven) in the resort, named after the position he plays in the Portuguese national team.

Through all the ups and downs, Sue has worked hard to make her business successful, helped by the fact that, despite being something of a globetrotter, she feels at home in Vilamoura. In terms of local attitude, Sue says she has not experienced any prejudice against her as a businesswoman, and would recommend Portuguese life and the property business to anyone, concluding, 'The Portuguese really want to be agreeable and have made me feel very welcome.'

Mackenzie Real Estate,
Loja 1B, Block B, Marina Plaza, 8125-401 Vilamoura, Algarve, Portugal
Tel: *+351 289 315784*
Fax: *+351 289 380354*
Mobile: *+351 963 137524*

GLOSSARY

A

administrador
administrator (for a community of property owners or a property development) *nm*

advogado
lawyer *nm*

aluga-se/aluguer
rent/for rent *nm*

alvará
a permit held by the builders that grants them permission to build *nm*

alvará de construção
construction licence *nm*

arquitecto
architect *nm*

Associação de Mediadores Imobiliários
Association of Estate Agents *nm*

associação de proprietários ou condóminos
community of owners in a community development *nf*

autárquica
community tax/rates payment *nf*

autorização de residencia
residence permit *nm*

B

bilhete de identidade
Portuguese identity card *nm*

buscas
checks *nf*

C

caderneta predial
contains tax registration of a property *nm*

caixa
national insurance *nm*

Caixa Nacional de Pensões
Portuguese National Pensions Centre *nm*

câmara municipal
town hall/local authority *nf*

cartão de contribuinte
tax card *nf*

cartão de eleitor
election cards *nf*

casa de campo
country house/chalet *nf*

casa de fazenda
farmhouse or house on a farm *nf*

casa de férias
holiday or second home *nf*

casa renovada
renovated house (old village house or cottage) *nf*

centro regional de segurança social
Portuguese social security centre *nm*

certidão de registro
property land registration certificate *nf*

certidão de teor do Registro Predial
(as above) land registration certificate/a Land Registry extract *nf*

conservatória do Registro Predial
Land Registry office *nm*

construtor/empreiteiro
builder *nm*

conta certa EDP
direct debit *nf*

contrato promessa de compra e venda
promissory contract *nm*

contribuição
contribution/payment *nf*

copia simples da escritura
copy of the escritura *nm*

D

declaração de início de actividad
declaration of the start of trading as registered for a business *nf*

domiciliação de pagamentos
standing order (eg, payment for bills) *nf*

domicílio fiscal
main residence for tax purposes *nm*

E

electricista
electrician *nm*

engenheiro civil
civil engineer *nm*

escritura de compra e venda
final contract and transfer of ownership to the buyer

escritura pública de compra e venda
the notarised deed of sale, transfer deed *nm*

estabelecimento individual de responsabilidade limitada (RIRL)
sole business trader *nm*

estimativas
estimate *nf*

F

facturas
bills/receipts *nf*

finanças
tax office *nf*

H

hipotecas
mortgage *nf*

I

imobiliária
estate agent *nf*

imposto
tax *nm*

imposto de mais valias
capital gains tax *nm*

imposto de selo
stamp tax *nm*

imposto municipal sobre transmissões (IMT)
property transfer tax replacing SISA tax *nm*

imposto municipal sobre Imoveis (IMI)
forthcoming replacement for *contribuição autárquica* *nm*

imposto sobre de sucessões e boações
inheritance/gift tax *nm*

imposto sobre o rendimento das

Business and Legal Glossary

BUSINESS AND LEGAL

pessoas colectivas (IRC)
corporate income tax *nm*

imposto sobre o rendimento das pessoas singulares (IRS)
Income tax *nm*

imposto sobre o valor acrescentado (IVA)
value added tax (VAT) *nm*

inventário
inventory *nm*

J

junta de freguesia
district council *nf*

L

licença de abertura
opening licence for a business *nf*

licença de construção
construction licence *nf*

licença fiscal/alvará
a business licence or permit *nf*

licença de habitação
local authority habitation licence *nf*

licença de obras
town hall building licence *nf*

licença de utilização
licence granted by the town hall stating what the building can be used for *nf*

lote (de terreno)
plot (of land) *nm*

M

matriz predial
financial register *nf*

Ministério de Emprego e Segurança Social
Portuguese Ministry of Social Security *nm*

Ministério do Trabalho
Ministry of Labour *nm*

minuta de aprovação
minute of approval provided by the notary *nf*

N

notário
notary *nm*

número de contribuinte
tax number *nm*

número de identificação fiscal (NIF)
fiscal identity number, used for tax purposes *nm*

número de identificação para estrangeiros (NIE)
foreigner's identification number *nm*

O

orçamentos
quote *nm*

Ordem dos Advogados
Portuguese legal association, the equivalent to the Law Society in the UK *nf*

P

parecer camarário
any previous information needed to grant hypothetical permission to build *nm*

plano da ordem costeira (POC)
coastal building law *nm*

planos directores municipais
municipal regime for building authorisation *nm*

potencia
power *nf*

predial registro
property registration *nm*

procuração pública
power of attorney or proxy *nf*

procuração com poderes gerais
general power of attorney *nf*

procuração com poderes limitados
limited power of attorney *nf*

propriedade horizontal
freehold title held for a property *nf*

R

regime do arrendamento
law governing property rentals *nm*

repartição de finanças
local finance department *nf*

rés-do-chão (1o andar)
ground floor *nm*

S

seguro
insurance *nm*

seguro de bens domésticos
home insurance *nm*

segurança social
social security *nf*

selo fiscal
official stamp (on a document) *nm*

serviço de estrangeiros e fronteiras
foreigners' service *nm*

SISA
property transfer tax (being replaced by *imposto municipal sobre transmissoes*)

sociedade anónima (SA)
business corporation *nf*

sociedade em nome colectivo (SNC)
general business partnership *nf*

sociedade por quotas (Lda)
private limited company *nf*

superintendente de vistoria
surveyor *nm*

T

taxa de juro
interest rate *nf*

testamento
will *nm*

V

valor tributável ou valor patrimonial
details the property's tax value and determines your property's rateable values *nm*

Z

zona de protecção terrestre
site protected against building development *nf*

81

The Regions

The Regions introduction

THE REGIONS

Profiles of Portugal's highly individual regions, the styles of property they offer and where to find the best value

Maps of Portugal	**84**
REGION GUIDES	
Algarve	**88**
Alentejo	**108**
Lisbon & Estremadura	**124**
Coimbra & the Beiras	**140**
Costa Verde & the North	**156**
Madeira	**172**

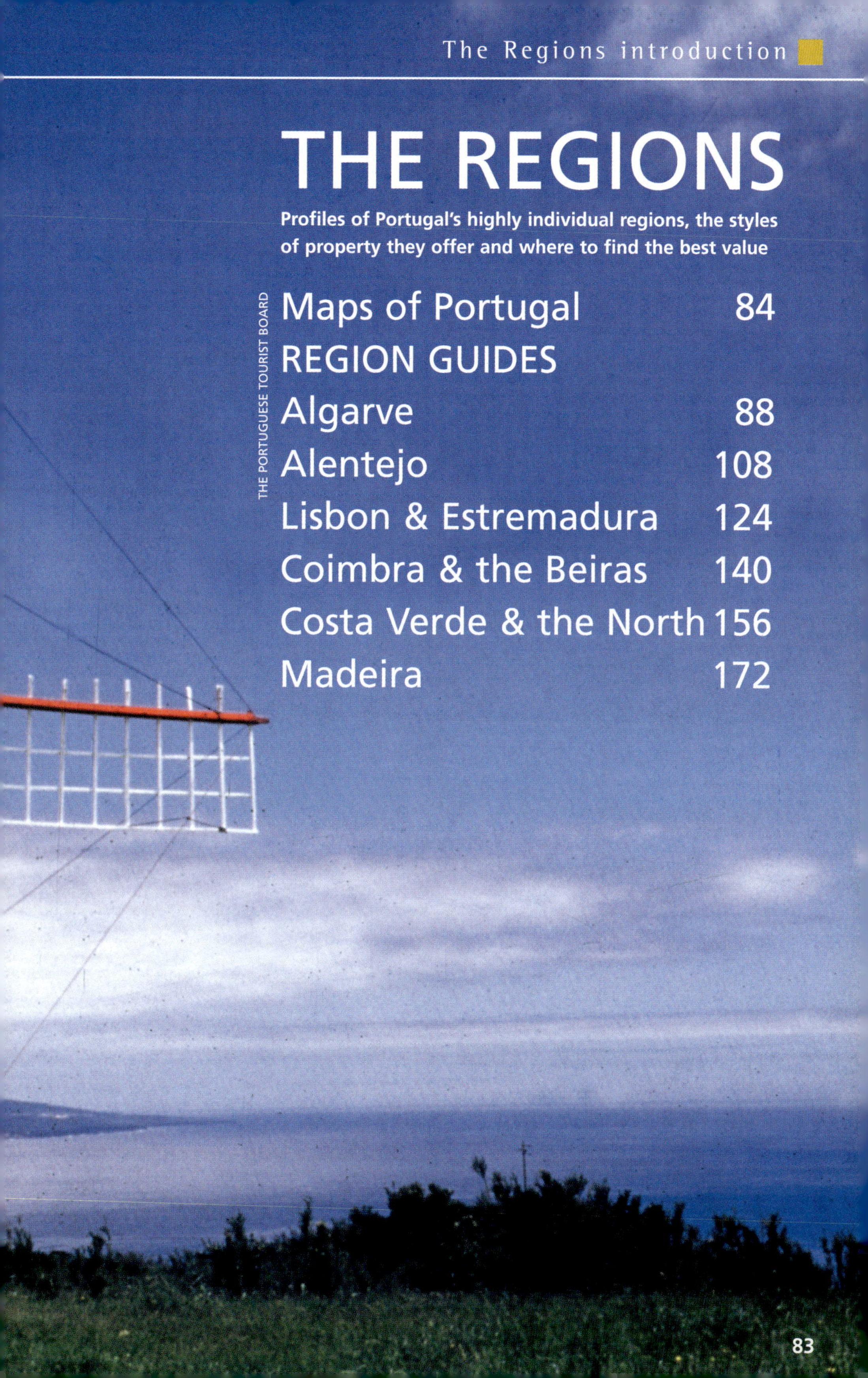

THE PORTUGUESE TOURIST BOARD

The Regions

Portugal Tour Map

The Regions

Region Map

THE PORTUGUESE REGIONS

The administrative make-up of Portugal has seen much evolution over the years. It was traditionally composed of seven provinces, which were later sub-divided into administrative regions. More recently, however, the government and tourism authorities decided, for statistical purposes, to split the country into five large regions (Algarve, Alentejo, Lisbon e Vale de Tejo, Beiras – Centro de Portugal, Porto e Norte de Portugal), with 19 smaller tourist regions within them.

It is these five administrative regions, along with the island of Madeira, that we have used for our Region Guides and Price Guide sections. We have altered the names slightly to reflect the most important areas for property buyers, so Beiras and Central Portugal becomes Coimbra & the Beiras, while Porto and the North becomes Costa Verde. The list below shows the five official regions and Madeira (with our region names in brackets if different) and their largest cities and towns within them.

THE REGIONS, FROM SOUTH TO NORTH

THE ALGARVE
Faro
Albufeira
Tavira
Lagos
Silves
Portimão

ALENTEJO
Portalegre
Évora
Estremoz
Borba
Beja
Sines
Santiago do Cacém
Mértola

LISBON E VALE DE TEJO
(Lisbon & Estremadura)
Lisbon
Estoril
Sintra
Cascais
Setúbal
Santarém
Leiria
Pombal

BEIRAS – CENTRO DE PORTUGAL
(Coimbra & the Beiras)
Castelo Branco
Coimbra
Viseu
Guarda
Aveiro
Figuera da Foz

PORTO E NORTE DE PORTUGAL
(Costa Verde & the North)
Porto
Braga
Guimarães
Bragança
Chaves
Viana do Castelo
Vila Real

MADEIRA
Funchal
Calheta
São Vicente
Machico
Vila Baleira (on Porto Santo)

The Regions

The Algarve

The Algarve coast is characterised by rocky coves, accessible only by steep steps or boat

THE ALGARVE

With some of the most beautiful sandy beaches in Europe, the Algarve has long been a draw for holiday-makers and second home-owners, but this region has plenty of other delights

THE PORTUGAL TOURIST BOARD

The Regions

The Algarve's rocky cliffs are punctuated by many sandy beaches, some broad and busy and others tiny and intimate

The Algarve

It's not all beaches and watersports in the Algarve, as its historic towns prove. Clockwise from top left: Tavira, Albufeira, Faro and Alvor

Portugal's Algarve region is situated on the southwestern corner of the Iberian peninsula, edged to the south and west by the Atlantic, to the north by the vast Alentejo region and to the east by the Spanish border. Its climate and trademark swathes of sandy beaches have contributed to its development and nowadays much of the region is geared to tourism.

The Algarve population quadruples in the months of July and August, with the majority of foreign visitors coming from neighbouring Spain and from the UK. Some resorts were hugely developed in the 1960s and 70s, mainly thanks to the boom in the package holiday trade and the opening of Faro airport in 1965, and this has led to some critics labelling some parts of the Algarve as a 'concrete jungle'. Certainly some resorts are overcrowded and overdeveloped, although more recent new-builds tend to be more sympathetic to the local styles and countryside. Of course, there are advantages to having this tourist infrastructure, and the area has over 20 top quality golf courses, many tennis and riding centres, and plenty of facilities for watersports.

The large majority of the region is unspoiled and supremely beautiful. Although a relatively small region, the Algarve plays host to various kinds of striking geographical features. These range from the hilly, inland, heather-covered moors, dotted with beech and pine trees, to the rocky, windy cliffs of the southwestern coast; from the peaceful coastal wetlands to the imposing peaks in the mountain ranges of Monchique and Caldeirão.

The history of the region is as varied as the landscape, and its location at the furthest flung corner of Europe has made it an important trading post. The first foreign traders in the area were Phoenicians and Greeks, but it was the Carthaginians who established permanent ports on the coast, such as that at Portimão. Later this area was occupied by the Romans, and their presence brought trade as well as wheat, vines and a road network to the area. In the early 700s, the region was invaded by the Moors and

The Regions

REGION INFORMATION

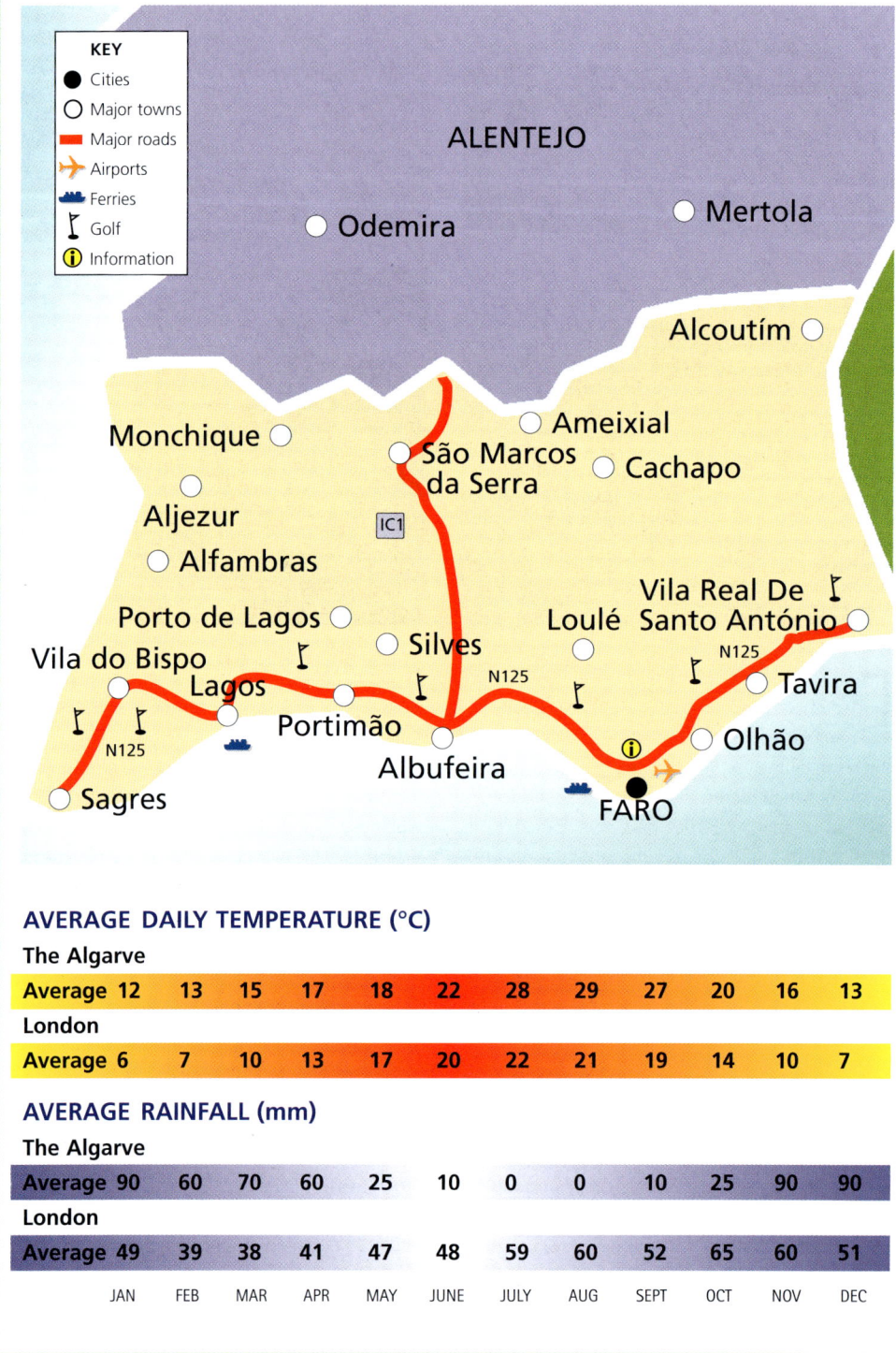

AVERAGE DAILY TEMPERATURE (°C)

The Algarve

Average	12	13	15	17	18	22	28	29	27	20	16	13

London

Average	6	7	10	13	17	20	22	21	19	14	10	7

AVERAGE RAINFALL (mm)

The Algarve

Average	90	60	70	60	25	10	0	0	10	25	90	90

London

Average	49	39	38	41	47	48	59	60	52	65	60	51

| JAN | FEB | MAR | APR | MAY | JUNE | JULY | AUG | SEPT | OCT | NOV | DEC |

The Algarve

GETTING THERE

AIR British Airways (0845 7733377; www.britishairways.co.uk) has several flights daily out of Gatwick, while **TAP Air Portugal** (020 7828 2092; www.tap.pt) flies daily out of Heathrow. **Easyjet** (0870 6 000 000; www.easyjet.com) offers flights to Faro from Stansted, Luton, East Midlands and Bristol, and **MyTravelLite** (08701 564564; www.mytravellite.com) flies from Birmingham. **Ryanair** (08712 460000; www.ryanair.com) flies from Dublin and **BMI Baby** (08702 642229; www.bmibaby.com) flies from East Midlands. Many other companies offer charter flights and holiday packages all year round.

SEA To reach the Algarve by sea, sail from Portsmouth to Bilbao with **P&O** (0870 600 0600; www.poportsmouth.com) or from Plymouth to Santander with **Brittany Ferries** (0870 536 0360; www.brittany-ferries.co.uk).

ROAD From Bilbao, take the A68 south and then the A1 to Burgos. (From Santander, take the N623 south to Burgos.) The N620 goes from Burgos, via Valladolid and Salamanca, to the Portuguese border at Fuentes de Oñoro, from where you join the IP5 and then the N17 to Coimbra then the A1 motorway to Lisbon. From here, access to the Algarve is easy.

RAIL Catch the **Eurostar** (0870 264 9899; www.eurostar.co.uk) to Paris and change for the TGV Atlantique. This takes you to Irún in Spain where you can take the Talgo to Madrid, then the AVE to Seville. Various local coach and train services journey between Seville and the Algarve region. For more details on services, contact **Rail Europe** (0870 584 8848; www.raileurope.co.uk).

CLIMATE SUMMARY

The Algarve region enjoys the hottest temperatures in Portugal, although many coastal resorts benefit from the cooling sea breeze, taking the edge off the temperatures somewhat. Daytime temperatures in summer can soar to 33°C, while the average daily temperature in winter is a comfortable 13°C.

The Algarve is the driest area of Portugal. It has most of its rainfall between November and March, with barely any rain from May to September. On average, the area has 325 days of sunshine a year.

This weather makes the Algarve the ideal location for beach holidays, although the hottest months of July and August are obviously the most busy. It is also a great destination for winter breaks – golfing holidays or otherwise – thanks to its gentle sun and infrequent scattered showers.

Lagos's beach offers kilometre after kilometre of soft, golden sand and perfect azure sea

they were to stay for 500 years, leaving their mark in the architecture and agriculture. It is also to the Moors that we owe the name 'Algarve', which comes from the Moorish 'el-Gharb' meaning 'western lands'.

By the 11th century, Christian soldiers were regaining territory from the Moors, and the last two regions to fall back into Portuguese hands were Alentejo and Algarve, reclaimed in the mid 13th century. The region's later history proved important in Portugal's overseas expeditions, with a navigation school being founded by Henry the Navigator (son of King João I) near Sagres in the early 1400s and many explorers setting off on their travels from this southwest corner.

The Algarve region can be neatly subdivided into three parts – western, central and eastern – and the most important cities in the region are Lagos and Portimão in the west, Albufeira and Faro in the centre, and Tavira in the east. Faro, the capital of the Algarve, is where the majority of visitors fly into, and it has its fair share of resorts built up on the coast. The most famous of these holiday developments is Quinta do Lago, with its rows of millionaires' villas and championship golf course. The town is dominated by its Sé cathedral, built in 1251 on the site of a previous Moorish mosque and the town is also characterised by its many panels of *azulejo* coloured tiles.

In western Algarve, you'll find Lagos, a historic city with a great nightlife and plenty of restaurants. It is well known for the quality famous of its sardine lunches, caught locally, of course! The most famous holiday resort in this area, meanwhile, is Praia da

The Regions

EMPLOYMENT CONTACTS

Portuguese Embassy:
11 Belgrave Square, London, SW1X 8PP; 020 7235 5331

British Embassy:
rua de São Bernardo 33, Lisbon; +351 213 924000; www.ukembassy.pt

Portuguese Trade Office (information about international companies with offices or who recruit English-speaking staff in the Algarve): 2nd Floor, 21-25a Sackville Street, London W1X 2LY; 020 7494 1441

International House (for details of English teaching vacancies throughout the Algarve region): rua Marquês Sá da Bandeira 16, Lisbon; +351 213 151496; www.internationalhouse.com

Cambridge Schools (employment for TEFL certificate holders): avenida da Liberdade 173, Lisbon; +351 213 124600; www.cambridge.pt

Ordem dos Medicos: (medical recruiting): avenida da Liberdade 65, Lisbon; +351 213 462725

Overseas Jobs Express (publication listing tourism-related jobs abroad): www.overseasjobsexpress.co.uk

Anglo-Portuguese News (Lisbon-based newspaper with jobs section): Apartado 113, 2765 Estoril; +351 214 661423

Faro Job Centre
rua Dr. Cândido Guerreiro, 41 R/c Edificio Nascentre 8000-318 Faro;
+351 289 890100

Rocha, whose developments have mostly gone up within the last decade.

Albufeira, on the central south coast, is probably the busiest resort on the Algarve. Most visitors head to its beaches and resorts, but it is worth visiting the historic town centre, where you can step inside the peaceful Misericordia Chapel. Tavira in eastern Algarve, about 20km from the Spanish border, is much quieter and less commercial than its fellow Algarve cities. Its fishing port dates back to Roman times although the industry still thrives today. Fishing plays a part in the restaurants of the town, some of the best being on rua José Pires Padinha, where you can sample some of the tastiest and freshest fish and shellfish in the Algarve. From Tavira, it's just a short trip to the tranquil Guadiana valley and also to Tavira island, where there is a much slower, more traditional pace of life.

Inland from these coastal centres, there are many beautiful countryside villages, impressive mountain ranges, beautiful lakes and areas of breathtaking natural beauty. While many people may overlook the Algarve as a built-up, commercialised region, if you are prepared to look more closely, you may find your slice of ideal Portuguese life here.

WORKING IN THE AREA

The Algarve area is possibly the easiest area to find work in without needing to learn Portuguese as there are many British expatriate communities here. That said, it is always recommended to have at least a basic knowledge of the language to get you ahead. With such a buoyant tourist economy, most jobs are in the service sector, in restaurants, bars, hotels and nightclubs. However, it is worth checking if these jobs are seasonal, as once the summer season is over, many staff may be no longer needed. Other tourist-related jobs can be found on the beaches, with many openings for qualified lifeguards and watersports experts. Again, however, these jobs are

The bustling city streets of Albufeira (top) contrast with the Algarve's idyllic beaches and coastline

The Algarve

BUYING IN THE ALGARVE

The Algarve remains the most popular destination for foreign investors and second home-seekers and also offers the widest range of properties to buy. These vary from studios and apartments in purpose-built blocks to detached villas in well tended grounds with a pool. As well as new-builds, there is the opportunity to buy into a slice of traditional Algarve life by buying a terraced or detached cottage, a townhouse on the seafront or a restoration project further inland.

Most of the homes offering restoration potential are in inland villages, but you can often find already renovated period properties in the main cities, in the centre of towns like Albufeira or Portimão. The prices of these kinds of houses, if fully restored, can reach £350,000 but it is also possible to find apartments in converted townhouses from £50,000.

If you're prepared to put in the investment and the hard work on renovating ruins, you can find old village houses from £25,000. If you want a property in generous plot of land, you should expect to pay from around £40,000. If, however, you seek something already renovated, a large villa with, say, private pool, gym, garage, gardens and sun terraces, prices can reach £500,000 and beyond.

Traditional Algarve architecture is characterised by whitewashed cube houses, decorated with brightly coloured *azulejo* tiles, with flat roofs that were historically used for drying fruit. While these houses don't come up on the market very often, it pays to keep your eyes open and your ear to the ground, as many homes in these quaint villages are sold privately.

If you prefer to go for a new-build, there are many developments springing up in the region, although they tend to be more sympathetic to regional architecture and the surrounding countryside than in the holiday property boom of 1970s. Most of the coastal towns and villages have holiday or apartment complexes, and prices range from £80,000 to £300,000 for a luxury seafront apartment. Many developments tend to be built in the Moorish style, with arched windows, chimneys and red tiled roofs. Most are fully equipped with air conditioning, marble floors and fitted kitchens and most complexes tend to feature communal swimming pool, garages or private parking, tennis courts and other facilities on site. You can expect to pay slightly more for an apartment built in one of the golf course developments, although the price obviously includes course fees.

WHAT YOU GET FOR YOUR EUROS

PROPERTY 1
AREA: Altura

A characterful and traditional country house with four bedrooms. Offering the best of both worlds, this property is just one kilometre from several beaches and boasts stables, orchards, lawns and extensive gardens. It is a great investment in a quiet location.

PRICE: 800,000 euros
UK EQUIVALENT: £533,330

PROPERTY 2
AREA: Albufeira

An impressive and well appointed villa with four bedrooms and four bathrooms in the much admired location of Cerro de Aquia. Near to all golf facilities, this is a beautiful family home with great rental potential. Competitively priced, this recently built property is definitely worth viewing.

PRICE: 688,000 euros
UK EQUIVALENT: £458,667

For more properties in the Algarve, turn to our Price Guide, starting on page 192

The Regions

The Algarve's picturesque coastline makes it a great place to explore by boat

The Algarve

The beautiful town of Silves with its Moorish architecture (top left), huge market hall (top right), ruined *castelo* (above) and thought-provoking statues (above left) was once the capital of the Moorish kingdom of El-Gharb

strictly seasonal and will only offer work over the summer months.

The construction industry can provide year-round work for builders, plumbers, electricians, painters and decorators. As the Algarve is being constantly developed and new homes are being built all the time, there is always demand in this area, especially as many British people often feel at ease giving the job to somebody who speaks the same language.

Another option is to buy into an existing business, especially one that is already owned by a Brit or an English speaker. Although this may smooth the language barrier, don't forget that you will still need to contemplate the Portuguese laws for the purchasing and running of the business. That said, it offers a huge amount of choice, from bars and restaurants to clothes shops, hairdressers, butchers and grocery shops.

Because Portugal belongs to the European Community, British nationals can work freely over there without the need of any work permit or visa, which makes it very easy for Portuguese companies to employ the British. Because of the importance of the English language in the Algarve, this is quite an advantage. Teaching is, of course, another possibility whether in any of the international schools in the

SNAPSHOTS

● Although the Algarve has attracted more tourist development than the rest of Portugal, parts of inland Algarve, such as the area around Alcoutím, are relatively untouched.
● Today known for its impressive *castelo* and 12th-century cathedral, Silves, just inland from the coastal town of Portimão and presiding grandly over the Rio Arade, was once the capital of the Moorish kingdom of El-Gharb or Algarve.
● Major classical music artists come to the Algarve for the annual International Music Festival.
● The public transport system is better in the Algarve than any other region of Portugal.
● Albufeira is one of the biggest Algarve resorts.
● To escape the crowds, head west of Lagos to explore the coast-hugging natural park.
● Many upmarket hotel, leisure and golf facilities are centred around Vilamoura, which is also home to the Algarve's largest nightclub.
● Armação de Pêra claims to have the region's largest beach. It also has pretty cave formations.

The Regions

area, or as a teacher of English to Portuguese pupils, who understand the need for good English in an area that is populated by so many British tourists and expatriates.

Another option is to enter the real estate business. More and more people continue to seek and buy properties in the Algarve, whether as permanent homes, holiday homes or investments, and these people obviously need an estate agent, often one who can speak English. Experience is important although not essential, but good communication skills and knowledge of the Portuguese house-buying system are a must. It is also worth noting that this line of work can be tough and very competitive, but there are opportunities available.

For those who want to work directly with holidaymakers, it may be possible to work in holiday resorts, either as an independent tour guide or working with a British-based tour operator. These companies are always looking for holiday reps, hotel staff, receptionists and waiters, although again the work is mostly during the summer season.

LEISURE TIME

There is so much to do in the Algarve that it is difficult to list all the options to fill your leisure time. Of course, the area is dominated by its coastline and seaside resorts and it is here that many pastimes are on offer. Whether you simply want to relax on a beach, or partake in one of the more energetic sports, such as windsurfing, jetskiing, surfing or sailing, almost every resort along the southern and western coast of the Algarve will oblige. There is also the option of taking fishing trips out of one of the main ports or smaller fishing harbours.

The sport most people will come here to take part in, however, is golf. The most difficult thing will be choosing from the many prestigious, expert-designed, championship courses that litter the Algarve area. Most courses welcome visitors, although many cater for tourists who come here on organised golfing holidays. These operate here all year round.

Despite the wealth of modern developments and busy resorts that line the coast, the Algarve is home to picturesque towns and plenty of history,

The Algarve region offers plenty to keep the children occupied and entertained, whether it's swimming with dolphins at one of the area's many aquariums (above) or visiting one of the ancient castles and fortresses, such as the Lagos *castelo* (below left)

The Algarve

One of the biggest draws to the Algarve region is its huge number of championship golf courses

and there are plenty of churches, castles and museums to visit. While in these towns, it's worth experiencing some of the region's many great restaurants. In some of the larger resorts, where there are pockets of expat communities, you will find Indian, Chinese and Thai restaurants alongside many traditional Portuguese and fish restaurants.

If you prefer sights of a natural kind, there are quiet, tranquil valleys that can provide satisfaction to lovers of nature and tranquillity alike, while the mountainous region, inland from Lagos, should provide plenty of options for the avid walkers and bikers among you.

As mentioned above, the Algarve has a huge number of quality golf courses, and in the last 30 years a variety of new developments have been built focusing primarily on golf and golfing holidays. *Quinta Do Lago at Almancil* (+351 289 390700) is a good example with its four courses, although *Vilamoura Golf Club* (+351 289 310341) offers four 18-hole championship courses and *Vale do Lobo* (+351 290 393939) has two. In the eastern Algarve, there is the newly opened Castro Marim course and

ACE OF CLUBS

The Algarve has a thriving golf community, and its eight main golfing centres are strung along its coastline from east to west at Sagres, Lagos, Portimão, Albufeira, Vilamoura, Almancil, Tavira and Santo António.

Keen golfers can choose between 25 courses, including the Penina championship golf course, designed by three-time British Open Championship winner, Sir Henry Cotton. It opened in 1966 as the Algarve's first course, and is now home to Portuguese Open Championships. It has two nine-hole loops, as well as a resort and academy course.

If you decide to try out a course, you will be in good company, as the Algarve received the award for the Worldwide Golf Destination of the year for 2000. The courses regularly attract famous UK footballers like David Seaman and former Arsenal striker Ian Wright. Famous players who began their careers at the Algarve Open Championships include Americans Hal Underwood and Tom Watson.

Fees for a round range from around 49 euros (£33) in low season up to around 110 euros (£70) during popular months. However, a course's peak season is dependent upon its location, so it is worth contacting a golf club before embarking on a golf holiday there. If you buy a property in Algarve, of course, you could just become a member!

The Regions

Whether you want to dive off rocky outlets or reflect in a Lagos park, the Algarve has it all

the 18-hole course at Quinta da Ria in Tavira. Of course, this is just a dip in the ocean of available quality courses in the area, and there are various others in development for the near future too.

As most courses are run to a very high standard, often hosting major golf tournaments, you are usually required to have a current handicap certificate in order to play. Green fees vary and very frequently they are subject to discounts for hotel residents or golfers with year memberships.

Watersports are big in the Algarve, thanks to the emphasis on coastal life in this region. While sports like waterskiing, surfing, windsurfing and sailing can be done as and when you want at the many beach resorts, it is also possible to book yourself on to courses to learn or improve your technique. Scuba diving is growing in popularity here, and although only those with PADI licence can attended organised diving trips, it is possible to study for your certificate here, with such schools as *Blue Ocean Divers* (estrada de Porto do Mos, Motel Ancora, Lagos; +351 282 782718).

Fishing is another activity widely available in the Algarve along the whole coastline and recently it has become possible to go either shark fishing throughout the whole year and big game fishing in August, September and October.

Those who prefer their activities on land rather than on sea should head to the hills, especially the areas around Monchique, to seek out the biking and hiking trails. There are many horse riding centres around the region, the most famous being Almancil's *Paraíso dos Cavalos* (+351 289 394189). For a slightly different take on sightseeing, you can take part in one of the various jeep trips that take you into the mountains. *Riosul* (+351 281 510200) are based in Monte Gordo and offer trips along the west coast, while *Zebra Safari* (+351 289 586860) takes you up into the hills behind Albufeira.

EATING AND DRINKING

This area of Portugal is renowned for its fresh fish, and many restaurants in all the coastal towns and cities feature speciality fish restaurants whose menus will no doubt feature the local favourite dishes of *pargo* (bream), *gambas* (prawns), *robalo* (sea bass) and *camarões* (shrimps).

As with much of Portugal's cuisine, Algarve gastronomy is not sophisticated but it is full of evocative flavours of the local produce and if you enjoy the taste of fresh seafood and locally produced

MOST FAMOUS FESTIVALS

Towns throughout the Algarve region hold various festivals throughout the year, but the most famous has to be Loulé's **Easter** celebrations. The weekend before the beginning of Lent is carnival time, and the whole town dresses up for street parades, music performances, singing, dancing and feasts in the street. On Easter Sunday, however, it's a more sombre affair, with the festival of **Nossa Senhora de Piedade**, when the townspeople gather to follow a two-kilometre-long procession through the streets from the Nossa Senhora chapel to the church in the town. A fortnight later, the procession takes place in the other direction, as the portrait is returned to its site in the chapel on top of the hill. The chapel nestles next to the newly built Igreja de Nossa Senhora da Piedade.

The Algarve

organic vegetables you are in the right place. Fish is normally cooked in simple methods, either grilled over charcoal or quickly pan fried, and simple dishes – such as sardines with crusty bread – are often the most delicious, as well as being healthy and full of flavour.

Some of the elaborate local dishes include *amêijoas na cataplana* (stewed clams, spicy sausage, ham, garlic and onions), *arroz de marisco* (seafood rice) and *bacalhau à bras* (salted cod, potatoes and egg), a dish eaten all over Portugal. Vegetable dishes includes the popular *arjamolho* (see below right) the Portuguese version of the Spanish *gazpacho*. Another interesting starter is *espadarte fumada* (smoked swordfish), which is served in wafer-thin slices, much like smoked salmon.

Restaurants in the Algarve offer generous portions, and diners can expect to start with a selection of entrees, such as fish paté, sliced bread with garlic butter, olives and an assorted plate with different salads, including octopus and tuna.

Among the local desserts to look out for are *pastel de nata* (custard tart), *doces de amendoa* (marzipan cakes) and *bolos Algarvio* (a cake made from almonds, eggs, sugar and cinnamon).

Vines have been grown in the Algarve region since Roman times, and these days the Mediterranean style climate of long hot summers and mild winters produces some very good quality bottlings. Both reds and whites are produced in the area, the majority from the Lagoa region, and while rich in flavour, their light nature makes the perfect

RESTAURANTS

Portimão is renowned for its seafood, specifically its sardine specialities. For a seafood regional culinary experience, try **Restaurante Retiro do Peixe Assado** (zona do Porto, Antiga Fabrica Feu; +351 282 418335) while a cheaper option are the freshly grilled sardines at **Flor da Sardinha** (cais da Lota; +351 282 424862).

As well as being renowned for its quality golf courses, **Hotel Quinta do Lago** (+351 289 350350) offers fantastic, if expensive, food. Whether you try the Ca d'Oro or Brisa do Mar restaurant, you're sure to taste the best the Italian chefs have to offer. For more down-home Portuguese cooking, try **Cabaz da Praia** in Albufeira (praça Miguel Bombarda; +351 289 512137) where you can taste fish soup and the delicious fish soufflé. Lagos has a large selection of restaurants, and the most prestigious of these is probably **O Galeão** (rua da Laranjeira 1; +351 282 763909), which serves luxurious dishes and its infamous lobster thermidore. For something more affordable, try **Restaurante Piri-Piri** (rua Lima Leitão 15; +351 282 763803) whose most popular dish is the spicy piri-piri chicken from which it takes its names. Dishes start from 7 euros (around £5).

RECIPE
Arjamolho

This classic cold tomato, garlic and breadcrumb soup is the Portuguese answer to *gazpacho* and is best served with ice cubes and a sprinkle of marjoram.

accompaniment to the region's fish dishes. For something with a bit more kick, try the notorious *medronho*, a spirit made from the strawberry tree and usually drunk neat.

FOR CULTURE VULTURES

When you think of the Algarve, culture isn't necessarily the first thing that springs to mind. However, aside from the golf courses and built-up resorts, the Algarve has plenty of history to share with its visitors. Many of the region's towns and villages, even the most commercialised, have a historic centre, and the area is rightly proud of its ancient ruins and beautiful churches.

Many towns in the area feature museums, the most famous probably being Faro's *Museo*

Traditional Algarve cuisine relies heavily on the region's abundance of fresh fish and shellfish

The Regions

Many of the region's whitewashed towns and villages are dominated by ornate churches and chapels

The Algarve

Among the Algarve's major sightseeing destinations are the pretty town of Tavira (top left and above left), the Roman mosaics of Estói (top right) and the caves at Albufeira (above right)

Municipal Arqueológico (largo Dom Afonso III; +351 289 897400). Here you can view an impressive collection of ancient artefacts, including remains of the ruined Roman settlement of Estói and the famous Neptune mosaic. Faro's medieval old town or *cidade velha* is home to a wealth of old buildings that cluster round its warren of narrow streets, including the impressive *câmara municipal* (town hall) and beautiful Bishop's Palace, decorated with *azulejo* tiles. Also worth a detour is the imposing church of Nossa Senhora do Carmo, known for its two imposing towers, its highly gilt interior and the Capela dos Ossos (bone chapel), whose walls are lined with the skeletons and bones. A few kilometres from Faro is Estói whose abandoned Palácio do Visconde and ruined Roman villa make for a pleasant day-trip.

In the eastern Algarve, the relatively unspoiled city of Tavira boasts many sights in its old town, including the intricately decorated 16th-century Igreja da Misericórdia, the fortified castle, the Roman bridge and the Convento da Nossa Senhora da Graça. While in the area, you should take a boat trip to Ilha de Tavira, just off the coast, with its sweeping sand dunes, scattering of trees and a wide range of wildlife.

Albufeira is obviously a draw for the tourists with its beaches and hotel towers, but the old town lends itself to a pleasant wander, while Silves has an impressive *castelo*, the 12th-century Sé cathedral and an archeological museum. Lagos, too, has various attractions, its town walls offering a great way to circumnavigate the town and the town museum showcasing all sorts of oddments and curios. And for more castles, try Castro Marim and Loulé, both of whose *castelos* play host to archeological museums. Other museums in the area include Faro's Museu da Marítimo, São Brás de Alportel's Museu Etnográfico featuring various local crafts and antiques, and Silves's Museu da Cortiça, devoted to the production of cork in the local area.

The Algarve plays host to many concerts and theatrical performances, mainly throughout the

The Regions

Fresh fruit, vegetables and fish can be found in abundance at markets throughout the Algarve

summer months, and watch out in tourist offices and on town noticeboards for outdoor and indoor events that are held in churches, palace grounds and castles throughout the summer.

SHOPPING: GIFTS AND GROCERIES

The Algarve offers a wide variety of shopping from grocery markets to modern malls and, thanks to the thriving expatriate communities of British residents here, it's possible to buy plenty of familiar British goods here as well as authentic Portuguese fare.

All towns and villages in the region have regular markets, the most famous being the huge Albufeira market, held on the first and third Tuesdays of each month. Here you can buy everything from meat and fish to organic vegetables, fruit, spices and household goods, although just being here for the busy atmosphere is enjoyable enough. Lagos's market is held on the first Saturday of each month, while those in Portimão and Tavira take place on Mondays. If you time your visit right, you may be lucky enough to catch the monthly agricultural fair held in Monchique. Here, as well as food and drink, you can seek out plenty of local specialities, from huge smoked hams to typical Algarvian wooden furniture. If you miss the fair, try to get here for the weekly Saturday market where you'll find local cheeses, traditional pottery and hand-made lace.

Of course, this being the most developed part of Portugal, the Algarve is home to plenty of modern developments with shopping centres and department stores. The most recently opened of these is the Algarve mall, just outside Albufeira. As well as 100 shops, the mall houses a nine-screen cinema, a bowling alley, fast-food restaurants and a huge hypermarket that offers good value food, drink and household goods. In addition, all the main cities and most large towns will have at least one main supermarket, as well as plenty of smaller grocery shops, butchers, bakers and fishmongers.

Whether you're keen to bring home an authentic souvenir of Algarvian traditional craftsmanship or you're on the look out for baked beans and tomato ketchup, there will certainly be an Algarve shop or market to suit your needs!

GETTING AROUND

The Algarve has Portugal's most developed network of public transport, used by many people on a daily basis, including trains, buses and of taxis. Trains in

HOLDING THE FRONT PAGE!

● Two Algarve newspapers serve the British population in the Algarve: *The Algarve Resident* (www.algarveresident.com) and *The News* (www.the-news.net).
● First published in 1989, *The Algarve Resident* is a weekly, and is the region's most widely read English newspaper. It sometimes also carries articles in other European languages.
● Around 5,000 copies of *The Algarve Resident* are distributed to around 13,000 readers.
● You can buy it in the shops or receive it by subscription – around 350 subscribers exist currently – at a cover price of 1.25 euros.
● *The News* is an subscription internet newspaper that is popular with many English speakers.

The Algarve

the Algarve are a great way of transport and are very cheap as well as being extremely reliable and punctual. The main Algarve train line runs from Villareal in the frontier with Spain to Lagos in the west and at Tuñes it links with the Lisbon line and thus with the rest of northern Europe. You can find out more about Algarve's train services from *Rail Europe* (0870 584 8848; www.raileurope.co.uk) or the local freephone information line (808 208208).

Buses in the Algarve area are also cheap, clean and pretty comfortable, and there are plenty of fast regional coach services that link most of the main towns of the region. Faro-based *EVA* (+351 289 899700; www.eva-bus.com) runs reliable local and regional services (its buses are yellow) as well as frequent services to Lisbon and Spain. There are also regional and national services operated by *Rede Nacional de Expreses* (+351 969 502050; www.rede-expressos.pt).

Its breathtakingly beautiful beach and rocky coves make Praia de Lagos a sunseeker's paradise

The Regions

Taxis in the Algarve operate within tight legislation and taxi fares tend to be pretty much the same between operators. However, as most taxis tend not to have meters, you should agree a price with the driver before getting in.

If you prefer to drive yourself around, most of the main car hire firms have offices at Faro airport, including *Hertz* (+351 289 818248), *Avis* (+351 289 810120) and *Budget* (+351 289 818888).

LOCAL LIFE

The further south you travel in Portugal, the more relaxed and laidback the attitude to life, and that is certainly the case here in the Algarve. People in this region are renowned for being hospitable and friendly and there is surprisingly little opposition from locals to the growing numbers of British buyers and visitors who continue to gravitate towards this region. It is taken for granted that tourism and the influx of foreign home owners keeps the economy buoyant and most people coming here will receive a warm welcome.

As with most areas of Portugal, life in the Algarve is punctuated by various festivals throughout the year, most tied to dates in the religious calendar. The week before Easter, known as *Semana Santa*, is characterised by processions and masses, the most extravagant of which is the procession of Mãe Soberana in Loulé on Easter Sunday itself. Loulé is also famous for its Battle of Flowers festival in February, while other towns celebrate May Day with music, dancing and feasts in the street.

Music is an important part of life here, as expressions of local character, and this is epitomised by the Algarve Music Festival that is held throughout May and June, taking in recitals, concerts and ballets. Traditional Algarvian dances include the *corridinho*, the *baile de roda* and the *baile mandado*, all of which feature a dancer whose movements are dictated by the *mandador* or conductor, and accompanied by jiggling triangles and accordions. The traditional Portuguese song *fado* is also popular here, although not as widely performed as it is in Lisbon or Coimbra.

In this region, bound on two edges by the sea, fishing has always played a big part in daily local life, and this is celebrated by other festivals, such as Faro's Feira da Nossa Senhora do Carmo on July 16. This date sees fireworks, parades, music and dancing on the seafront.

Generally, life in the Algarve is relaxed and laidback, although obviously benefiting from all the advantages that the modern tourist developments bring: restaurants, shops, hospitals, parks and clean beaches. The nearer the main coastal resorts, the busier it is, and the summer months are obviously when the region receives its most visitors, but there are plenty of places to escape to for peace and quiet and tranquil scenery if the high life isn't for you.

SPECTATOR SPORTS

Football is followed with a fervour by locals in the Algarve region, even though its teams aren't as successful as those in the more northerly regions or in the capital Lisbon. There are various professional clubs in Faro, Lagos, Portimão and Vila Real de

Displays of traditional folk dancing can be experienced at the many local festivals and carnivals

The Algarve

USEFUL CONTACTS:
EDUCATION, HOSPITALS, UTILITIES, TOURIST OFFICES AND SERVICE PROVIDERS

SCHOOLS
If you are moving to live in the Algarve long-term, it is recommended that you enrol your children in a local school. However, there is a wide choice of English and international schools in the area. These include **Algarve International School** (Barros Brancos, Apartado 80, Lagoa; + 351 282 342547), **Barlavento English School** (rua Silva Lopez 28, 2º Fte, Lagos; +351 282 789206), **Colegio Internacional de Vilamoura** (Apartado 856, Quintinhas, Vilamoura; + 351 289 321585) and **Escola Internacional de São Lourenço** (Sitío da Rabona 445, Almancil; +351 289 398328). For more information about schooling and education, contact the **Ministry of Education** (Gabinete Relações Internacionais, avenida 5 de Outubro 35-37, Lisbon; +351 217 950330; www.minedu.pt).

SERVICES
You will need to make sure you get your new home connected up with utilities, so these contacts should prove useful: **Portugal Telecom** (+351 213 540020; www.telecom.pt), **CPPE** (+351 213 525353; www.edp.pt) for electricity, and **EPAL** (+351 213 466541; www.epal.pt) or **Lusagua** (+351 217 928670; www.lusagua.pt) for water. Many homes simply use bottled gas, but one company to contact is **Galp Energia** (+351 217 242500; www.galpenergia.com).

HOSPITALS
There are many hospitals in the Algarve, including **Lagos Hospital Distrital** (rua Castelo Governadores Lagos; + 351 282 761094), **Portimão's Hospital Distrital** (avenida Boavista Praia Vau; + 351 282 418498), **Faro's Hospital Distrital** (rua Leão Penedo; + 351 289 891100) and **Tavira's Clinica Portanova** (avenida Doutor Eduardo Mansinho; +351 281 324112).

TOURIST OFFICES
You can find a tourist office in almost every town in the Algarve, but here is a selection of the main *turismos*: **Albufeira** (rua 5 de Outubro; +351 289 585279), **Faro** (rua da Misericórdia 8-12; +351 289 803604), **Lagos** (rua Vasco da Gama; +351 289 463900), **Portimão** (cais de Comercio e Turismo; +351 282 416556) and **Tavira** (rua da Galeria 9; +351 281 322511).

POLICE
The national emergency number is **112**. Every tourist resort in the Algarve has a small police station, but you may find that the larger city stations have English translators. Contacts worth having are those of the stations in **Albufeira** (estrada Vale de Pedras; +351 289 515420), **Faro** (largo de São Sebastião 18; +351 289 801828) and **Lagos** (largo Covento Nostra Señhora da Gloria; +351 282 762809).

MORE INFO
You can get more information about everything from police stations and schools in the area to visas and immigration from the **British Consulate** in the Algarve (largo Francisco A Mauricio; +351 282 417800) or from this website (www.rtalgarve.pt).

San Antonio. There is much excitement in the area about 2004's European Football Championships that are being held in stadia all round the country, and much of the current development is to cater for the influx of fans from all round the world who will no doubt descend on the Algarve and the rest of Portugal in their thousands next summer. One of the most outward signs of this development is the recently built Estádio Intermunicipal, just outside Faro on the way to Loulé.

Many golf and tennis tournaments are held at the various clubs dotted around the Algarve, and it is not uncommon to see golf, tennis and football stars mingling with the locals at bars, clubs and trendy nightspots in some coastal towns, especially in Albufeira and Faro.

The other popular sport is bullfighting. Although different to Spanish bullfights, the Portuguese version does not allow the bull to be killed in the ring. Less bloodthirsty, the performances are focused on the skill of the horsebacked *cavaleiro* who attempts to plant *bandarilhas* (barbed darts) in the bull's back. Hundreds of people flock to watch the fights in the Algarve's bullrings, usually held at weekends throughout the summer months.

> For a guide to property prices in the Algarve, turn to our Price Guide, starting on page 192

The Regions

ALENTEJO

The sprawling Alentejo region, with its rolling countryside, is home to a wealth of historic monuments, from Roman temples to medieval castles and beautiful churches

Évora's Roman temple is just one of the ancient monuments dotted around the Alentejo area

The Regions

Many of Alentejo's hillside towns feature white-washed houses and magnificent views

Alentejo

The white-washed, red-rooved houses built on the hillside at Mértola are overlooked by the imposing 13th-century castle and keep

Alentejo comprises roughly the bottom half of Portugal excluding the far southern area of the Algarve. Its name comes from the Latin for 'beyond the Tagus', owing to its geographical position away from the river Tagus (called the Tejo in Portuguese), which runs from the north of the country and ends at Lisbon. This huge expanse of land has its eastern border with Spain, and touches the Ribatejo in the west, the Algarve in the south, Beira Baixa in the north and the Atlantic in the east. It is split into two halves – Alto in the north and Baixo in the south – and covers one-third of the entire country.

Its characteristic rolling, hilly landscape dotted with granite-built medieval villages, is often called 'the bread basket of Portugal', and it has a significant agricultural importance in Portugal's economy, with some wheat, barley, cork and olive plantations continuously used since Roman times. By contrast, western Alentejo relies heavily on busy fishing and port towns, such as that of Sines.

The Alentejo region was an important part of the Portuguese empires of both the Romans and the

SNAPSHOTS

- When Portugal changed over to the euro in 2001, the government employed Catholic priests to explain the impact of the changes to those living in the slow-moving, inland rural areas.
- Beja has spawned one of Portugal's most famous and controversial books, the *Five Love Letters of Portugal*, reportedly written by the nun Sister Mariana Alcoforado to Count Chamilly, a cavalry officer from France. Translated in 1669 into French, the original letters have never been traced.
- The Mira estuary at Vila Nova de Milfontes is rumoured to have been used by Hannibal and the Carthaginians to shelter from storms.
- Beja is now the only district of Alentejo to have a communist government; they have been ousted elsewhere in the region, following the 1974 revolution when workers without land took collective ownership of *latifúndios*.

The Regions

ALENTEJO REGION INFORMATION

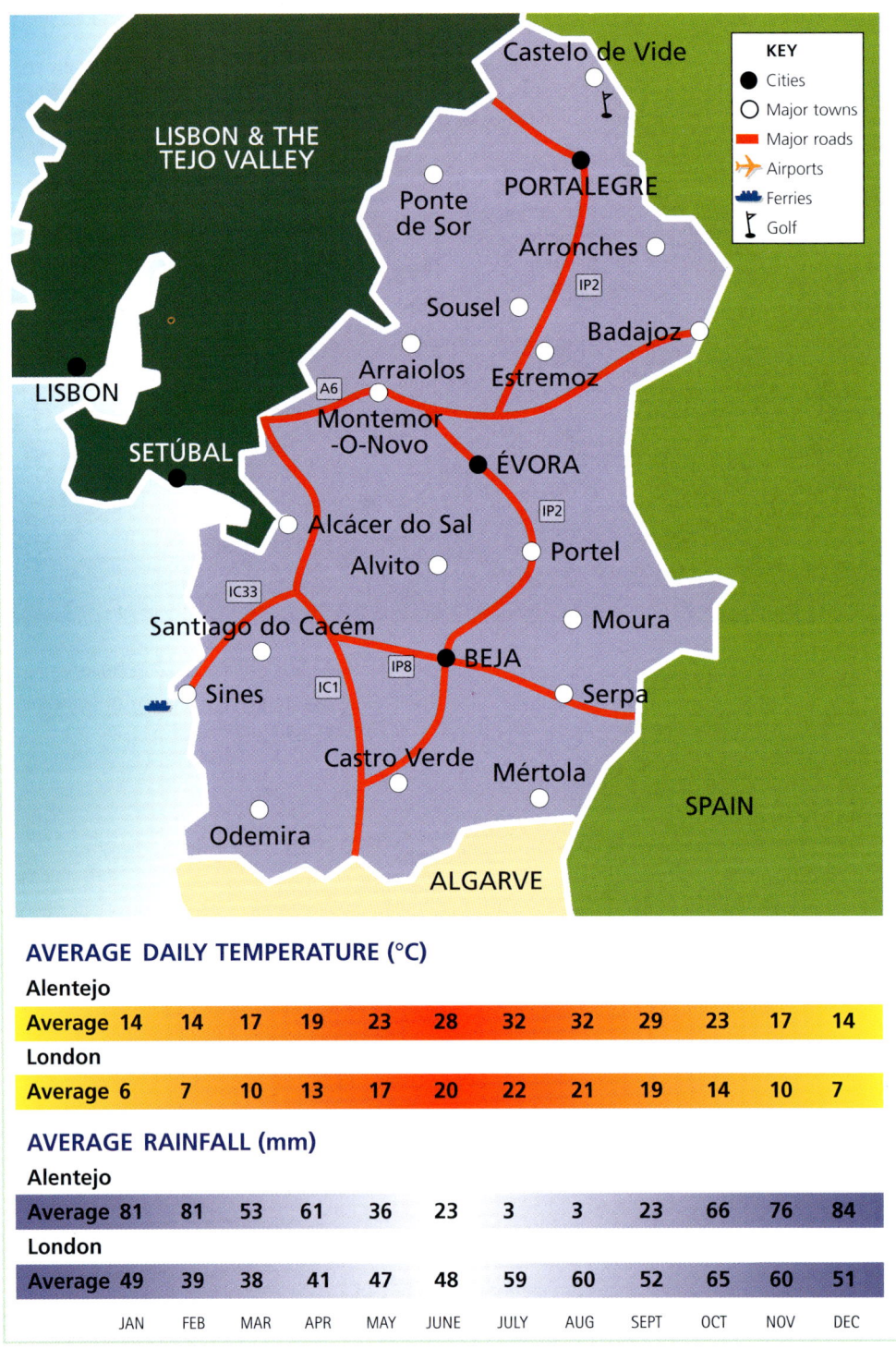

AVERAGE DAILY TEMPERATURE (°C)

Alentejo											
Average 14	14	17	19	23	28	32	32	29	23	17	14
London											
Average 6	7	10	13	17	20	22	21	19	14	10	7

AVERAGE RAINFALL (mm)

Alentejo											
Average 81	81	53	61	36	23	3	3	23	66	76	84
London											
Average 49	39	38	41	47	48	59	60	52	65	60	51
JAN	FEB	MAR	APR	MAY	JUNE	JULY	AUG	SEPT	OCT	NOV	DEC

Alentejo

GETTING THERE

AIR Alentejo's lack of international airports means that you're left with a choice of flying into Lisbon or Faro and making the rest of the journey by car, train or coach. **TAP Air Portugal** (020 7828 2092; www.tap.pt) and **PGA Portugália Airlines** (0870 755 0025; www.pga.pt) fly from Gatwick and Manchester to Lisbon and Faro, while **British Airways** (0845 773 3377; www.britishairways.co.uk) flies from London Gatwick and Heathrow.

SEA You can travel by ferry into the Spanish port of Bilbao with **P&O Ferries** (0870 600 0600; (www.poportsmouth.com) or sail to Santander with **Brittany Ferries** (0870 536 0360; www.brittany-ferries.com).

ROAD From the northern Spanish ports, it is a direct drive along the N1 to Madrid, then to Mérida, Badajoz and over the border into Alentejo. For travel to the Alentejo by coach, contact **Eurolines UK** (0870 574 3219; www.eurolines.co.uk).

RAIL The Alentejo region is served by train lines from Lisbon, Faro and Madrid, with most visiting the main towns of Évora, Beja and Portalegre. Other local lines run services to many of the smaller regional towns. For more information on train travel to and in the Alentejo region, and the rest of Portugal, contact **Rail Europe** (0870 584 8848; www.raileurope.co.uk).

CLIMATE SUMMARY

Alentejo enjoys a Mediterranean climate, and it's no surprise that this area provides grapes for one-third of Portugal's entire wine-making industry.

The summers here are undeniably hot, with the temperatures often averaging over 30 degrees Celsius, making air conditioning a common feature in most shops and offices, as well as plenty of homes. The winters here, in contrast, are cool, mild and wet. The further north and inland you go in the region, where the terrain is semi-arid and the winds are dry, the warmer the temperatures. The coast south of Lisbon, however, is cooler, thanks to the sea breezes, although it still provides plenty of great tanning opportunities. But those wanting to dip a toe in the sea should watch out, as the ocean is surprisingly colder than the waters of the Med. Most visitors come to the region outside the hottest (and busiest) months of July and August, when they can appreciate the warm spring and autumn and the legendarily kind and mild winters.

Evidence of the traditional rural life is still to be found in villages all around Alentejo

WWW.STRAWBERRYWORLD.COM

Moors, and many towns here – such as Beja, Estremoz and Portalegre – have a rich historic heritage. Even after the Portuguese won the country back from the Moors, Alentejo remained a thriving region, and today is littered with medieval settlements, including the spa village of Castelo de Vide and Borba, with its stunning 15th-century Nossa Senhora das Neves church.

Alentejo's main tourist draw is the ancient capital, Évora. Classified as a UNESCO World Heritage Site, it boasts prehistoric cave paintings and neolithic stone monuments, as well as impressive Roman, Moorish and Christian remains. These include the enormous fortified Sé cathedral, built in the 12th century, the remains of the Roman temple dedicated to the goddess Diana, a large selection of beautiful churches and the grand Palácio dos Duques de Cadaval, a medieval castle that became home to the Cadaval Dukes, formerly the grand home of two Portuguese kings.

WORKING IN THE AREA

Although one of the largest regions of Portugal, the Alentejo isn't naturally blessed with a wealth of jobs for the foreign immigrant. That said, the main industries that keep the area going are agriculture and wine-making. Whether you have experience or not, you should find some employment (albeit seasonal) in the olive, cork, wheat or eucalyptus plantations, or perhaps on sheep and pig farms that

The Regions

EMPLOYMENT CONTACTS

Portuguese Embassy:
11 Belgrave Square, London, SW1X 8PP; 020 7235 5331

British Embassy: rua de São Bernardo 33, Lisbon; +351 213 924000; www.ukembassy.pt

Portuguese Trade Office (for information about international companies with offices in the Alentejo region): 2nd Floor 21-251 Sackville Street, London, W1X 2LY; 020 7494 1441

The British Council (for general employment advice): rua Luís Fernandes 1 - 3, Lisbon; +351 213 214500

Cambridge Schools (employment for TEFL certificate holders): avenida da Liberdade 173, Lisbon; +351 213 124600; www.cambridge.pt

International House (for details of English teaching vacancies): rua Marquês Sá da Bandeira 16, Lisbon; +351 213 151496; www.internationalhouse.com

Employment & Vocational Training Agency: rua Vasco da Gama 7, Évora; +351 266 760500

Job Centres
IEFP Portalegre: rua 31 de janeiro 96; +351 453 30373
Centro de Emprego Beja: praça da República 1-4; +351 843 29086

Centro Regional de Segurança Social (social security office for information about benefits): rua Dom Manuel da Conceição Santos 51, Évora; **+351 266 7409430**

Overseas Jobs Express (newspaper listing tourism-related jobs abroad): www.overseasjobsexpress.co.uk

Anglo-Portuguese News (English paper published in Lisbon with job adverts): Apartado 113, Estoril; +351 214 661423

Instituto Portugues da Juventude (opportunities for youth and voluntary work): avenida da Liberdade 194, Lisbon; +351 213 179200)

International Friendship League (voluntary positions in the Alentejo area): rua Ruy de Sousa Vinagre 2, Alcochete, Lisbon; +351 212 341082)

Ordem dos Medicos (advertising medical posts): avenida da Liberdade 65, Lisbon; +351 213 462725

Ordem dos Advogados (legal posts): largo Domingos 14, Lisbon; +351 218 823550)

IAPMEI (offers support for small to medium-sized enterprises): rua Rodrigo da Fonseca 73, Lisbon; +351 213 864333

ICEP (for details about investing in Portuguese trade and tourism): avenida 5 de outubro 1010, Lisbon; +351 217 930103; www.portugal.com

---

are prevalent in the area. These jobs can be anything from harvesting to running your own farm, but you have to be prepared for hard work. The wine industry does open its doors to foreign employees, and whether you dream of simply picking grapes or becoming a wine-maker, there are opportunities to be found here.

There are also some jobs to be had in tourism, either as English-speaking tour guides (in the larger Alentejo towns) or in tourist offices, although a grasp of Portuguese will help greatly, as you will no doubt be dealing with mostly native tourists.

Other industries include the thriving marble trade (the Alentejo region has been known for its quality marble since Roman times), as well as stone quarries, construction and energy companies, some of which have headquarters or offices in the UK, in which case it may be easier to apply from home before arriving in the area. If you already work in one of these industries, your experience will go a long way, but bear in mind that you will no doubt be expected to have at least started to learn the language, if not have some degree of fluency.

For those with teaching qualifications, in Portuguese or in English (especially if you hold a TEFL certificate), there are some jobs in education. These will mostly be in local schools, but if you're willing to travel between the region and Lisbon, it would be possible to get a post in one of the capital's various international schools.

Giving domestic help as a maid, cleaner or au pair is always an option, although it's not as popular here as in the neighbouring Algarve region. However, it's worth scouring the local papers for available posts. One growing area of employment, though, is in the building and carpentry trade. With many second home buyers extending their search from the Algarve to the inland Alentejo areas or the coast

Alentejo

BUYING IN ALENTEJO

This huge area of Portugal, by its very nature, offers a mass of property types, from seaside villas near the coast, to rambling farms in the country and apartments in the busier towns. The one thing Alentejo doesn't yet have a lot of, however, is modern developments of flats or villas, although these are becoming more popular in the south of the region, mainly thanks to the interest shown by house buyers spreading their search north from the Algarve.

Many second home-buyers look to the country, where homesteads set in sprawling areas of land can be had for relatively little outlay. For instance, a farm property with around 18,000m² of land sells for around 210,000 euros (about £140,000). Typical of the area are the long, low, stone- and clay-built properties, often with characteristic red rooves, offering a cooling environment in the hot summers and warmth in the cool winters. These homes are usually sturdy and built to last, so make for great investment propositions.

Those looking to set up a tourist-related business in this area, such as a B&B or horse trekking centre will be pleased to know many of the houses here come with a generous amount of land, ideal for building extra guest accommodation or adding a swimming pool. There are also occasional chances to buy large properties, perfect for converting into hotels, such as the 23-room farmhouse shown below.

Of course, properties do come up for grabs in the city's main towns, and a decently proportioned townhouse in a town like Elvas and Portalegre can cost in the region of 240,000 euros (about £160,000). In many traditional villages, such as Castelo de Vide, you will find the distinctive whitewashed homes with red clay tiled rooves, and these come slightly cheaper.

This region combines history with good links to Lisbon and Algarve and is definitely one of Portugal's up-and-coming areas.

WHAT YOU GET FOR YOUR EUROS

PROPERTY 1

AREA: Portalegre

DESCRIPTION: Requiring renovation, this traditional village house offers 23 rooms, and features a courtyard and enormous garden. Located in a large town near the Spanish border, this property affords splendid views and is extremely characteristic. This property offers the future owner enormous potential.

PRICE: 157,600 euros
UK EQUIVALENT: £105,065

PROPERTY 2

AREA: Ourique

DESCRIPTION: Located close to the coast and within easy reach of Lisbon, this beautifully constructed villa boasts four bedrooms, and also features a two-bedroom guest house within the grounds. The two houses are set within 23 acres of pleasant gardens and woodlands. It also has a swimming pool.

PRICE: 550,000 euros
UK EQUIVALENT: £366,665

For more properties in Alentejo, turn to our Price Guide, starting on page 192

The Regions

Fields of sunflowers are a common sight in this area, where agriculture plays an important role

Alentejo

The coastal resort of Vila Nova de Milfontes is dominated by the ivy-covered medieval castle that was originally built as a Moorish fortress

south of Lisbon, there are various opportunities for working on new-builds or renovation projects. This can either be in an existing firm or as a self-employed freelancer, and you may find yourself working for English-speaking home owners.

Medical posts are often available at one of Alentejo's five main hospitals, but again it's important that you have a grounding in the language. And for those with more of a sports background, there are possibilities for gaining employment at one of the region's golf courses or working with horses at the many trekking centres.

LEISURE TIME

The dramatic landscape of the Alentejo means there are plenty of outdoor pursuits to take part in here, and, as mentioned above, one of the most popular pastimes is horse riding. There are many trekking trails scattered around the hillsides, and one company that organises group or individual horseback tours of the region is *CDA Portugal* (Apartado 116, Milfontes; +351 283 998106; www.cdaportugal.com).

Golf-lovers will, unfortunately, only find two 18-hole courses in the region, although they are of a great standard. You should take your clubs to the *Marvão Golf Club* (Quinta do Prado, San Salvador d'Aranmenha, Marvão; +351 245 993755; www.portugalgolfcourses.com), a course that is dramatically set in São Mamede Natural Park. The second option is the course at *Tróia* on the Lisbon coast (Complexo Turistico de Tróia, Setúbal; +351 265 494112; www.portugalgolfcourses.com/troia.html).

Walking is another great outdoor pastime, and Alentejo's four nature parks make great destinations for those after a strenuous hike or a gentle stroll. The most adventurous should head for the four famous peaks – Fria, Marvão, Castelo de Vide and São Mamede – of the *Serra de São Mamede Natural Park* (+351 245 203631), while other options include the *Parque Natural das Serras de Aire e Candeeiros* in Portalegre (+351 243 999480), the *Parque Natural da Arrábida* (+351 265 541140), stretching from Setúbal's peninsula to the Tagus valley, and the *Parque Natural do Sudoeste Alentejano e Costa Vicentina* (+351 283 322735). For general details of the large array of organised hikes and walking tours on offer around

The Regions

RESTAURANTS

The **Adega do Alentejano** in Évora (rua Gabriel Vitor do Monte Pereira 21a; **+351 266 744447**) is a great stop if you want to sample well prepared regional dishes. Don't miss the *à la carte* option, which costs 10 euros including wine.

Also in Évora, the **Cozinha de Santo Humberto** restaurant (rua da Moeda 39; +351 266 704251) is a more upmarket proposition, serving local specialities for around 20 euros per person. It is a firm favourite with the locals, which is always a good sign. The knuckle of pork (known locally as *chispe assado de Santo Humberto*) is a must-try.

With an impressive wine list, the **São Rosas**, (largo de Dom Dinis 11, Estremoz; **+351 268 333345**) is a restored medieval inn that is widely regarded as Estremoz's best eatery. It offers a well priced tourist option *ementa turistica* for 15 euros.

In Elvas, **Canal 7** (rua dos Sapateiros 16; **+351 268 623593**) offers budget meals from 6 euros, while in Sines, **Varanda Oceano** (Largo Nossa Senhora Salvas, Sines; +351 269 633135) specialises in shelfish dishes, and has a quirky 1930s-style interior. The staff are friendly, but be prepared to order in Portuguese.

CLASSIC DISH
Porco com ameijoas a alentejana

Pork served with clams is a popular local, dish and tastes delicious washed down with a local red wine.

the region, contact *Portugal Walks* (+351 282 698676; www.portugalwalks.com).

Sines's secluded beaches at Praia do Somouqueira are great for watersports, while for good surfing, you should visit São Torpes beach in Porto Covo. Hot-air ballooning is also popular in this area, with *Hemisférios* (+351 919 445868) offering flights (costing around 150 euros) around the Setúbal area.

EAT, DRINK AND BE MERRY

There is a wide variety of dishes and distinctive flavours in this part of Portugal, with many national dishes named after the region. The most famous is *porco com ameijoas a alentejana* (see *Classic Dish* box, above), along with *carne de porco à alentejana* (pork with coriander) and *sopa alentejana* (a tasty bread, garlic, coriander and olive oil soup, topped with a poached egg). Another favourite starter in the region is the traditional *gazpacho*, a tomato and garlic soup served cold and topped with chopped cucumber, peppers and a drizzle of olive oil. Tasty main courses worth sampling are *borrego ensopado* (a lamb stew in a rich gravy), *cabrito assado* (roast kid with paprika, garlic and red wine), *ensopado de borrego* (spicy lamb stew with bread) and other rich stews, the best being those from Castelo de Vide, Nisa, Arronches and Arraiolos.

Other regional favourites that might not sound immediately appetising are *chispe de coentrada* (pigs' trotters with coriander) served in Baixo Alentejo and *miolos salteados* (sautéd brains) from Alto Alentejo. Meanwhile *coelho em vinho* (rabbit fried in oil and served in a wine sauce) is another Alentejan speciality. Fish dishes served in Alentejo include *caldeirada*, a stew of fish with potato and served with cheesy bread.

Speaking of bread, as Alentejo is the so-called bread basket of Portugal, many dishes, including the aforementioned *sopa alentejana* feature bread in some form or another. Popular here are hearty, bread-based, porridge-like dishes, called *açorda*. Rich, thick and very filling, the dish comes in many guises, including the very popular *açorda de marisco* (bread, eggs and shellfish). Most meals in the region's restaurants are served with a helping of the traditional *pão alentejano*, or peasant bread, but if this all sounds too filling, you should try some of the region's smaller treats. These include *morcelas de Niza* (blood sausages), *chouriços de Beja* (spicy

It's not all rugged landscapes as Alentejo is also home to a couple of popular golf courses

DAVID HEADLAND ASSOCIATES

Alentejo

Much of the region's wine is aged in oak barrels in cellars like this one in Estremoz

sausages) or *cacholeira* (sausage made with pig's liver, blood-soaked meats and other offal), although all three may require a brave constitution!

Those with a sweet tooth will enjoy the huge variety of cakes the area produces, including the *palha* from Fabrantes, the Imperial cakes of Almeirim, the almond paste and egg cakes available at cafes in *Évora Bolo Joana* (Santa Clara convent, Évora), the convent pastries of Portalegre and Beja and *queijada*, an Alentejan cheesecake. All of them are well worth trying over a coffee.

Of course, this area is known for its wine-making, and there are plenty of local bottlings to be tried.

WINE

The Alentejo has the ideal climate for growing grapes, and the vines and wines of this area are held in national and international esteem. Portugal's most famous estate, the Quinta do Carmo, is found in this area. Alentejo produces mostly full-bodied red wines that taste fruity and fresh when young and more richly flavoured when left to age. The red grapes of Aragonês (Tinta Roriz, Tempranillo), Trincadeira (Tinta Amarela), Periquita (Castelão Francês) and Alfrocheiro Preto dominate, but white wines are improving, and the Síria (Roupeiro) grape is thought to be the best.

The Regions

The most well known and enjoyable are those from famed winemaker João Ramos. Top of the list to try are the Trincadeira 2000 (a young rich wine), the tasty Syrah 2000 (with an intriguing herby flavour) and his figurehead wine, the Marques de Borba Reserva 1999. When dining out, variety and quality is assured when a bottle is marked *vinho regional* (regional wine).

FOR CULTURE VULTURES

If you want to take a break from the outdoor sports, or if you've eaten your fill in the local restaurants and cafés, then there's a huge range of museums and galleries throughout the Alentejo. The most famous place to experience a bit of culture is in Évora. With its many churches and Roman baths, there is plenty to see, and that's before you've even considered the Museu de Arte Sacra da Sé, the sacred art museum in the cathedral. There's also the collection of paintings, sculpture and archeological objects in the *Museu de Évora* (largo do Conde de Vila Flor; +351 266 702604) and the range of portraits and ancient religious texts kept in the Salas de Exposiçõ in the *Palácio dos Duques de Cadaval* (largo Conde de Vila Flor; +351 266 704714).

Other archeological artefacts can be found at various locations throughout the region, including the *Museu Etnográfico* in Serpa (+351 284 540100), the *Museu Visigótico* in Beja (largo de Santo Amaro; +351 284 321465) or the museum housed in the Romanesque-Gothic church at San João de Alporão. To see the ancient structures *in situ*, try the Roman ruins at Pisões, or perhaps the 15th-century Amoreiras aqueduct in the fortress town of Elvas.

This is a region of splendid castles as well, such as the impressive 13th-century *castelo*, also in Elvas,

CORK

Almost as ubiquitous as the vineyards are Alentejo's plantations of cork trees, although some farmers complain that their cork trade is under threat thanks to the recent rise in the popularity of plastic corks. The highly skilled process of stripping cork trees has been carried out in Alentejo for centuries, but it's no simple feat. A cork tree has to mature for 25 years before it is first cut. Once they are old enough, the trees are 'harvested' every nine years, when skilled cork workers peel back the outside bark to reveal the cork inside. The cork is carved off the tree and the remaining trunk turns a reddish brown, before growing back again. A well tended tree will give cork for up to 100 years.

However, now that many wineries are choosing to use plastic corks, those in the trade feel it could endanger their future and are campaigning for corks to still be used. Another argument is that cork plantations provide a perfect habitat for rare wildlife, including the Iberian lynx and Bonelli's eagle. Think about that next time you reach for the corkscrew!

the medieval *castelo* at Portalegre and the 14th-century fortress of Queen Isabel (later made a saint) in Estremoz. Many of these castles are worth the detour alone, but some also host museums charting their and the local town's history, many being free to browse around. Other historic sites in the area include the Duke's Palace and Nossa Senhora da Esperança monastery at Vila Viçosa, the chapel of São Salvador do Mundo at Elvas and Portalegre's São Bernardo convent.

For a slightly different taste of local culture, try a couple of the more intriguing museums of the area, namely the *Museu da Tapeçaria* in Portalegre (rua da Figueira 9; +351 245 307980) dedicated to the town's famous tapestry factory, and Serpa's *Museu do Relógio* (praça da República; +351 284 543194; www.museudorelogio.pa-net.pt) in the Mosteirinho convent, home to over a thousand clocks!

SHOPPING: GIFTS AND GROCERIES

One of the most popular locally made souvenirs to look out for in Alentejo is pottery, especially the colourful figures usually portraying rural scenes with

These brightly coloured clay figurines make for perfect Alentejan souvenirs

Alentejo

The architecture of the region takes in the curved lines of the Manueline style (above), scattered and untidy hillside towns (top right) and *azulejo* tile-covered frontages (right).

animals or harvested crops. Pedro Corval and Évora in particular are known for their earthenware, pottery and decorative plates, and the best place to pick them up is at the handicraft fair held in Estremoz at the beginning of May.

Other rural crafts that make wonderful presents are embroidery and hand-made carpets, particularly the beautiful rugs produced by the craftsmen at Arraiolos. Leather goods can also be found in plentiful supply throughout the region, and it's worth keeping an eye out for quality handbags, wallets and purses.

Most towns in the area have a weekly market, and the Rossio Saturday morning market is particularly renowned for selling a wide range of local produce including fruit and vegetables, fish and meat, and the flavoursome local goat's and ewe's milk cheeses. You'll find a choice of food shops wherever you go, but if you're after supermarkets, look out for the Pingo Doce chain found throughout Portugal, and also the large Modelo and Intermarché supermarkets on the outskirts of Portalegre.

POPULAR LOCAL FESTIVALS

This area, like all others in Portugal, celebrates many festivals, most in conjunction with saints' days or the celebrations of Holy Week or *Semana Santa*. However, probably the most renowned festival in Alentejo is **Colete Encarnado** or running of the bulls, which takes place in Évora each September. Bulls are released in the town's main square and chased through the streets until the bulls (or their chasers) are exhausted. Dangerous, yet exciting, it's certainly worth seeing... but make sure you keep your distance!

GETTING AROUND

A comprehensive bus service makes getting around the Alentejo easy. *Rodoviária Nacional* (+351 266 769410) operates three buses per day between Beja and Évora, while other bus services throughout the region are run by *Belos Transportes* from Évora and Estremoz (+351 266 769410) and *Eva Transportes* from Beja (+351 284 313620). Services to the region from Lisbon are mainly run by *Rede Nacional de Expressos* (+351 213 545439). The company also

The Regions

The Alentejo region is littered with ancient remains such the Templo Romano in Évora (above) but also various dolmens, menhirs and neolithic tombs throughout the countryside (right)

runs a bus service from Faro in the Algarve through Alentejo to Lisbon three times a day, with stops at various towns in the region.

If you prefer to hire a car, you'll find a *Hertz* office in Évora (+351 266 701767) and a *Europcar* office in Beja (+351 284 328128).

LOCAL LIFE

Alentejan life is heavily influenced by history and tradition, whether it's through the local festivals or the winemaking process. Many towns are devoted to the wine trade, and hold celebrations of the harvest and the first bottlings, but one thing all places here have in common is their festivals. These include religious celebrations such as processions through narrow village streets, like those held in Vidigueiria or the slaughtering of lambs at Easter in Castelo de Vide. St John's Day sees massive celebrations in Évora in June, while Elvas celebrates St Matthew's Day in September with markets, dancing and bullfights. Agricultural fairs and markets are also popular in most of the larger towns in the area, and on various weekends throughout the summer you will see town squares and streets filled with all attractions: stalls selling local fare; pens of cows, pigs and sheep; and schoolchildren putting on displays of folk dancing and music.

With many local people here making their living from agriculture and handicrafts, this is not exactly a prosperous region, and neither does it receive much income from tourism, except perhaps on the coast and in Évora. The result is that life tends to be quiet and relaxed... one of the many reasons people are beginning to discover Alentejo as a perfect location

Alentejo

USEFUL CONTACTS:
EDUCATION, HOSPITALS, UTILITIES, TOURIST OFFICES

SCHOOLS
For information on Portuguese schools, contact **The British Council** (rua Luís Fernandes, 1-3, Lisbon; +351 213 214500), who have a full list of English speaking schools in Portugal. You can also contact the **Departmento do Education** in Alentejo's capital, Évora; (+351 266 757900). For details of private English schools, the **Ministério da Educação** (avenida 5 de outubro 35-37, Lisbon; +351 217 950330; www.min-edu.pt) is a great source for general information.

SERVICES
Many homes, both old and new, will rely on bottled gas, and this can be obtained from a range of companies, including **Marques Raso**; (+351 219 830157). One bottle lasts a week. For phone connections, contact **Portugal Telecom**; (+351 213 540020; www.telecom.pt); for electricity contact **CPPE** (+351 213 525353; www.edp.pt) or **EPAL** (+351 213 466541; www.epal.pt) and for water services, get in touch with **Lusagua** (+351 217 928670; www.lusagua.pt).

HOSPITALS
The Alentejo Regional Health Administration is an essential contact (praça 1º de Maio 4, Évora; +351 266 758770; www.arsalentejo.pt). There are various hospitals in the area, including Évora's **Hospital do Espírito Santo** (largo Senhora da Pobreza; + 351 266 740100), Beja's **Hospital José Joaquim Fernandes** (+351 284 310200) and **Hospital Distrital** (rua Dr António FC Lima; +351 284 310200), Portalegre's **Hospital Doutor José Maria Grande** (avenida Santo António; +351 245 301000), Elvas's **Hospital de Santa Luzia de Elvas Morada** (rua Mariana Mart; +351 268 622225) and Serpa's **Hospital São Paulo de Serpa** (largo de São Paulo; **+351 284 544715**). It is usually possible to get by with English in these hospitals, as most medical staff have some command of English, but be prepared to learn some stock Portuguese 'health' phrases.

TOURIST OFFICES
There are only a few tourist offices (called *turismo*) in Alentejo, but they are all situated in key historic spots. They can be found in **Portalegre** (rua 1o maio 7; **+351 245 300770**), **Beja** (praça da Republica, **+351 284 310150**), **Évora** (Posto de Turismo, praça do Gerlado 73; **+351 266 742534**) and **Elvas** (Serviços de Turismo, Câmara Municipal; +351 268 622236). If you're not in one of these towns and you want to find out information, from within Portugal, about museums, galleries and other tourist attractions in the Alentejo region, then you can always call the freephone 'green tourist line' or **Linha Verde Turista** (+351 800 296296). If your Portuguese isn't perfect, simply ask for one of their many English-speaking operators.

POLICE
Portugal's emergency number for police, fire brigade (*bombeiros de incendio*) and ambulance (*ambulancia*) services is **112**. However, it might be worth making a note of police station contacts for **Mértola** (rua Dr Afonsa Costa; +351 286 612127), **Beja** (largo Dom Nuno Álvares Pereira; +351 284 322022), **Évora** (rua Francisco Soares Lusitano; +351 266 746977) and **Estremoz** (Câmara Municipal; +351 268 334141).

MORE INFO
To get more information about immigration, relocation and visas, contact the **British Embassy** (rua São Bernardo 33, Lisbon; +351 213 924000; www.uk-embassy.pt).

for a second home or a getaway. That said, most towns will have local discos and bars where the nightlife can be fun if not boisterous.

SPECTATOR SPORTS
This is probably the one area of Portugal where bullfighting actually overtakes football in popularity, where, strangely enough, most local people support either Porto or Lisbon teams. Most towns have a bullring, where fights are held most weeks throughout the summer months. Although in Portuguese bullfights it is illegal to kill the bull during the fight, certain Alentejan towns are asserting their independence (and making headlines) by killing the bull in public. Whatever your views, they are certainly a lively diversion… but you have been warned!

> For a guide to property prices in Alentejo, turn to our Price Guide, starting on page 192

The Regions

LISBON AND ESTREMADURA

The Portuguese capital is a popular tourist spot thanks to its stunning position and colourful history, while the neighbouring regions of Estremadura and Ribatejo are full of spectacular beaches, quaint inland villages and impressive monasteries

PORTUGUESE TOURIST BOARD

Lisbon spills down the hillside towards the waterfront on the river Tagus

The Regions

Lisbon's famous Discoveries Monument commemorates the Portuguese expeditions made throughout the centuries

Lisbon and Estremadura

The busy centre of Portugal's capital city (left), with its packed streets and tall townhouses complemented by the genteel seaside resort of Cascais (top left) and the beautifully verdant inland town of Sintra (above)

The city of Lisbon and the regions of Estremadura and Ribatejo lie on the western coast of Portugal, about two-thirds down the country. Lisbon is set at the mouth of the river Tagus (Rio Tejo), which splits the country in two distinct halves. And it is this geographical split that resulted in the name Estremadura, it being the furthest area away from the northern Douro region (*extrema Dourii*) when the lands north of the Tagus were part of the Christian kingdom of Portugal.

After the Algarve, Lisbon is probably Portugal's second most visited area by foreign tourists, but even today it retains a charm and friendliness somewhat lacking in other far busier European capitals. The city is built on seven hills and was originally peopled by the Phoenicians, although it rose in prominence when the Romans established a busy port and fishing centre here around 150BC. Most of the city was destroyed by the huge earthquake and the ensuing fires of 1755 and while many houses of the Alfama district survived, most areas were rebuilt in the 18th century on a grid plan, as can still be seen in the Bairro, Baixa and Chiado quarters. Not long after the city had begun to recover from the disaster, it was occupied by Napoleonic forces until a combined army of Portuguese, English and other soldiers succeeded in freeing the city in 1811. In recent years, Lisbon has enjoyed much attention, and the success and wealth that comes with it; it was voted European City of Culture in 1994, played host to Expo 98 and its football stadia will host many games in the 2004 European Football Championships.

The city boasts many impressive sights, including the Castelo de São Jorge, which sits atop one of the seven hills, the Sé cathedral in the Alfama district, the Mosteiros (monastery) dos Jerónimos and the famous Tower in Belém. More modern attractions are the Oceanarium in the Parque dos Nações (built for Expo 98) and the 1960 monument to the Discoveries in Belém.

There are also plenty of attractions outside the city. To the south, for instance, are the quiet yet beautiful beaches of the Costa da Caparica and the nature reserve at the mouth of the river Sado. To the west are the seaside resorts of Cascais (now highly developed for tourism) and Estoril (bearing traces of its elegant past), while inland is the attractive hilly town of Sintra, with its extravagantly designed, multi-coloured palaces and houses.

Further into the Estremadura region are the windswept coastal towns of Ericeira, Peniche and

The Regions

REGION INFORMATION

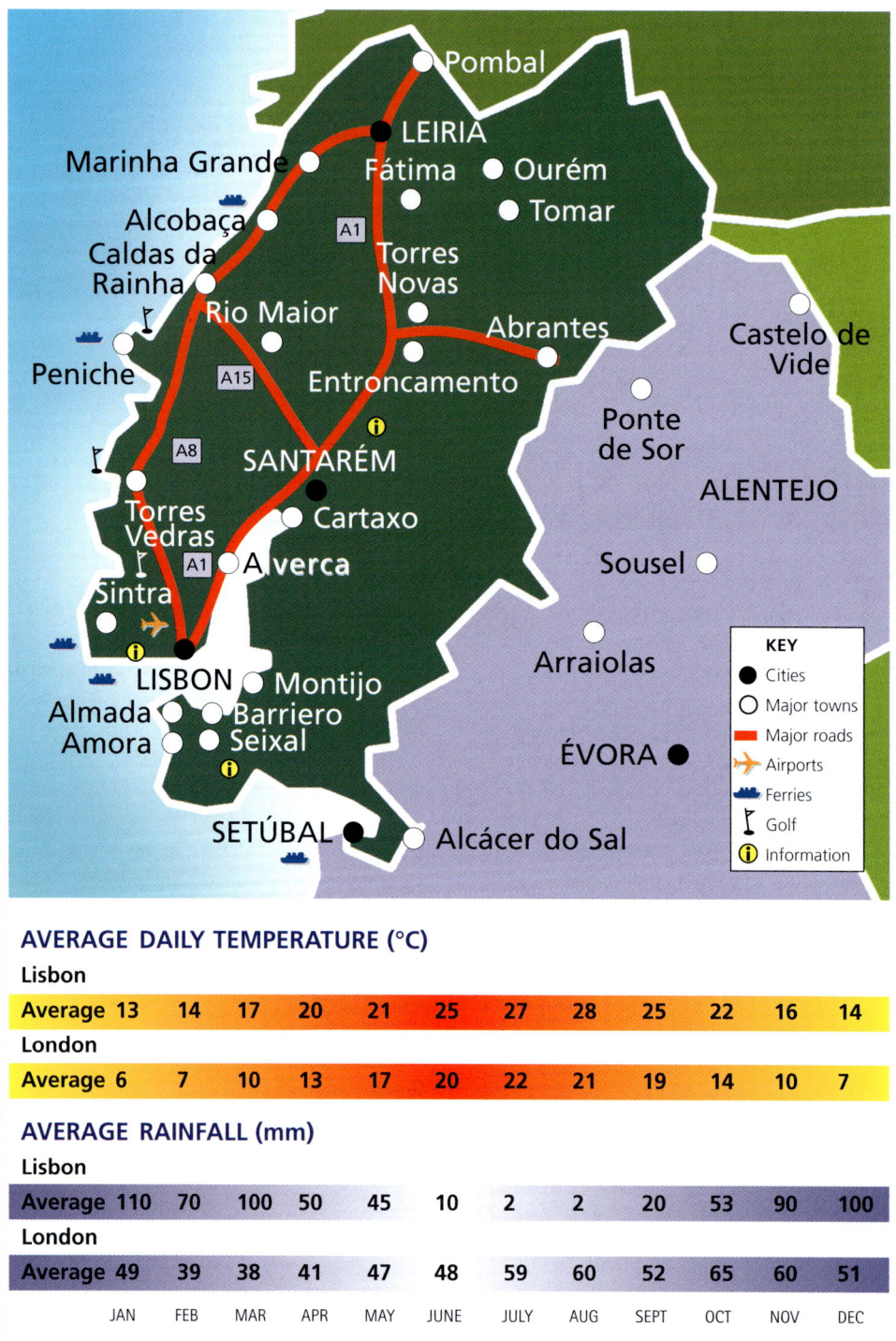

AVERAGE DAILY TEMPERATURE (°C)

Lisbon											
Average 13	14	17	20	21	25	27	28	25	22	16	14
London											
Average 6	7	10	13	17	20	22	21	19	14	10	7

AVERAGE RAINFALL (mm)

Lisbon											
Average 110	70	100	50	45	10	2	2	20	53	90	100
London											
Average 49	39	38	41	47	48	59	60	52	65	60	51
JAN	FEB	MAR	APR	MAY	JUNE	JULY	AUG	SEPT	OCT	NOV	DEC

Lisbon and Estremadura

GETTING THERE

AIR British Airways (0845 7733377; www.britishairways.co.uk) flies into Lisbon from London Heathrow, while **TAP Air Portugal** (020 7828 2092; www.tap.pt), the Portuguese international airline, flies into Lisbon from both Heathrow and Gatwick. **PGA Portugália Airlines** (08707 550025; www.pga.pt) is Portugal's domestic airline, but also operates flights between Lisbon and Manchester.
SEA Most visitors driving into Portugal will take the ferry to northern Spain and drive down from there. The two main options are to travel from Portsmouth to Bilbao with **P&O** (0870 600 0600; www.poportsmouth.com) or from Plymouth to Santander with **Brittany Ferries** (0870 536 0360; www.britanny-ferries.com).
ROAD From this coast, it's around a 1,000km drive to Lisbon. From Bilbao, take the A68 south and then the A1 to Burgos. (From Santander, take the N623 south to Burgos.) The N620 goes from Burgos, via Valladolid and Salamanca, to the Portuguese border at Fuentes de Oñoro, from where you join the IP5 and then the N17 to Coimbra. Just west of Coimbra, join the main A1 motorway and continue south to Lisbon.
RAIL Take the **Eurostar** (0870 264 9899; www.eurostar.co.uk) from London Waterloo to Paris, where you change for the TGV Atlantique, which takes you as far as Irún in Spain. Here you change for the Sud-Expresso that heads for Coimbra and then Lisbon. Check with **Rail Europe** (0870 584 8848; www.raileurope.co.uk) for timetables, prices and more details.

CLIMATE SUMMARY

The Lisbon regions are blessed with a comfortable climate with mild winters and warm summers. Most of this region's rain falls between November and March, leaving the summer months dry and hot, with barely any rain in July and August. Temperatures are higher on the coast, although tempered by sea winds, while in Lisbon the temperature in summer is made bearable by evening river breezes. Most visitors come in the summer months to take advantage of the sun-drenched beaches, but visiting in late spring or autumn will mean you can avoid the crowds, as well as take advantage of the extended summer. April, May and June are characterised by long, crisply warm days, while September and October can be thought of as an Indian summer, with lazy, languid heat. Watch out for the bitterly cold winter weather in some of the Ribatejo's hill towns, however.

Rossio Square in Lisbon is just one of the legacies left by the rebuilding of the city on a grid pattern after the disastrous earthquake of 1755

FRANCISCA NAVARRO-GARCIA

Nazaré, all popular with watersports fans, while the protected Berlenga islands, just off the coast from Peniche, attract nature lovers and divers. Óbidos, a former port but now about five miles inland, features quaint narrow streets lined with white-washed houses and pretty squares, while Caldas da Rainha is the site of natural hot springs, developed into a hospital in the 15th century. Also worth seeing in the area are the monastery and royal palace of Mafra, the beautiful Mosteiro da Batalha monastery and the amazing 12th-century monastery at Alcobaça.

The Ribatejo region is often considered dull, being littered with factory towns. However, it does offer the region capital of Santarém and its many pretty churches, the breathtaking Convento de Cristo in Tomar and the Catholic shrine at Fátima.

Altogether this area has much to offer, whether you want busy shops or historic sights, watersports or birdwatching, and it's no wonder that it's becoming more and more popular with foreign house buyers, determined to secure themselves a slice of this historic corner of Portugal's culture.

WORKING IN THE AREA

As is the case with almost anywhere in Portugal, except perhaps in the enclaves of British expatriates in the Algarve area, finding work opportunities in Lisbon and the Estremadura and Ribatejo areas will depend to some extent on your knowledge of the

The Regions

EMPLOYMENT CONTACTS

Portuguese Embassy:
11 Belgrave Square, London, SW1X 8PP; 020 7235 5331

British Embassy:
rua de São Bernardo 33, Lisbon; +351 213 924000; www.ukembassy.pt

Portuguese Trade Office (for information about international companies with offices in Lisbon, Estremadura and Ribatejo): 2nd Floor, 21-25a Sackville Street, London, W1X 2LY; 020 7494 1441

International House (for details of English teaching vacancies): rua Marquês Sá da Bandeira 16, Lisbon; +351 213 151496; www.internationalhouse.com

Cambridge Schools (offering employment opportunities for TEFL certificate holders): avenida da Liberdade 173, Lisbon; +351 213 124600; www.cambridge.pt

Centro Emprego (job centre): rua Conde Redondo 129a, 1100 Lisbon; +351 213 188300

Overseas Jobs Express (publication listing tourism-related jobs abroad): www.overseasjobsexpress.co.uk

Anglo-Portuguese News (Lisbon-based newspaper with a jobs section): apartado 113, Estoril; +351 214 661423

Ordem dos Medicos (organisation for recruiting of medical staff): avenida da Liberdade 65, Lisbon; +351 213 462725

language. Fluent Portuguese speakers will be limited only by their existing skill base, and even then would be able to take on a training or a junior role learning the ropes in pretty much any working environment. Other people coming to this area might be on a transfer within one of the large European firms that have offices or factories in the Lisbon and surrounding area. If this is the case, you may be able to get by speaking English, although it wouldn't hurt to get some grounding in the basic pleasantries and office fundamentals.

Obviously Lisbon itself, as well as towns along the coastline south and north of the city, offers job opportunities within the tourist trade, and this can include anything from opening your own *pousada* (an upmarket B&B/hotel) or running a bar to joining a tour guide agency or working as an English-speaking helper in a tourist office. In addition, there are many tourist-orientated shops, cafés and services that may be looking for English-speaking help, although again it really does help to have a grounding in the language for your own benefit.

In the coastal towns, there will be opportunities again to get involved with the tourist trade, either through the surf shops and sporting activities on the beach, or in shops or cafés in the towns. Elsewhere in the region, there are some opportunities to work in the industries in Ribatejo or in agriculture, whether in vineyards, orchards or olive groves or running a countryside hotel near one of the main tourist towns, such as Sintra or Mafra. And, as with anywhere in Portugal, this region, Lisbon especially, always has opportunities for English teachers.

LEISURE TIME

In terms of finding things to do with your leisure time, Lisbon and the Estremadura and Ribatejo regions are not short of opportunities. As mentioned above, the wealth of history in this area means a startling array of castles, forts and gardens to visit. And that's before you've even considered the huge number of galleries, concerts, museums, houses, churches and *fado* clubs offered by Lisbon itself. Needless to say, Lisbon is also home to some fantastic restaurants that offer a wide variety of local food and drink specialities.

Culture aside, the coastal resorts of this area boast facilities to cater for any watersport fanatic's

Lisbon is packed with impressive monuments

Lisbon and Estremadura

BUYING IN LISBON

Lisbon's property market offers the buyer everything from very expensive new development properties to the south of the Tagus and the suburbs of western Lisbon, to blocks of flats and small apartments located above a commercial property. Although providing a broad range of options, it is worth bearing in mind that if you do buy in Lisbon, you are likely to pay twice as much as you would anywhere else in Portugal. Once you leave Lisbon, there is a tremendous change in the property market and the houses available. The Portuguese love for new things means that Leiria and Santarém offer many recently renovated and renovation properties, some of which can be real baragins.

There are numerous beach properties avaliable on Leiria's west coast, most of these being resale homes as you get further from Lisbon. Therefore if you intend to buy here, be prepared for properties that require roofing or need other running repairs. In Lisbon city centre, a two-bedroom apartment costs 285,000 euros (about £190,000), while a luxury five-bedroom villa in Foz do Arelho costs only 264,000 euros (£176,000), highlighting how expensive it is to acquire property in Lisbon. A renovation property in Foz do Arelho can cost 47,500 euros (£31,600), while Cabaços in Leiria offers a granite house in disrepair for 42,000 euros (around £28,000). At the other end of the scale, a luxury property in Cascais with 10,000m^2 of grounds costs 2,200,000 euros (£1,460,000).

Prices vary depending on the property's proximity to the capital, so be prepared to part with a significant amount of cash if you buy a home in or around Lisbon.

WHAT YOU GET FOR YOUR EUROS

PROPERTY 1

AREA: Penha Longa

DESCRIPTION: Located in a sought after area on the outskirts of Lisbon, this villa offers five bedrooms and a living/dining area with a fireplace. Featuring a separate study and a modern kitchen, the home also boasts a large master bedroom with walk-in closet. As well as a large garage and storage area, this home also benefits from mature gardens and glorious views. Easily accessible from Lisbon centre.

PRICE: 1,800,000 euros
UK EQUIVALENT: £1,200,000

PROPERTY 2

AREA: Mafra

DESCRIPTION: This three-bedroom, two-bathroom house offers beamed ceilings, a stone fireplace and dramatic views. Combined with this are modern luxuries such as central heating and a new kitchen. With mature gardens, this home is in the village of Mafra on Lisbon's outskirts. Accessible for the capital and the coast, this is an excellent property that exudes comfort and luxury.

PRICE: 250,000 euros
UK EQUIVALENT: £166,665

For more properties in and around Lisbon, turn to our Price Guide, starting on page 192.

The Regions

The 16th-century Torre de Belém sits on the river Tagus and offers fantastic views to the city from its crenellated balconies

PORTUGUESE TOURIST BOARD

Lisbon and Estremadura

need, whether it be jet-skiing or windsurfing, sailing or swimming. Walking, too, is a popular pastime in this area, particularly in the hilly inland areas of Estremadura or in the peaceful Tagus estuary. Nature lovers will also find this a dream region, with lots of nature reserves and national parks to explore.

Most activities in Lisbon involve visiting historic sights or museums, or perhaps watching one of the three local football teams. However, there is a sailing club, the *Clube Naval* (Cais do Gás, Letra H, Cais do Sodré; +351 213 469354) on the river Tagus that proves very popular at weekends.

Further afield are more outdoor options, with a wide choice of golf courses. These include the testing course at the *Complexo Túristico de Tróia* (Carvalhal, Grândola; +351 265 494112; www.troiahotels.com/en/golf.html), the impressive *Belas Clube de Campo* (Alamedo do Aqueducto, Cascais; +351 219 626640; www.belasgolf.com), the championship *Clube de Golfe in Estoril* (avenida da República; +351 214 680176) and the *Quinta da Marinha* near Cascais (+351 214 680100), which also offers tennis, swimming and horseriding.

On the coasts both north and south of Lisbon, people take advantage of the huge rollers and

This area offers all kinds of pastimes, from paragliding and football to the cafés of Belém and the aquarium at Parque das Nações

SNAPSHOTS

● Lisbon residents are somewhat oddly nicknamed *alfacinha*, which means 'little lettuces'.
● In March, the Lisbon area plays host to the Super Bock Super Rock festival.
● Don't miss the Cristo Rei, a huge statue of Jesus with outstretched arms, similar to that overlooking Rio de Janeiro. Situated in Cacilhas, south of the river Tagus, it offers fantastic views.
● The Lisbon area is packed with UNESCO World Heritage sites. These include the town of Sintra, the Torre and the Mosteiro dos Jerónimos in Belém, the 12th-century town of Tomar and the monasteries of Alcobaça and Batalha.
● Lisbon became the capital of Portugal in 1255.
● Instead of taking an expensive tour round Lisbon, catch the number 28 tram, which will carry you through the old Bairro Alto and Alfama districts.
● Industry in the Estremadura and Ribatejo region relies heavily upon on timber, grain, fruit and wine, as well as copper, iron, coal and marble exports.

The Regions

RESTAURANTS

In the Alfama area is the much lauded **Casa do Leão** (largo do Chão de Feria; +351 218 824242), situated within the Castelo de São Jorge. The menu features high quality fish dishes, as well as other Portuguese specialities. A cheaper but still good quality option is **Bota Alta** (travessa da Queimada 37; +351 213 427959) in the Bairro Alto quarter. Popular with locals, Bota Alta's menu includes various salt cod dishes and home-made sausages. For a truly luxurious option, dinner at **Lawrence's Hotel** (rua Consiglierí Pedroso; +351 219 105500) in Sintra offers local specialities served in the luxury of this 18th-century inn that has played host to royalty. Rumours abound of fantastic meals in countryside hostels that cost little more than pocket money, and many of the far-flung *pousada*s provide high quality meals. One worth a visit is **Trindade** (praça Dom Alfonso Henriques 22; +351 262 582397) in Alcobaça, which offers various fish dishes and home-made local specialities.

CLASSIC DISH
Bolo de rei

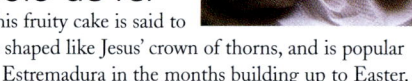

This fruity cake is said to be shaped like Jesus' crown of thorns, and is popular in Estremadura in the months building up to Easter.

EAT, DRINK AND BE MERRY

Portuguese may not be the most famous cuisine in the world, but whether you're eating in a chic restaurant in Lisbon's Alfama district or in a secluded farmhouse kitchen in the hills, you can be sure of hearty, well prepared, fresh local produce, centred around fish on the coast and local meats and sausages further inland.

The cuisine of Lisbon and its environs is known for its reliance on *bacalhau* (salted cod), with *bacalhau à Brás* (salted cod fried with potatoes and eggs) and *pataniscas* (salt cod fritters) featuring on many menus. Another local speciality is *pastéis de Belém*, a sweet pastry whose recipe was developed (and kept secret) by the monks of the Mosteiro dos Jerónimos. Another sweet Estremadura speciality is the *bolo de rei* (king's crown) cake, served between Christmas and Easter (see left).

To accompany your meal, you'll invariably be offered local wines, with Bucelas whites and the Colares reds (from near Sintra) being the best choices. And while most Portuguese meals are rounded off with the ubiquitous glass of port, known as *vinho do Porto*, in the Lisbon area you'll also be able to partake of the local (very strong!) *ginjinha* cherry brandy.

FOR CULTURE VULTURES

As mentioned elsewhere in this chapter, the cultural life of this region centres on the capital itself, which is crammed with concert halls, theatres, art galleries and museums. It's worth noting that most museums offer free entry on Sunday mornings, while throughout the year, various festivals (including the Festa da Primavera in March and the BaixAnima

Atlantic winds for surfing, windsurfing and yachting. The best beaches for all three are Praia das Maçãs, Praia Grande and Praia do Guincho, where the World Surfing Championships have been held in the past. Deep-sea fishing is also a popular pastime, and some areas, around Sesimbra in particular, provide ocean fishing trips. If you'd rather *look* at the sealife than catch it, snorkelling and scuba diving can be arranged, being particularly popular in the waters surrounding the Berlenga islands.

The countryside all round the Estremadura and Ribatejo regions offers plenty of opportunity for mountain biking, hiking and horseriding, and all three pursuits can be arranged from most of the towns in the area. Gradually becoming more popular in the area are the more extreme sports of canyoning, abseiling, rock-climbing and kayaking, and specialist tour operators offer adventure weekends and holidays. Ask at the local tourist offices for more details and contacts.

Take advantage of Lisbon's café culture... best experienced in one of the impressive squares

Lisbon and Estremadura

Even in the smallest, humblest cafés you'll find performances of the uniquely Portuguese tradition of *fado*, usually involving a guitarist (or two), a vocalist and an appreciative audience

Festival from July to September) lead to free, often impromptu, performances of music and dance in the streets.

Lovers of fine arts and the performing arts have no shortage of options in this part of Portugal. Among the many museums of Lisbon, the *Museu de Arte Antiga* (rua das Janelas Verdes; +351 213 912800; www.mnarteantiga-ipmuseus.pt) should be at the top of your list. Situated in the Belém area, it houses hundreds of examples of Portuguese art, as well as other European works, all in the striking surroundings of an elegant 17th-century palace. The second most important cultural venue in Lisbon is the *Fundação Calouste Gulbenkian* (avenida de Berna 45a; +351 217 823000; www.gulbenkian.pt), which houses a huge collection of ancient artefacts, artworks and sculpture, bequeathed to the city by the Armenian millionaire Calouste Gulbenkian. Concerts by the resident choir and orchestra are held in the open-air theatre within the Foundation's grounds.

Opera and ballet performances are put on at the *Teatro Nacional de São Carlos* (rua Serpa Pinto 9; +351 213 465914; www.saocarlos.pt) while the *Teatro Nacional Dona Maria II* (praça Dom Pedro V, Baixa; +351 213 472246; www.teatro-dmaria.pt) is home to the national theatre company. Orchestral

FADO

Lisbon has a lively nightlife scene, with plenty of bars and clubs. For a slice of authentic Lisbon entertainment, though, the *fado* clubs are the place to go. *Fado*, meaning 'fate' in Portuguese, is a style of song performed by a a vocalist accompanied by one or two guitars. The music reflects the sentimental, often wistful, lyrics usually based around the Portuguese tradition of *saudade*, a nostalgic longing for the past or the impossible: missing someone, a never forgotten kiss, a longing for home or a happy memory. Traditional *fado* and the specific Lisbon style of *fado castiço* can be heard in various cafés, restaurants and specialised clubs around the city, one of the best being **Clube de Fado** (rua de São João da Praça, Lisbon; +351 218 882694; www.clube-de-fado.com) in the Alfama quarter. Here, for just 7 euros, you can hear professional *fado* singers performing traditional and more modern songs…but prepare to be moved!

The Regions

concerts are held at the *Teatro Camões* (Parque das Nações; +351 213 474049), home to the Portuguese Symphony Orchestra, while for a more dramatic theatrical experience, you should seek out the open-air plays hosted in the ruined Convento do Carmo, uphill from rua Garrett, in the summer months.

SHOPPING: GIFTS AND GROCERIES

Probably the best shopping in the whole of Portugal is to be found in Lisbon. There's something here for everyone, from the chic boutiques in the Chiado district to the tiny gift shops in the narrow streets of the Alfama area. Lisbon also boasts several large shopping malls, including the Amoreiras in the centre of town (which is also home to a ten-screen cinema and 50 or more restaurants), the Vasco Da Gama centre in the newly built Parque das Nações and the enormous Colombo complex (again, housing a ten-screen cinema) near the Benfica football stadium.

As for speciality gifts, here, as elsewhere in Portugal, you'll find *azulejo* tiles for sale everywhere, although other local treats to look out for are the green, cabbage-leaf plate and dish designs of Caldas da Rainha, hand-painted ceramics in Lisbon (from shops in the Baixa quarter), lacework from Nazaré and the local wines as well as, of course, the omnipresent port.

Lisbon hosts a number of different markets in various areas of the city, the most renowned being the huge *Mercado da Ribeira* (avenida 24 de Julho, Cais do Sodré), which becomes a flower market in the afternoons, and the Feira da Ladra flea market (it actually means 'thieves' market') held on Tuesdays at Campo de Santa Clara in Graça. Supermarkets can be found all round the city –

Above left: As well as the large main markets, you'll find plenty of stalls on the streets of Lisbon
Above: One of the best ways of getting round the city is by the unmissable trams

watch out for the omnipresent Pingo Doce chain – while the huge El Corte Inglés (a Spanish department store chain) on avenida António Augusto de Aguiar has a large food hall.

GETTING AROUND

Travel around Lisbon is made easy, with a choice between train, metro, tram and buses as well as the *elevadores*, saving the effort of climbing up the city's steep hills. There are various options for travelling around the city, the best of which is the Lisboa Card.

POPULAR LOCAL FESTIVALS

Saint Anthony is adopted by most Lisboêtas (Lisbon residents) as their patron saint, despite the fact that Saint Vincent is their official protector, and this means that the most lively religious festival in the city is that of **Santo António** on **June 12-13**. The two days of celebration combine a mixture of pensive religious reflection and vibrant shows of joyous singing and dancing, as well as eating and drinking. The *festa* begins with the **Marchas Populares** (march of the people), where the congregations of the various city churches walk along the avenida de Liberdade. While most people progress on to church services, there is also much fun to be had on the streets where parties, concerts and barbecues are held in the various neighbourhoods. Locals decorate their windows, balconies and streets with flowers and streamers, while musicians sing and dance throughout the streets and everyone eats and drinks their fill.

Lisbon and Estremadura

It comes in 24-, 48- and 72-hour versions, and gives free travel on all public transport, plus free entrance to a selection of museums and sights. Most buses and the trams around the city are operated by *Carris* (+351 213 613054; www.carris.pt).

Travelling in the region is best undertaken by train, although some towns in the area, such as Mafra, remain without a station. Heading deeper into the Estremadura and Ribatejo usually involves one of the various bus and coach services, most of which originate in Lisbon. For instance, the service from Rossío station delivers you to various towns, including Caldas da Rainha, Óbidos and Leiria. Details of train services can be found from *Caminhos de Ferro Portugueses* (+351 218 884025; www.cp.pt) or *Rail Europe* (0870 584 8848; www.raileurope.com). Meanwhile, some companies, including *Citirama* (avenida Praia da Vitória; +351 213 558564) and *Top Tours* (avenida Duque de Loulé 108; +351 213 521217) offer coach tours around the Lisbon region.

If you want to drive yourself around the Estremadura and Ribatejo regions, you can hire cars through a number of well-known companies, with *Avis* (+351 218 435550), *Europcar* (+351 218 473181), *Hertz* (+351 218 492722) and *Budget* (+351 218 478803) all having offices at Lisbon airport.

EXPLORERS

Throughout history, Lisbon has played a key role in Portugal's seafaring exploits, with maritime schools established here with support from the royal court. The earliest of the explorers was the son of King John I, **Henry the Navigator** (1394-1460) whose expeditions to Africa and the Madeiran islands opened up new trade routes. **Vasco da Gama** (1469-1524) was the first explorer to make the journey to Asia around the Cape of Good Hope, setting off from Lisbon in July 1497 and arriving in Calcutta the following May.

Probably the most celebrated Portuguese explorer, however, is Fernão Magalhães (1480-1521), better known as **Ferdinand Magellan**, the first to organise an expedition around the world. A member of the royal court, he made various voyages to India, Africa and Malaysia from Lisbon. His most famous journey, actually funded by Charles I of Spain, was to Brazil, round the southern tip of South America, through what's now called the Magellan Straits, across the Pacific, to the Philippines (where Magellan died in 1521), then back to Africa and north to Portugal.

All these explorers, as well as many other leaders of Portuguese expeditions, are commemorated by the Memorial to the Discoveries (right) erected in 1960 on the waterfront in Belém, proof that Lisbon is rightly proud of its seafaring past.

The rocky coastal cliffs include the famous Boca do Inferno or 'Mouth of Hell' near Cascais

FRANCISCA NAVARRO-GARCIA

The Regions

LOCAL LIFE

As with most parts of Portugal, the highlight of religious traditions are the festivals or *festas* of the Popular Saints in June. These celebrate the feast days of Saint Anthony, Saint John and Saint Peter, with the festival of Saint Anthony being particularly lively in Lisbon (see the *Popular Local Festivals* box, on page 136). Other festivals in the city include the Festival dos Oceanos, celebrated in the coastal towns in mid August, and various music and jazz festivals, the most popular being the Jazz In August festival hosted by the Calouste Gulbenkian Foundation.

Outside Lisbon, Sintra plays host to the Festival de Música in June and July, while the *Semana Santa* celebrations in Óbidos involve religious processions throughout the week leading up to Easter. Nazaré is home to the Nossa Senhora pilgrimage that takes place in early September, involving processions, music, dancing and bullfights, while Santarém is famous for its Feira Nacional da Agricultura, which features bullfights and exhilarating bull-running through the streets to rival that in Spain's Pamplona.

SPECTATOR SPORTS

The most popular spectator sport in the Lisbon area is football, where the city's three teams – Sporting (Sporting Club Portugal, or SCP), Benfica (Sport Lisboa e Benfica, or SLB) and Belenenses (Clube de Futebol 'Os Belenenses', or CFB) – have a long-standing rivalry. Football will again become the focus of Portugal's attention in 2004 when the country plays host to the European Championships, with some of the matches being played at Benfica's recently renovated *Estádio da Luz* (+351 217

Look closely at this region's wonderful architecture and you will find some intriguing surprises

Lisbon and Estremadura

USEFUL CONTACTS:
EDUCATION, HOSPITALS, UTILITIES, TOURIST OFFICES

SCHOOLS

If you are taking children young enough to pick up the language quickly, it should be possible to enrol them in your nearest Portuguese school. However, there are some schools that either teach some lessons in English or deal with pupils whose first language is not Portuguese: **American International School of Lisbon** (Apartado 10, Carnaxide, Lisbon; +351 214 861860; www.ecis.org/aislisbon/); **St Dominic International School** (rua Outeiro da Polima Arneiro, São Domingos da Rana, Parede, Lisbon; +351 214 440434); **Queen Elizabeth's School** (rua Filipe Magalhães 1, Alvalade, Lisbon; +351 218 486928) and **Cascais International School** (rua das Faias, Lt. 7 Torre, Cascais; +351 214 846260). For more information about school and education, contact the Portuguese **Ministry of Education** (Gabinete Relações Internacionais, avenida 5 de Outubro 35-37, Lisbon; +351 217 950330; www.minedu.pt).

SERVICES

One of the first things to do when you move into your Portuguese home is to get the utilities connected. Contact **Portugal Telecom** (+351 213 540020; www.telecom.pt) for phone connections, **CPPE** (+351 213 525353; www.edp.pt) for electricity, and **EPAL** (+351 213 466541; www.epal.pt) or **Lusagua** (+351 217 928670; www.lusagua.pt) for water. Many homes here don't have piped gas, but one company that deals with gas and other services is **Marques Raso** (+351 219 830157).

HOSPITALS

Hospital Inglês (rua Saraiva Carvalho 49, 1350 Lisbon; +351 213 955067) and the **International Health Centre** in Cascais (largo Luís Camões, 2750 Cascais; +351 217 140607) have some English-speaking staff. There are plenty of other hospitals in the region, though, including those in **Alcobaça** (rua Alfonso de Albuquerque; +351 262 590400); **Caldas da Rainha** (rua Diário de Notícias; +351 262 830300); **Cascais** (rua Padre Loureiro; +351 214 827700); **Ericeira** (Centro de Saúde, rua Prudéncio Franco da Trinidade; +351 261 864100); **Peniche** (rua General Humberto Delgado; +351 262 780900); **Setúbal** (avenida dom João 11; +351 265 522133) and **Sintra** (Centro de Saúde, rua Dr Alfredo Costa 34; +351 219 106685).

TOURIST OFFICES

Most towns have a small tourist office called a *turismo*, usually located near the town hall or within a museum. The main offices for this area are the **Turismo de Lisboa** (+351 210 312700; www.tourismlisbon.com), located in the **Welcome Centre** on Lisbon's praça do Comércio, the **Regional Tourist Office** in Óbidos (rua Direita 45; +351 262 955060) and the **Costa Azul Tourist Office** in Setúbal (travessa Frei Gaspar 10; +351 265 539120; www.costa-azul.rts.pt).

POLICE

The emergency number, as in the rest of the country, is **112**. Most large towns have their own police station, although it's worth noting the details for **Lisbon's** (rua Capelo 13; +351 217 654242).

MORE INFO

You can get more information about everything from schools and visas to emigration details and setting up a business from the **British Embassy** in the city centre (rua Sao Bernardo 33, Lisbon; +351 213 924000; www.uk-embassy.pt).

219540) and the *Estádio Nacional* (+351 214 197212), outside the city. Many of Portugal's biggest football stars play outside their home country, but that doesn't dampen the fans' support of the game, with almost every small town in this region having their own teams and pitches.

While it is not as fanatically supported in Portugal as it is in neighbouring Spain, there is a steady following for bullfighting. The main bullfighting venue in the region is Lisbon's red-brick *Campo Pequeno* (+351 217 932442), built in the 1890s. Late-night fights are held here every week during the June-September season, while at other times the arena is used to host concerts and other performances. Nazaré also has a well attended bullfighting season, with fights held every weekend in the bullring in Sítio. And the towns of Santarém and Vila Franca de Xira are also renowned for their bullfights, with the latter's bullring featuring an adjoining museum.

> For a guide to property prices in and around Lisbon, turn to our Price Guide, starting on page 192

The Regions

COIMBRA & THE BEIRAS

Coimbra & the Beiras

The ancient university town of Coimbra and the northerly Beira regions offer the visitor or resident everything from scenic mountain ranges, dense forests and peaceful nature reserves to bustling cafés, lively festivals and historic castles

PORTUGUESE TOURIST BOARD

The beautiful university city of Coimbra, overlooking the lazy river Mondego

The Regions

The historic village of Piódão boasts typical granite buildings and attractive ecclesiastical architecture

Coimbra & the Beiras

The Beiras region has much more to offer than just the city of Coimbra, with the beaches of Figueira da Foz (left), striking windmills (centre) and Aveiro (right), known as the Venice of Portugal

Situated in the north of Portugal, stretching across from the Atlantic to the Spanish border, this region is made up of the Beira Litoral, Beira Alta and Beira Baixa. It's a region of contrasts, taking in the mountains of the Serra da Estrela park and the sandy stretches of coast. Dominating the area, however, is Coimbra, home to one of Europe's oldest universities.

Coimbra, the capital of Beira Litoral, was actually Portugal's capital until the late 13th century. In ancient times, the Romans developed the town alongside the rival settlement of Conímbriga, south of the river Mondego, and the remains of the latter – including a stretch of road, baths and aqueducts – can be visited today. In the eighth century, Coimbra became a Moorish outpost, although the city was won back for Portugal by the mid-1060s. In the 12th century, the university was founded and although it was moved between here and Lisbon, it came back to Coimbra for good in the 1500s. Nowadays, the city enjoys the hustle and bustle of student life, and is dominated by the university buildings and the cathedral on top of the hill and the three convents across the river.

The other Beira capitals are Castelo Branco and Viseu, the latter being known for its stunning cathedral. Up in the mountains are pretty spa towns, such as Luso and Caramulo, as well as the country's highest peak, stunning waterfalls and a rich variety of wildlife, while the area's long history as a frontier between Portugal and Spain means a rich heritage of castles and fortified towns, such as Sortelha and Covilhã. Back near the coast is the pretty town of Aveiro, intersected by a series of canals, which were traditionally used by the locals. They harvested the kelp from these channels in colourful boats.

Wherever you are in this diverse, historic and charming region, you can be sure of a warm welcome, great food and beautiful scenery.

WORKING IN THE AREA

Taking the Beira regions as a whole, there isn't a wide variety of employment opportunities in this area of Portugal, especially in the more lowly populated interior towns and countryside. That said, however, if you put your mind to it, you will find potential for work.

Coimbra is the most obvious place to look, being the hub of the whole region. Although it sometimes gets overlooked by visitors in favour of Porto or Lisbon, Coimbra has a buoyant tourist trade. Most services in the city cater for Portuguese and Spanish tourists, which brings up potential work in the cafés, shops and restaurants for those with Portuguese or Spanish as a second language. There are also many jobs associated with the university, from the most obvious posts like lecturers and librarians, right down to canteen workers, housekeepers and security guards. These posts are usually advertised on the university website and in local papers.

The Regions

REGION INFORMATION

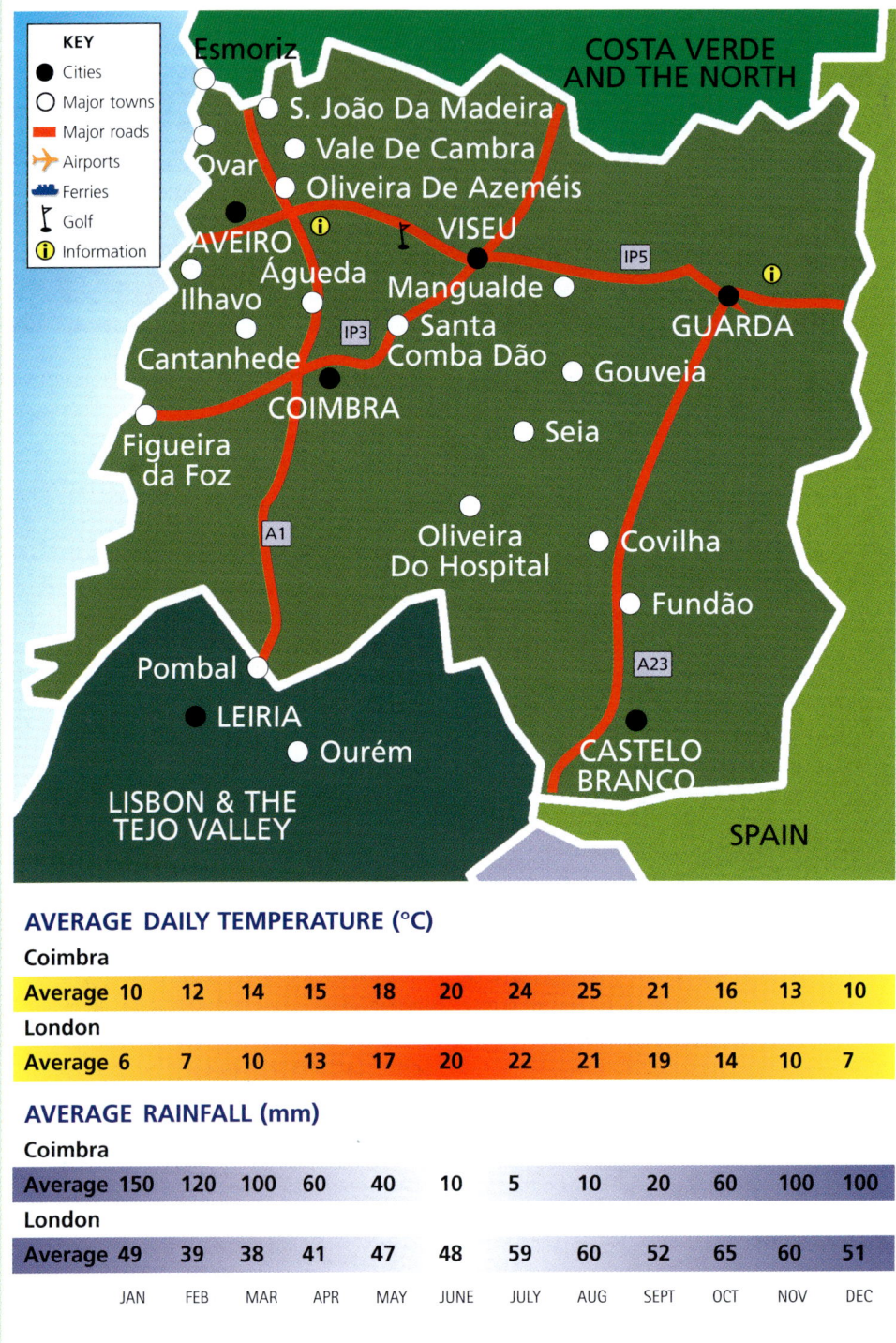

AVERAGE DAILY TEMPERATURE (°C)

Coimbra

| Average | 10 | 12 | 14 | 15 | 18 | 20 | 24 | 25 | 21 | 16 | 13 | 10 |

London

| Average | 6 | 7 | 10 | 13 | 17 | 20 | 22 | 21 | 19 | 14 | 10 | 7 |

AVERAGE RAINFALL (mm)

Coimbra

| Average | 150 | 120 | 100 | 60 | 40 | 10 | 5 | 10 | 20 | 60 | 100 | 100 |

London

| Average | 49 | 39 | 38 | 41 | 47 | 48 | 59 | 60 | 52 | 65 | 60 | 51 |

| JAN | FEB | MAR | APR | MAY | JUNE | JULY | AUG | SEPT | OCT | NOV | DEC |

Coimbra & the Beiras

GETTING THERE

AIR British Airways' daughter airline **GB Airways** (0845 7733377; www.britishairways.co.uk) operates twice-weekly flights from London Heathrow to Porto, while **TAP Air Portugal** (0845 601 0932; www.tap.pt) flies direct to Porto or via Lisbon from London Gatwick.

SEA If you intend to take your car to the region, you'll need to catch one of the ferries to northern Spain. **P&O** (0870 600 0600; www.poportsmouth.com) sails from Portsmouth to Bilbao, while **Brittany Ferries** (0870 536 0360; www.britanny-ferries.com) sails from Plymouth to Santander.

ROAD From Bilbao, take the A68 south and then the A1 to Burgos. (From Santander, take the N623 south to Burgos.) The N620 goes from Burgos, via Valladolid and Salamanca, to the Portuguese border at Fuentes de Oñoro, from where you join the IP5 and then the N17 to Coimbra.

RAIL Eurostar (0870 518 6186; www.eurostar.co.uk) operates from London Waterloo to Paris, where you'll need to catch the **TGV Atlantique** for Irún in Spain. Here, take the **Sud-Expresso to** Coimbra. **Rail Europe** (0870 584 8848; www.raileurope.co.uk) can provide you with full timetables, prices and more details.

Coimbra and the Beiras area is renowned for its vibrant markets, full of a variety of fresh produce

CLIMATE SUMMARY

The region encompassing the three Beira districts could be seen as a cross-section across the breadth of Portugal, and therefore has no one definitive climate. The more mountainous areas of the Beira Alta and Beira Baixa can be up to ten degrees cooler than the Beira Litoral areas. And even in the Litoral region, the areas inland around Coimbra will be slightly warmer than the actual coast, which is pummelled by often strong Atlantic winds.

Most of the region's rain falls between December and March, when there is also snowfall on the higher land in the Serra da Estrela.

Summers on the coast are hot and rarely humid, making the season from May to September perfect for beach lovers. In the mountains, the summer months (light rain and mist excepted) make it perfect for hiking and horse-riding, while the snow in the mountains makes the winter attractive for skiers.

There isn't such a well established British expat community here as there is in the Algarve or Lisbon, so fully English-speaking jobs aren't as common, but there are occasional opportunities for UK builders, tour guides and the like to find work for a British employer.

Of course, the upside of Coimbra's growing popularity as a destination for holiday-makers and second home-owners alike, is that there are some opportunities for starting your own business, whether as a restaurateur, property developer, hotelier or shopkeeper. The trade may not be as lucrative as it is in Lisbon, Porto or the Algarve, but the lower cost of living may well balance things out. It's also possible to look towards the mountains of the Serra da Estrela where you can take advantage of the tourist industry that is fed by both the winter ski season and the summer hiking season.

With much of the Beira Baixa and Alta regions being predominantly agricultural, you may find work on farms, orchards and vineyards, although these jobs are usually seasonal and poorly paid. However, there are certain openings in the region (mainly in the three regional capitals: Coimbra, Castelo Branco and Viseu) for those with TEFL and other English-teaching qualifications, as well as for au pairs and translators.

LEISURE TIME

As can be said with most of Portugal's regions, the Beiras offer something for everyone, whether it's

The Regions

EMPLOYMENT CONTACTS

Portuguese Embassy: 11 Belgrave Square, London, SW1X 8PP; 020 7235 5331

British Embassy: rua de São Bernardo 33, Lisbon; +351 213 924000; www.ukembassy.pt

Portuguese Trade Office (for information about international companies with offices in the Beira regions): 2nd Floor, 21-25a Sackville Street, London, W1X 2LY; 020 7494 1441

Jornal de Coimbra (local newspaper): rua da Sofia 95, Coimbra; +351 239 852777; www.jornaldecoimbra.pt

University of Coimbra (for teaching posts): www.uc.pt

International House (for details of English teaching vacancies): rua Marqués São da Bandeira 16, Lisbon; +351 213 151496; www.internationalhouse.com

Cambridge Schools (employment for TEFL certificate holders): avenida da Liberdade 173, Lisbon; +351 213 124600; www.cambridge.pt

Overseas Jobs Express (publication listing tourism-related jobs abroad): www.overseasjobsexpress.co.uk

modern art or motorboat racing, bird watching or ballet. However, the main emphasis is on outdoor life. In the mountains of the Serra da Estrela Natural Park, there is a lively ski season, as well as opportunities for hiking and walking in summer. Meanwhile, on the coast, sunbathers and watersports fanatics alike are equally well catered for. Nature lovers can take advantage of the Beiras' peaceful and undisturbed valleys and forests, where many of Europe's rarest animals and birds make their home, while those after a bit of adventure can partake of the many organised kayak, abseiling and rock-climbing clubs.

Not everything happens outdoors here though. Coimbra, being a university town, has a lively nightlife and plenty of restaurants that would give even the best in Lisbon a run for their money. And, of course, the *fado* here is supposedly superior to that sung in Lisbon, although you can make up your own mind by attending one of the many *fado* clubs in the city. As well as art galleries, concerts and dance, Coimbra is also home to various music festivals, but if it's sport you want to watch, check out one of the Beira's local football teams who are followed with a passion by the locals.

As mentioned elsewhere in this chapter, the Beiras are the perfect region in which to partake in outdoor activities. The most popular pastimes are walking and hiking, with many visitors bringing their walking boots to make the most of the trails and paths that criss-cross the inland valleys. The adventurous should try the testing slopes of the

A perfect region for outdoor activities, tennis is just one of the sports you can take part in here

DAVID HEADLANDS ASSOCIATES

BUYING IN COIMBRA & THE BEIRAS

Coimbra & the Beiras offers an incredible array of properties to suit every buyer's taste and budget. Property is available at a reasonable price, from spectacular coastal properties for £490,000 to inexpensive ruins at £35,000. Demand for property is clearly higher on the west coast of the Beiras, with areas of eastern Portugal such as Guarda and Castelo Branco experiencing a limited amount of market activity and a non-existent expat community. Urban relocation is also an option for anyone interested in investing in the Coimbra area. Compared to the cost of purchasing in the Lisbon area, a townhouse in Arganil can cost as little as 50,000 euros (£33,300). For those desiring to renovate, the Coimbra area is the ideal place to seek a renovation project. Available in their droves, renovation properties are cheap and located in some truly stunning rural or urban areas. From a disused watermill at 60,000 euros (£40,000) to a small ruin near Elvas for 25,000 euros (£16,665), the Beiras have it all.

Another bonus of moving to the Beiras region is the peace offered by the rural surroundings. A buyer has to be particularly happy with their own company and that of their companions to move to the more secluded areas of the Beiras but essentially there is a huge availability of property for those who aren't too fussy or who have the capital to carry out renovations. New developments are springing up in the coastal areas, especially those close to the Lisbon coast. Yet there have been no drastic changes in this region's property market in recent years. Still a relative secret, property is affordable for such a stunning area.

WHAT YOU GET FOR YOUR EUROS

PROPERTY 1

AREA: São Martinho do Porto

DESCRIPTION: A two-bedroom property with delightful views across an expansive valley to the distant hills. With a well manicured garden surrounded by shady pine trees and flagstone paths, the grounds offer privacy as well as a welcome escape from the afternoon heat. Within easy reach of a sandy beach in a quiet, sheltered bay, this home is a great prospect. The town is located right on the seafront and within easy reach of the motorway.

PRICE: 195,000 euros
UK EQUIVALENT: £130,000

PROPERTY 2

AREA: Bodiosa

DESCRIPTION: This detached property requires an owner willing to renovate. Located near the main road and within easy reach of Viseu, this property is ideally located for those seeking a quiet, peaceful lifestyle. Coimbra as a region offers many historic attractions, and is far removed from the hustle and bustle of the Algarve. Combining historic interest with beautiful countryside, this great value property offers huge potential and is ideal for a family home.

PRICE: 30,000 euros
UK EQUIVALENT: £20,000

For more properties in Coimbra & the Beiras, turn to our Price Guide, starting on page 192

The Regions

Many of this region's historic buildings are complemented by stunning, well manicured gardens

PORTUGUESE TOURIST BOARD

Coimbra & the Beiras

Serra da Estrela park, while those after a less taxing walk should head for the tranquil Buçaco forest, where you'll come across the occasional clearing or ruined chapel.

Whereas golf dominates other parts of Portugal, here tennis is more popular, and those after a game should contact two of the best clubs in the area, at Coimbra (avenida Urbano Duarte; +351 239 403469) and Figueira da Foz (avenida 25 de abril; +351 233 422287). In winter, the mountains play host to skiing, snowboarding, tobogganning and snow-hiking, with most activities bookable at Torre (+351 275 334933).

When the snow clears, there are plenty of adventure sports on offer in the mountains, including abseiling, rock-climbing, kayaking and canyoning, while those who prefer to see the countryside from horseback can take part in organised treks and trips in the Choupal forest near Coimbra or around the marshlands near Aveiro.

Back towards the coast, surfing and windsurfing are on offer for the beginner and experienced alike from the beaches at Buarcos, Praia de Cabedelo and Praia de Gaia, as well as on the Quiaios Lakes, while sea fishing trips are on offer off Cape Mondego.

A region of contrasts, the Beiras offer splendid architectural heritage (top left), the beaches of Ericeira (top right), the district capital of Viseu with its impressively dominating cathedral (above right) and the quaint village of Monsanto (above left)

SNAPSHOTS

● The university for which Coimbra is famous was actually founded by King Diniz in Lisbon in 1292. It was moved to Coimbra twice, the first time (temporarily) in 1308 and the second time for good in 1540.
● In the 1300s, Prince Pedro, son of King Alfonso IV, fell in love with his wife's lady-in-waiting, Inés de Castro. When his wife died, he had four children with Inés but his father wanted him to marry someone else (for political reasons) and had Inés murdered in Coimbra.
● Piódão, near Coimbra, claims to be the longest continually inhabited town in Portugal.

The Regions

RESTAURANTS

One of the most intriguing settings for a quick meal in Coimbra is in the **Café Santa Cruz** (praça 8 de Maio; +351 239 833617). The café is situated in what used to be a chapel, and you can take your *bica* (the Portuguese take on expresso) or your lunch surrounded by stained glass windows, wood panelling and an intricately vaulted ceiling. If you are after something more substantial, try the **Trovador restaurant** (largo da Sé Velha 15; +351 239 825475). As the address suggests, it sits on the main square in the shadow of the old cathedral, where it serves tasty local dishes as well as simple lunch snacks. Although it can get busy in the touristy summer seasons, if you come here on a Friday or Saturday night, you can enjoy some of the best *fado* in Coimbra, along with all the locals. Many of the coastal resorts specialise in fish restaurants, with the **Restaurante Dory Negro** in Buarcos near Figueira da Foz (largo Caras Direitas 16; +351 233 421333) serving everything from lobster to the delicious but reasonably priced *arroz de marisco* seafood and rice dish. One of the most glamorous places to eat in the region, however, is at the **Palace Hotel Buçaco** in Luso (+351 231 937970; www.almeidahotels.com). It doesn't come cheap, but you can eat wonderfully prepared, high quality food, served in sumptuous surroundings with attentive service and an extensive choice of wine from the enormous cellar.

Serving up local delights

A selection of Beira sweet treats

CLASSIC DISH
Leitáo á Bairrada

In the Coimbra region roast suckling pig, with crispy crackling, is a local speciality. Eaten hot or cold.

The Portuguese produce a variety of sausages, two of which are the *linguiça* and the *chouriço*

EATING AND DRINKING

Despite the differences between the many areas of this vast region, from the coast to the mountains, from wooded valleys to bustling towns, the one constant is the food, which mostly takes its lead from the hearty fare of the mountains, with rich stews, roasted meats and dishes of beans. That's not to say these are the only things on the menu; far from it. So, for instance, in the coastal towns of Figueira da Foz and Aveiro, you'll find plenty of restaurants that make great use of fresh fish and shellfish, while in the chic eating places of Coimbra you'll find something for everyone from Chinese to European, including some stylish places that combine an intriguing fusion of European and South American cuisine.

Here and in towns throughout the region, however, you will always find a place where you can tuck into suckling pig, cured hams, roast kid, bean stews and chestnuts. Also popular in the mountains

Coimbra & the Beiras

are the soft but strong-tasting *queijo da serra* sheep's cheese, honey and *pão de milho* corn bread.

To accompany your meal are plenty of good quality local wines, made in the Dão region. Compared by some drinkers to French Burgundy, Dão wines are strong flavoured reds, with a smooth after-taste and rich fruitfulness. As well as gracing restaurant wine lists, the wines can also be tried in various vineyards around the region. For something stronger to round off a meal, you should try the *aguardente*, a liqueur made from juniper berries, which tastes surprisingly different from gin.

FOR CULTURE VULTURES

Being a university town, there are many cultural spectacles put on throughout term-time, ranging from choral concerts in the old cathedral to exhibitions of student's art and sculpture and *fado* evenings in the various clubs around town. And, as Coimbra has been elected Portugal's 'Capital of

Above and top left: Fish appears at most meals especially in the coastal town of Figueira da Foz
Above right: Here, as elsewhere in Portugal, markets offering fresh produce are hugely popular

The Beiras, in keeping with national tradition, are known for their salted cod *bacalhau* recipes

The Regions

MOST FAMOUS FESTIVALS

The most famous festival of the region must be Coimbra's **Queima das Fitas** ('Burning the Ribbons'), held at the start of May. The tradition comes from the ribbons that the university students wear or attach to their briefcases to denote which faculty they study in. The festival, which marks the end of exams and of the academic year, includes the burning of these ribbons, but also entails a parade of decorated floats, special *fado* evenings, a series of concerts… as well as streets filled with merry students who make the most of the free cases of beer given away by the event's sponsors!

Culture' for 2003, there are many visual arts and music events being organised specifically for this year, including sculpture in the streets and photography shows.

Sights you can see all year round include the Machado de Castro museum in Coimbra, which houses many examples of sculpture, textiles, furniture and Portuguese paintings, and the famed *Museu de Francisco Tavares Proença Júnior* (+351 272 344277) in Castelo Branco. Situated in the Bishop's Palace, the museum contains local Roman artefacts, as well as various examples of antique *colchas*, the intricately embroidered silk bedspreads for which the town is well known. For a slightly different museum experience, try the one dedicated to the wool industry, the *Museu de Lanficios* in Covilhã (+351 275 319700).

If, however, you enjoy culture of a more spiritual kind, there are many impressive religious buildings around the area, including the imposing Sé Velha church in Coimbra and the inspiring Igreja de Santa Maria church in Covilhã. The most famous, however, is the gothic cathedral at Viseu. Dominating the town on a rocky outcrop, the dark Renaissance front is set off by the rose window, while the beautiful interior decoration includes a carved ceiling and stunning altarpieces. While inside, head for the chapterhouse, with its displays of 17th-century *azulejos* (decorative tiles) and the Sacred Art museum.

SHOPPING: GIFTS AND GROCERIES

The city of Coimbra is a great shoppers' destination, with a wide variety of clothes, food and souvenir shops, as well as the many bookshops (thanks to the student population) on rua Ferreira Borges.

If you are looking for more specialised local crafts, Castelo Branco is worth a visit for its traditional *bordado* embroidery. The traditional bedspreads are these days mostly made for the tourist trade, and the best place to buy is from the workshop next to the previously mentioned *Francisco Tavares* museum (+351 272 344277). You should also seek out the delicate china made in Vista Alegre, which can be bought from the gift shop next door to the *Museu Histórico* (+351 234 320755).

For wood carvings, especially the pretty, intricate figurines, try the rua Direita in Viseu, and for mountain souvenirs – woollen hats and slippers, honey, cured hams and Serra da Estrela cheese – try the O Mundo Rural shop in Gouveia, which sells all these and other local crafts. The main food market in Coimbra is located on the rua Nicolau Rui Fernandes. Most towns in the area also host a weekly market from which it is possible to obtain a variety of fresh produce.

WWW.LEITMOTIF.COM

Coimbra's bustling market attracts a huge cross-section of shoppers, from students looking for cheap fresh meals to locals and tourists alike

Coimbra & the Beiras

GETTING AROUND

The city of Coimbra is served by the Ecovia university buses, with two lines covering most of the city. Tickets can be bought on board the buses. For more information about the city's bus and *elevadores* services, contact *Serviços Municipais de Transportes de Coimbra* (+351 239 941441). To travel to the Roman site at Conimbríga from Coimbra, catch one of the *AVIC Mondego* (+351 239 820141) services, although they are few and far between. Rodoviário offer various bus routes around the whole region, with *Rodoviário da Beira Interior* (Rodrigo Rebelo 3, Castelo Branco; +351 272 340120) serving towns towards Castelo Branco and Covilhã and *Rodoviário da Beira Litoral* (avenida Fernão de Magalhães, Coimbra; +351 239 855270) heading coastwards.

There are three main train lines that serve the region, most converging on Coimbra. One travels south to (and across) the Ribatejo border and north to Curia, Aveiro and Porto; another heads north and east to Luso, Viseu and Guarda; and the third travels east and south to Covilhã, Fundão and Castelo

Life in the Beiras is very traditional and, Coimbra aside, slow-paced. All around the region you will see women in traditional black headscarves and men locked in fervent discussion at the local café

PARQUE NATURAL DA SERRA DA ESTRELA

The **Serra da Estrela** park is probably best known as being home to Portugal's highest mountain, the Torre, but it's also where the source of this region's longest river, the Mondego, can be found. There are many reasons why visitors come to the park, whether it's skiing in winter, hiking in summer or enjoying the local hospitality and hearty specialities. However, many others come here to spy the rare creatures that make this countryside their home. These include many rare species, such as the alpine swift, wolves, mountain gecko and peregrine falcon. Whatever you do, don't forget your binoculars!

The Regions

The Beiras boast amazing architecture from the church of Alcobaça (above centre), Tomar's convent (top centre) and Buçaco's monastery (above left) to the Roman ruins at Conímbriga (above, far right)

Branco. For more information, contact *Rail Europe* (0870 584 8848; www.raileurope.co.uk).

LOCAL LIFE

The pace of life in the Beiras really depends on where you are, and contrasts between the lively culture and youthful feel of the university town of Coimbra – particularly boisterous at the end of the summer term – and the peaceful tranquillity of the deserted mountainsides and dense forest of the natural parks of Serra da Estrela and Serra da Malcata.

Many towns in the region hold regular celebrations to commemorate saints' days or festivals, with the most lively being Coimbra's Festa da Reinha Santa in July, Figueira da Foz's Festas da Cidade at the end of June and Viseu's Feira de São Mateus, which sees music, food and fireworks celebrations continuing from the middle of August and into September. In addition to these is Figueira's well known Festival Internacional de Cinema in early September, where the red carpet is rolled out for national and international film stars alike.

WALLED CITIES

Many towns in the eastern reaches of the Beiras are fortified, owing to their vicinity to the border with Spain. The best known is **Almeida**, with its star-shaped medieval walls, built in the middle of the 17th century. This and the walled town of **Trancoso**, as well as other local fortress towns, are surprisingly low on the list of most visitors priorities, and therefore their breathtaking, imposing nature can be appreciated in tranquil surroundings.

USEFUL CONTACTS:
EDUCATION, HOSPITALS, UTILITIES, TOURIST OFFICES AND SERVICE PROVIDERS

SCHOOLS
There is a distinct lack of schools offering lessons in English in this area, although there is a generous amount of schools teaching (as opposed to teaching in) English in Coimbra, Viseu and Figueira. The best thing to do is enrol children in a local school and encourage them to pick up the language quickly. For more details about education, contact the Lisbon-based **Ministry of Education** (Gabinete Relações Internacionais, avenida 5 de Outubro 35-37; +351 217 950330; www.minedu.pt) or perhaps contact the **Portuguese Embassy in London** (11 Belgrave Square, SW1X 8PP; 020 7235 5331). If you really can't do without a bit of British education, try the library in Coimbra, run by the **British Council**, which has a large range of English-language books and information (rua de Tomar 4; +351 239 853704).

SERVICES
One of the first things to do when you move into your Portuguese home is to get the utilities connected. **Portugal Telecom** (+351 213 540020; www.telecom.pt) for phone connections, **CPPE** (+351 213 525353; www.edp.pt) for electricity, and **EPAL** (+351 213 466541; www.epal.pt) and **Lusagua** (+351 217 928670) for water. Many homes don't have piped gas, but one company that deals with gas and other services is **Marques Raso** (+351 219 830157).

HOSPITALS
Coimbra's hospital is actually part of the university (praça Professor Mota Pinto; +351 239 400400). The region's other main hospitals include **Aveiro Hospital** (avenida Artur Ravada; +351 234 378300), Castelo Branco's **Hospital Amato Lusitano** (avenida Pedro Cabral; +351 272 322133), Figueira da Foz's **Hospital Distrital** (+351 233 402000), Guarda's **Hospital Sousa Martins** (avenida Reinha Dona Amalia; +351 271 222133) and Viseu's **São Teotónio Hospital** (avenida Dom Duarte; +351 232 420500). Many of the region's other main towns will have a smaller *centro de saúde* (health centre).

TOURIST OFFICES
The main tourist office in **Coimbra** is on the praça da República (+351 239 832591) where you'll find useful city maps and information, but there is another *turismo* in Coimbra dedicated to the whole Beira region (largo da Portagem; +351 239 855930). Other *turismos* in the area include those at **Figueira da Foz** (avenida 25 de Abril; +351 233 422610), **Aveiro** (rua João Menonça 8; +351 234 423680), **Castelo Branco** (Câmara Municipal, Alameda da Liberdade; +351 272 33039), **Viseu** (avenida Calouste Gulbenkian; +351 232 420950), **Guarda** (praça Luis de Camões; +351 271 505530) and the regional tourist office for the **Serra da Estrela national park** (rua Dom Sancho, Guarda; +351 271 225454).

POLICE
As with the rest of Portugal, the emergency phone number for police, fire and ambulance services is **112**. The main police station in Coimbra is in the centre of the city (rua Olimpico Nicolau Rui Fernandes; +351 239 822022).

SPECTATOR SPORTS
In the Beira regions, football is hugely popular, with even the smallest towns in the interior boasting a football field. The two most fervently followed teams in the area are Académica and SC Beira Mar, both of which ended the 2002-3 season in Portugal's top division, the SuperLiga. Beira Mar are based at Aveiro's Estádio Mário Duarte stadium, although the team will be relocating to a brand new stadium at nearby Tabueira next year, as part of the upgrading and expansion plans for the Euro 2004 European Football Championships. Académica play at the Estádio Municipal in Coimbra, which is also getting a facelift for Euro 2004.

Bullfighting is pretty popular in this region, with Figueira's bullring being most popular, particularly during the Festas da Cidade in June. Other spectator events include surf competitions all along the coast and the World Beach Football Championships held at Figueira in July and August.

> **For a guide to property prices in Coimbra & the Beiras, turn to page 192 for our Price Guide**

The Regions

Costa Verde & the North

COSTA VERDE & THE NORTH

The oldest and arguably most beautiful of Portugal's regions, Costa Verde is both a quaint secret hideaway and Portugal's industrial powerhouse. Offering a unique blend of the historic and modern, this region gives residents and visitors a real taste of the changing face of Portugal

PORTUGUESE TOURIST BOARD

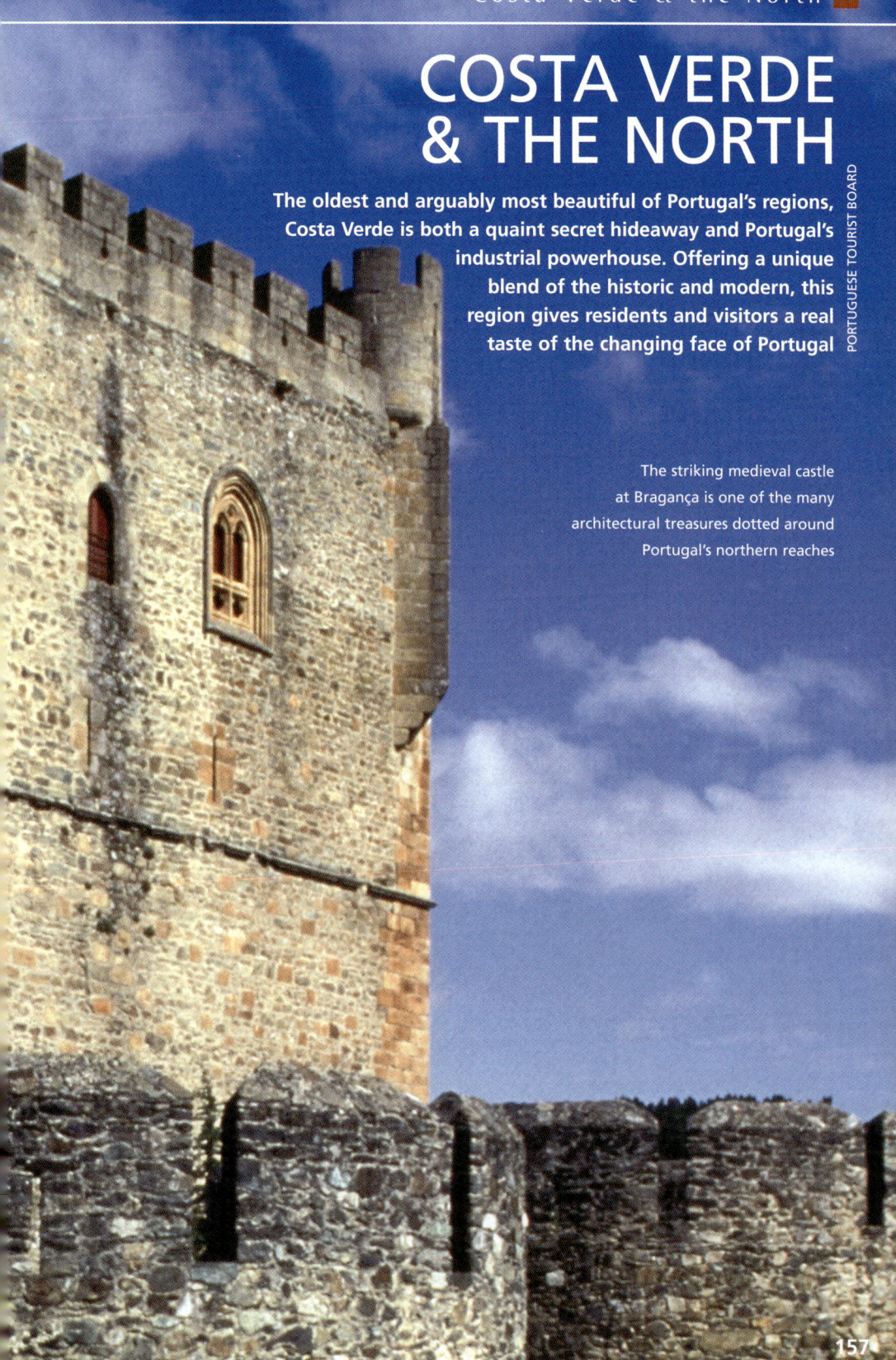

The striking medieval castle at Bragança is one of the many architectural treasures dotted around Portugal's northern reaches

The Regions

Most visitors to northern Portugal visit the city of Porto on the Douro river

Costa Verde & the North

The north of Portugal boasts a verdant landscape such as that at Pont de Lima (top left) and historic towns like that of Guimarães (above)

The area that comes under our broad banner 'Costa Verde & the North' comprises Porto (known to the Portuguese as Oporto), the Douro and Minho regions and Trás-os-Montes. It takes up the entire area north of the Douro river, bordering with north Spain and the Atlantic.

Porto is Portugal's second largest city, and its historic importance and wealth of ancient buildings have resulted in it being classed as a UNESCO World Heritage site and it was voted the 2001 European capital of culture. The city dominates the region of Douro, Portugal's industrial centre, grown rich from centuries of trade. The rest of the Douro is a blend of fishing ports, industrial zones and beach resorts. Unashamedly commercial and proud of its traditional work ethic, the local saying here is 'Coimbra studies, Braga plays, Lisbon shows off and Porto works'! And, of course, much of that work goes into the area's infamous port trade, evidenced by the Douro valley hillsides lined with vineyards.

Established by the Romans, and once Portugal's capital, the city of Porto was later given to Henri of Burgundy on his marriage in 1095, and in 1111, its status grew with the building of its cathedral. Porto was also the starting point for a number of Atlantic explorers, such as Henry the Navigator, who discovered the Azores and reached Sierra Leone and the African coast. Porto finally gained its independence from the French and the British, with 1822 seeing the first elected liberal constitution and 1878 seeing the first republican deputy elected.

The Minho was the birthplace of the first Portuguese king, who stated 'Portugal nasceu aqui' (Portugal was born here), as it was from Braga in 1139 that he retook Portugal from the Moors. Home to the country's main religious centres, Braga was founded by a Celtiberian tribe and transformed into a prosperous town under the Romans, due mainly to its position on the trade route.

Trás-os-Montes, literally meaning 'beyond the mountains', is known as Portugal's lost domain. In contrast to the richness and fertility of the Douro and the Minho, the area is remote and untamed and hard to farm. Although modern-day initiatives are now beginning to make an impact upon Trás-os-Montes, to all intents and purposes it remains a

The Regions

REGION INFORMATION

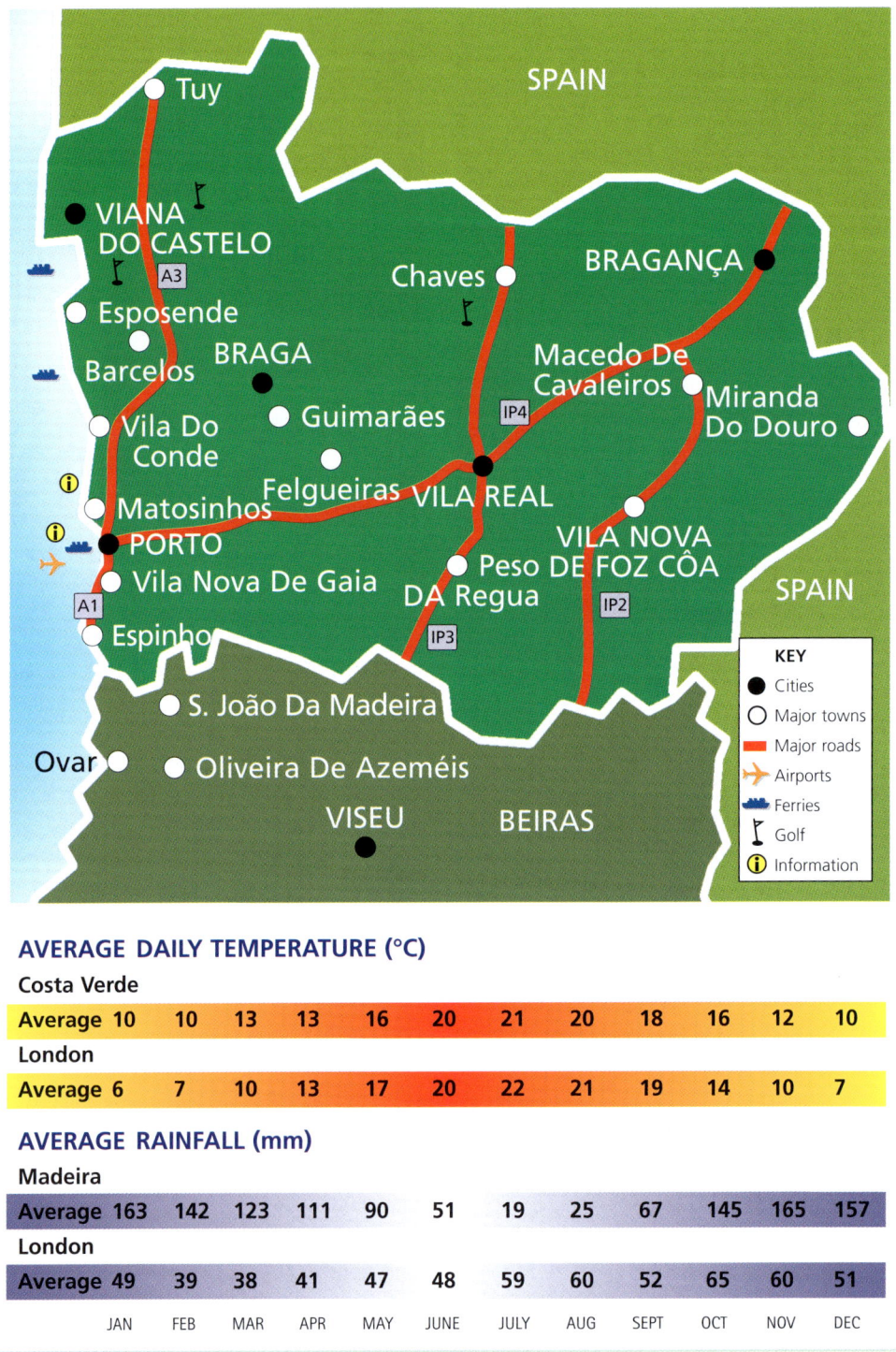

AVERAGE DAILY TEMPERATURE (°C)

Costa Verde

Average	10	10	13	13	16	20	21	20	18	16	12	10

London

Average	6	7	10	13	17	20	22	21	19	14	10	7

AVERAGE RAINFALL (mm)

Madeira

Average	163	142	123	111	90	51	19	25	67	145	165	157

London

Average	49	39	38	41	47	48	59	60	52	65	60	51
	JAN	FEB	MAR	APR	MAY	JUNE	JULY	AUG	SEPT	OCT	NOV	DEC

Costa Verde & the North

GETTING THERE

AIR The easiest way to get to this area is to fly into Porto, with major operators offering regular flights. **British Airways** (0845 773 3377; www.ba.com) and **TAP Air Portugal** (0845 601 0932; www.tap-airportugal.pt) both fly out of London to Porto. **British Airways** flies from London Gatwick to Porto once a day, **TAP** flies from Heathrow to Porto twice a day and **Portugália Airlines** (0870 755 0025; www.pga.pt) offers flights from Manchester to Porto once a day.

SEA By ferry, the only way to reach Portugal is to take a ferry from Portsmouth to Santander or Bilbao in northern Spain. **P&O Ferries** (0870 242 4999; www.poportsmouth.com) goes to Bilbao, while **Brittany Ferries** (0870 536 0360; www.brittany-ferries.com) sails to Santander.

ROAD From North Spain, it is roughly 750km to Porto. Take the A68 south, and then the A1 to Burgos. From there, take the N620 to Valladolid, and the N122 will take you across the border to Bragança. Once in Trás-os-Montes, the IP4 goes to Vila Real, from where the A4 goes on to Porto. From Porto, the N101 goes to Braga and the IC1 runs along the coast into Minho.

TRAIN Take a train through France to Irún in Spain. Once in Irún, an overnight service will take you on to Coimbra, and then a local Portuguese service will take you from Coimbra to most other stations in the area. **Rail Europe** (0870 584 8848; www.raileurope.co.uk) provides full details on international rail travel.

CLIMATE SUMMARY

Costa Verde enjoys a similar climate to the rest of Portugal, but its proximity to the mountains surrounding Trás-os-Montes makes it colder and wetter than elsewhere in Portugal. The north experiences more rainfall than anywhere else in the country, especially in the northwest, where the Atlantic has its strongest influence, and where the weather is damper and milder, with up to 2,000mm of rain falling each year. Of course, this amount of rain should come as no surprise when you consider the name 'Costa Verde' means 'green coast' and, indeed, the climate supports the region's agricultural fertility, nurturing the region's abundant production of grapes, and making it the most important area for Portugal's port and wine trade. It is best to visit this area between May and September, when the temperature is at its highest and the rainfall at its lowest.

Porto has a lively nightlife, especially on those evenings when a laser display takes place

wilderness of stone houses, crop fields and desolate moor lands.

There is a sharp natural north-south divide that exists within this remote rural province, with the south, known as *terra quente* (hot land) experiencing a Mediterranean climate, peppered with olive groves and vineyards. In contrast, the *terra fria* (cold land) offers bitter winds and an arid landscape of which a local proverb says 'Nine months of winter and three months of hell'. Meanwhile, covering twice the area of the Minho, yet possessing only half the population, Trás-os-Montes is perfect for those seeking a little solitude.

The Costa Verde offers many historic attractions and tourist centres, and this is especially apparent in Porto, with its diverse architecture. The city offers an array of attractions, from cultural sites to great restaurants and nightlife. Bragança in the Minho, meanwhile, is known as Portugal's ecclesiastical capital, and is definitely worth a visit by fans of religious architecture, while the Douro valley offers beautiful scenery and stunning tours, on both two and four wheels and in walking boots.

WORKING IN THE AREA

As Costa Verde has a famously low population, tourism is only really an option in major towns and cities. However, over recent years the Portuguese government has been investing heavily in the development of many of these northern towns and industries – as well as tourists – are beginning to come here more. Throughout the tourist season, there are always jobs available in bars, cafés, hotels

The Regions

EMPLOYMENT CONTACTS

Portuguese Embassy:
11 Belgrave Square, London, SW1X 8PP; 020 7235 5331

British Embassy:
rua de São Bernardo 33, Lisbon; +351 213 924000; www.ukembassy.pt

Job Centres
Although primarily a service for Portuguese nationals, job centres have an obligation, imposed by the EC regulations, to be of assistance to nationals of other EC countries. However, they are reluctant to help anyone who is unable to communicate in Portuguese. It is, therefore, recommended that if you are planning to move to Portugal and intend to support yourself through employment, you should ensure you have a job lined up prior to departure, especially if you cannot speak the language.

The Portuguese equivalent of the UK job centres are the *centros de emprego*, of which there are about 83 countrywide. In addition to operating a series of work placements, they also give assistance to entrepreneurs wanting to invest in the country. **IEFP**: Delegación Regional del Norte (rua Eng. Ezequiel Campos, Porto; +351 226 176336); **Centro de Emprego de Viana Do Castelo** (rua Pedro Homem de Melo 52-60, Viana do Castelo; +351 588 29018); **Centro de Emprego de Chaves** (largo 8 de Julho 7, Chaves; +351 276 340330).

Ministry for Social Security and Work (to find out more about finding work or claiming benefits in the northern regions of Portugal): praça de Londres 2, 16º andar, Lisbon; +351 218 424100; www.msst.gov.pt.

Portuguese Trade Office (for details about international companies with offices in Costa Verde): 2nd Floor, 21-25a Sackville Street, London W1X 2LY; 020 7494 1441

International House (English-teaching organisation with schools in Porto, detailing vacancies teaching English): rua Marechal Saldanha, Porto, +351 226 177641, www.ihporto.org

Overseas Jobs Express (UK-based jobs newspaper with listings of tourist-related jobs abroad, with a section on Portugal): www.overseasjobsexpress.co.uk

Anglo-Portuguese News (English newspaper with jobs section): apartado 113, Estoril; +351 214 661423)

TEFL International (for finding jobs as English teachers throughout Portugal): 367/11-12 Yaowarat Rd, Muang, Phuket Town, Phuket, Thailand; e-mail: general@teflcourse.com

This region's rocky hillsides offer great opportunities for abseiling, rock-climbing and canyoning

and all the usual tourist hotspots, particularly in Porto, Braga and Bragança. And, as elsewhere in Portugal, there are always jobs available for English teachers, especially TEFL certificate holders.

The main industries in the North are cork, ceramics (Barcelos is the ceramics capital of Portugal), fishing and wine. Many people in this area are employed by these industries, although you will obviously struggle to find employment in such industries unless you have a decent grasp of the language. However, it's worth finding out about international companies who may have offices in the region that might employ English speakers.

LEISURE TIME

Portugal's northern region offers much to the discerning and active traveller. If you choose to buy in this region, the Minho offers you glorious and quiet sandy beaches, while the surrounding national parks and mountainous regions make this area great for hiking, cycling and rock-climbing. The Douro

Costa Verde & the North

BUYING IN COSTA VERDE

The northern towns offer idyllic locations for your new home

If you're looking for a house in this region, you'll find most northern areas offer old properties built from granite, but with the introduction of more modern architecture, there are many newer developments in large towns and cities. Many areas offer ruins for renovation purposes rather than the custom-built villas of the Algarve and Lisbon, and generally prices are much lower than in the south, where demand is higher and the weather is more reliable with less rainfall. Generally there is more farmland in the remote areas and resale town properties rather than new builds. However, this may soon change with the influx and growth of tourism and the injection of cash into the area.

WHAT YOU GET FOR YOUR EUROS

PROPERTY 1

AREA: Porto

DESCRIPTION: This mansion, located in the centre of Porto, is arranged over three floors with a living space of 1,000m². It is a totally unique historic property that requires interior renovation yet has a protected façade. Ideal as a business premises or as a holiday home, this house is truly a piece of history, offering the buyer enormous potential. Located on the river front, this property offers stunning views and is well situated for access to all amenities.

PRICE: 1,600,000 euros
UK EQUIVALENT: £1,066,665

PROPERTY 2

AREA: Caminha

DESCRIPTION: A luxurious colonial-style villa, Casa Olivos is perfectly located just outside of Caminha, and only six kilometres from the local beaches. This beautiful home offers a peaceful environment with fantastic views and a delightful garden. Set in grounds that measure one hectare, this property was built in 1992, and has five bedrooms, two bathrooms and an office. It also features a second house.

PRICE: 598,000 euros
UK EQUIVALENT: £398,665

For more properties in Costa Verde, turn to our Price Guide, starting on page 192

The Regions

The red rooves and steeples of Porto often look on the verge of spilling into the Douro

Costa Verde & the North

offers spectacular boat trips, while Porto's city centre offers luxurious and upmarket shopping. Some of Portugal's best markets are located in the north, offering a variety of fresh produce.

Dripping with culture, Porto, Chaves and Guimarães offer many attractive historical sites, while the lush greenery of the Minho produces some of Portugal's best wines. Porto's riverfront and concert halls offer an active nightlife, while during the day, there are plenty of galleries, museums and churches to mill about in. Generally speaking, this area's abundance of historic buildings and natural beauty means residents and visitors alike are never short of things to do.

Organised outdoor activities, including walking and biking, are a booming industry in Portugal. The north of Portugal offers the best walks, the most demanding being the network of trails in the Parque Nacional da Peneda-Geres in the Minho and the Parque Natural de Montesinho in Trás-os-Montes. Near Vila Real is the Parque Natural do Alvão, which, although tiny, offers a variety of walks. Many private companies offer guided walks, two of which are English-run: *Portugal Walks* (+351 965 753033; www.portugalwalks.com) and *Rotas do Vento* (+351 213 649852). *Quercus* (+351 217 788474) also offers trips to areas of environmental interest.

Mountain biking is one of Portugal's fastest growing sports, with the Minho and Trás-os-Montes offering great riding trails and many centres renting mountain bikes to tourists. Most natural parks have cycling routes, and one of the best ways to get around them is in the company of the *Oporto Mountain Club*, one of Portugal's oldest cycling clubs, which organises cycle rides. An especially popular cycle route is through the Marão area, where port grapes are grown. The national parks of Serra de Montesinho and Serra do Geres also offer cycle routes, as well as walking trails.

For watersports lovers, Porto and Viana do Castelo have fine beaches for surfing and windsurfing. The best are Praia do Moledo in Caminha, Afife in Viana do Castelo, Esposende in Barcelos, Povoa de Varzim and Vila do Conde. For information on sports carried out under the sea, such as scuba diving and snorkelling, the *Portuguese Federation for Underwater Activities* (rua Frei Manuel Cardoso

River rafting is just one of the adventure sports offered by tour companies throughout the gorges of the northern region and the national parks

39; +351 218 460174) organises various expeditions in the area. Canoes and kayaks, for navigating the Rio Lima, can be hired from the *Clube Nautico* (+351 258 944499), while canoeing is also available in the Peneda-Gerês National Park.

The Minho and Beira Alto are home to eight championship golf courses. One of the best known is *Ponte de Lima* (Quinta de Pias, Fornelas, Ponte de Lima; +351 258 743414), which is a typical mountain course in the northern Minho region, close to vineyards and fruit gardens.

Many areas in Minho and Trás-os-Montes also have facilities for horseriding, while in the Vale de Lima, the *Clube Equestre* (+351 258 942466), *Centro Equestre Vale do Lima* (+351 258 743620) and the *Hipodromo de Ponte de Lima* (+351 258 762784) organise horse trekking. Swimming is also popular in the area, the most picturesque spot being

The Regions

RESTAURANTS

The most established resturaurant serving port in Porto is **Vinho do Porto** (+351 226 097793), located by the Jardim do Palácio de Cristal. The average cost per glass is 0.8 euros, and the friendly waiters will help you choose from their wide range. **Adega Vila Mea** (rua dos Caldeireiros 62, near Clerigos; +351 222 082967) serves various local specialities using fresh fish, and meals average about 12.50 euros. The very popular **Taberna de Bebobos** restaurant (cais da Ribeira 24-25; +351 222 053565) serves traditional cuisine at an average of 17.50 euros (£11.50) per meal while **Capa Negra** (rua do Campo Alegre 191) is famed city-wide for its meat sandwich (6-8 euros), and you also can choose fish and lobsters direct from the fish tank. Snacks from 4 euros and meals from 7.50-15 euros. **Oriental** (largo do Toural) is an excellent budget option, and offers very good regional specialities, as well as the usual fare. Featuring superb views over the square, prices start at under 7.50 euros, **Vira Bar** (largo Condessa do Juncal 27) is a well regarded restaurant with church-like surroundings and stained glass windows. For 13-20 euros, you can get the full works. **O Aldeão**, (rua Dom Pedro de Castro 7), popular and reasonably priced, is a restaurant offering a daily-changing menu with meals from 7.50 euros, while **O Espadeiro** (avenida Almeida Lucena, +351 259 322302) is a restaurant going strong for 30 years with meals starting at 12.50 euros.

CLASSIC DISH
Peixe Oporto

This dish of baked fish with a port wine sauce is a classic of the region, particular to Porto.

speciality is tripe made into a rich stew, and the inhabitants of Porto are known as *tripeiros* (tripe eaters). *Rabanadas*, *papos-de-anjo* and *barrigas-de-freiras* are varieties of sweetmeats eaten here, while *francesinha* is a hot sandwich containing beef, sausage and ham covered with melted cheese and a peppery tomato sauce. Another of Porto's specialities is *bacalhau a gomes de sa*, a creation of salt cod, potato and onion layers topped with eggs and olives. Funnily enough, one of the specialities of the Costa Verde region is a green one, name *caldo verde*, a traditional soup made from green cabbage and spicy sausage. Meanwhile, in Guimarães you'll find the local specialities of *chispalhada de feijão* (beans, sausage and pigs' trotters) and *papas de sarabulho* (a soup made from shredded pork and pigs' blood, and thickened with bread).

The dish traditionally eaten at Christmas in Chaves is octopus, while Trás-os-Montes is famous for a more robust and warming diet of pork, roast goat and veal, seasoned with nuts and dried beans. Trout, too, is used in much of the region's cooking, one such dish being *truta de barroso*, trout stuffed with ham, fried in bacon and served with potatoes.

Examples of sugary northern cakes are *toucinho do ceu*, rich, with almond and cinnamon flavours, *torta de Viana,* a sponge roll with a sweetened egg filling, and *sopa dourada,* a sponge cake covered with ground almonds and egg yolk, created in Viana do Castelo.

As far as drinks are concerned, Porto is of course infamous for its port production, with many port lodges in the area where you can taste and buy. Northern Portugal is also well known for its wine production, with the Minho producing *vinhos*

the rocky beach at Senhora da Ponte, just south of Mondim de Basto. Costa Verde offers a variety of sandy beaches and many larger towns have swimming pools. The Peneda-Gerês National Park, a wilderness park in the far north near the Spanish border, has many short-distance walking trails with places to swim along the way.

EAT, DRINK AND BE MERRY

The region has a rich tradition of producing wonderful soups, meats and cakes. Porto's regional

One of the specialities you'll find in the region is the extremely tasty egg dessert of *trouxas de ovos*

PORTUGUESE TOURIST BOARD

Costa Verde & the North

verdes or "green" wines, high in acidity, refreshing and lightly sparkling, made from exceedingly ripe grapes. Two of the best known labels are Dom Crespo and Alvarinho de Monção. Douro wines are fruity and of excellent quality, with strong colours and some of the best known labels are Acácio, Evel and Floral. Portuguese red wine is drunk chilled, and the best is the Dão, which comes from south Douro. Lamego, meanwhile, is renowned for its Champagne-like sparkling called *Raposeira*.

FOR CULTURE VULTURES

Porto's hills are home to some of the world's oldest prehistoric cave art, known as the Foz Coa, recently restored and open to the public. In Porto itself, the *Fundação de Serraives* is a contemporary art gallery, housing a fabulous collection, while throughout the year Porto is home to various art, film and jazz festivals. The Ribeira riverfront is home to most of Porto's bars, restaurants and nightclubs, and is a lively and dynamic area, while the cathedral or Sé quarter is more sedate, dominated by the cathedral but also featuring the amazing walls covered in *azulejo* tiles at the São Bente train station and the Renaissance church of Santa Clara. There are also many theatres in Porto, and the major venues are

Although most northern towns are sturdily constructed from granite, there is plenty of graceful architecture to be experienced here as well, including the church at Bragança (top left) and Guimarães castle in the Minho (above left)

TELLING PORKIES

One of the most curious sights you'll find here, particularly in the Trás-os-Montes region, are a number of crudely carved granite pigs known as *berroes* or *porcos*. Some are over 2,000 years old, and many have been dated back to the second and third centuries, but there is no specific answer as to why they are found within the region.

Most locals assume it has some sort of connection with the use of this land in these rural areas for pig farming over the centuries, but there may be more to it. Some people believe they are fertility or prosperity symbols, farm guardians or representations of Iron Age gods. Whatever their purpose, these mysterious pigs are now to be seen in museums in Bragança, Chaves and Miranda do Douro and within Bragança's citadel. One even sits in the square of the tiny village of Murca in Vila Real.

The Regions

the *Teatro Nacional São João* (praça da Batalha; +351 222 086634), the *Auditório Nacional Carlos Alberto* (rua das Oliveiras; +351 223 395050) and the *Belmonte Puppet Theatre* (rua Belmonte; +351 222 083341). Also highly recommended is a tasting and tour of the Port Lodge in Vila Nova de Gaia.

For venturing outside the city of Porto, the Douro train line is recommended for its stunning views of the Douro valley and terraced hillsides, while another means of seeing the sights is to take a cruise down the historic Douro, known as the "river of gold".

When visiting the Minho, the areas of Guimarães and Braga are recommended. Guimarães is a maze of cobbled streets and medieval monuments, while Braga is described as Portugal's answer to Rome, a city packed with religious architecture, including the country's oldest cathedral. The city is actually home to over 300 religious buildings and sanctuaries, including Bom Jesus, an extravagant Baroque building, the Citania de Briteiros, a magnificent pre-Roman fort, and the Pitões das Junais monastery dating from 1147. Between Braga and the coast lies Barcelos, a town famed for its production of ceramics and the famous Barcelos cockerels. The Minho is home to various museums, including the

Even the most ordinary streets in many towns will feature panels of the beautifully colourful and often hand-painted *azulejo* tiles

PORTUGUESE TOURIST BOARD

MOST FAMOUS FESTIVALS

This region sees a wide range of festivals throughout the year, with most activity happening throughout **Holy Week**, which is marked by processions and masses, such as the famous Easter week festival in **Braga** and the procession and feast held near Jardim de São Lazaro in **Porto**. In Braga. In **Vaca das Cordas**, the centuries-old tradition of the running of the bulls is also held around this time of year.

In June, Porto holds its famous celebrations of **São João** (June 23-24) and **São Pedro** (June 29), marked by street dancing and decorations. Meanwhile, in Ponte de Lima, look out for the **Feiras Novas** (New Fairs) which have been held here since 1125 and these combine a market and fair, with folk dances and fireworks.

On August 24 is the **São Bartolomeu festival** with a procession in **Foz do Douro**, where locals dress up in paper clothes, walk the streets and end up in the Douro river!

The festival of **São Nicolay** is held on December 6, with Porto children waiting for Santa Claus's arrival by boat at the Cais de Estiva. On December 8 the **Nossa Senhora da Conceição** public holiday, is rounded off by a night procession in the streets.

Museu Arqueológico Martins Sarmento in Guimarães (rua Paio Galvão, +351 253 415969), housing thousands of years' worth of ancient artefacts, including those from the nearby Celtic settlement of Briteiros.

Trás-os-Montes has many highlights, including the Solar de Mateus palace and the Roman remains at Panoias. The Corgo river valley is a stunning area, green and lush and packed with pretty villages and vineyards. The town of Chaves, close to the Spanish border, features a Roman bridge and spa, while the unique pentagonal citadel of Bragança, near the northern border with Spain, offers a bird's eye view over the peaceful Parque Natural de Montesinho.

SHOPPING: GIFTS AND GROCERIES

In Porto, the best shopping areas are Central and Baixa and the civic centre where chic, fashionable shops are located, in particular along the rua de Santa Catarina. The Boavista quarter in Porto is home to the huge and diverse Bolhão market, while on weekdays, a fruit and vegetable market is held

Costa Verde & the North

Porto has a lively cultural scene, and one of the best and most ornate venues to take in a concert is at the beautiful São João National Theatre

along the cais da Ribeira, and a weekly flea market on Saturday mornings along the rua das Fontainhas.

Both Braga and Barcelos play host to a large *mercado municipal* (town market) but, if you prefer, there is the Pingo Doce supermarket in Braga's shopping centre (on avenida da Liberdade) or various grocery shops on rua São Marcos in Braga. Supermarkets can be found in Barcelos (rua Filipa Borges), Guimarães (rua Paio Galvao) and Viana do Castelo (rua Martim Velho).

In Bragança, flea markets take over the municipal stadium (avenida Abade de Bacal) on the 3rd, 12th and 21st of each month. In the backstreets of the city, there are mini *mercados* (grocery stores), while the Feira das Cantarinhas is the biggest market of the year, a traditional street fair of handicrafts held on May 2–4 every year.

GETTING AROUND

To get yourself around the city of Porto, you've got the options of bus, tram, taxi or the ever-expanding metro system that is predicted to eventually reach the northern suburbs. However, you should find that most of the city's attractions are within walking distance of the centre, even if there are some steep hills to be negotiated! Most rail services in the northern regions start or end at Porto, with most

THE BARCELOS COCK

The Barcelos cock is a motif seen all over Portugal, especially in the form of pottery, and is named after the town of Barcelos, located in the Minho, 20km west of Braga. Its origins lie in a 16th-century legend: a traveller from Galicia, making the pilgrimage to Santiago de Compostela stopped at the town of Barcelos, where he was accused of stealing silver from a landowner and sentenced to death. The prisoner requested a meeting with the judge to protest his innocence and said that if the cockerel the man was about to eat, stood up on his plate and crowed, it would prove the pilgrim's innocence. The judge ignored the plea but as the prisoner was hanged, the cockerel, or so the legend goes, did indeed stand up and crow. Hurrying to the gallows, the judge found that the pilgrim had miraculously survived due to a loose knot in the noose. Years later, the Galician supposedly returned to the town and carved the Cruzeiro do Senhor do Galo, now housed in Barcelos's Museu Arqueológico.

The Regions

The Costa Verde region has a wealth of castles, built in a wide range of architectural styles, to explore; many are set in lush, verdant gardens

international and main national lines departing from Campanhã station outside the centre. For local services around the city suburbs and the regions, you'll have to head for São Bento station... but don't be distracted by the *azulejo* tile tableaux and miss your connection! All train tickets can be bought at São Bento, and you can find out more from *Caminhos de Ferro Portugueses* (local number: 808 208208).

The city's bus services are run by *STCP* (local number: 808 200166), with most services departing from the main stops at praça da Liberdade and in front of São Bento train station. Buses in Vila Real are organised by *AV Tamega* (+351 259 322 674), whose lines also serve Chaves, Lamego and the Minho. Services in the quieter Trás-os-Montes region are operated by *Cabanelos* (+351 222 005637), whose routes to and from Porto run from the main terminal on rua da Ateneu Comercial. Other towns in the North are served by *REDM/Rede Expressos* (+351 253 516229), *Arriva* (+351 253 423501) and *Rodonorte* (+351 253 412646) running to Amarante, Vila Real and Bragança.

If you prefer to drive yourself around the region, hire a car from one of the main companies who have offices at Porto's airport and in Braga: *Avis* (+351 222 055947), *Europcar* (+351 222 057737) and *Hertz* (+351 223 395300).

LOCAL LIFE

Northern Portugal is a highly religious and traditional area, where its people observe many festivals, whose economy relies on the wine and port trade. Of course, port is the major export for this region, but on the coast, at Viano do Castelo in particular, fishing is the main industry. Northern Portugal is also famous for its ceramics, the best known being the terracotta style from Barcelos and the dark grey Bisalhães style from the Trás-os-Montes area.

In between the many religious festivals, the pace of life here, outside the bustling city of Porto, is fairly slow, and in many mountain towns you will see housewives sitting outside their homes, making bobbin lace, embroidering linen tablecloths or

Costa Verde & the North

USEFUL CONTACTS:
EDUCATION, HOSPITALS, UTILITIES, TOURIST OFFICES AND SERVICE PROVIDERS

EDUCATION
If moving to Portugal with school age children, the recommendation is that they are entered into an international school, unless they're young enough to pick up the Portuguese language. International schools in Porto include **The British School** (rua da Cerca 326, Foz do Douro; +351 226 166660) and the **CLIP-Oporto International School** (esplanada Rio de Janeiro; +351 226 166790). For older pupils, try the **CLIC-Colegio Luso Internacional do Centro** (rua Dom João Pereira, Venancio, Marinha Grande; +351 244 503710), the **Lusiada University** (rua Dr Lopo de Carvalho, Porto; +351 225 570800) or **Portucalense University** (rua Dr Antonio Bernardino de Almeida, Porto). For more details about education in northern Portugal, contact the **Ministry for Education** (avenida 5 de Outubro, Lisbon; +351 217 950330; www.min-edu.pt) or the **Northern Ministry for Education** (+351 225 191100). For more detailed information on education and regional information in general, contact **The British Council** in Lisbon (+351 213 214500; www.pt.britishcouncil.org) or in Porto (rua do Breyner 155, Porto; +351 222 073060; porto.enquiries@pt.britishcouncil.or).

HOSPITALS
The two main hospitals in Porto are the **Hospital Pedro Hispana** (rua Dr Eduardo Torres; +351 229 391000) and the **Hospital Geral of Santo Antonio** (rua Vicente Jose Carvalho; +351 222 077500). Braga has a main hospital called the **Hospital São Marcos** (largo Carlos Amarante; +351 253 603800) as well as the **Hospital Maria Pia,** (rua da Boavista 827; +351 226 099674). There is also the **Hospital Maternity Julio Dinis** (largo da Maternidade, +351 226 087400) in Porto.

SERVICES
Connecting your utilities is an essential part of buying a home. Once you have moved in, contact **Portugal Telecom** (+351 213 540020; www.telecom.pt) for phone connections, **CPPE** (+351 213 525353; www.edp.pt) and **Ren** (+351 218 470180) for electricity, and **EPAL** (+351 213 466541; www.epal.pt) and **Lusagua** (+351 217 928670; www.lusagua.pt) for water. Most properties don't have piped gas, as there is no network available, but **Marques Raso** deals with gas (+351 219 830157).

TOURIST OFFICES
Porto's main tourist office is in the town centre (praça Dom João I 43; +351 222 057514), but there is a smaller office at **Carneiro airport** (+351 229 412534). There is another *turismo* office in the old town (rua do Infante Dom Henrique 63; +351 222 009770). The **City Council Tourism Office** is in the centre of Porto (rua Clube dos Fenianos 25; +351 223 393470; www.portoturismo.pt) and **Porto city council** is also a useful source of information (praça General Humberto Delgado, +351 222 097000; www.cm-porto.pt).

POLICE
The number for emergency services is **112** but you can contact the **Tourism Police** direct (+351 222 081833).

---

tending their tapestries. Some locals still wear traditional dress, although most people just bring it out for the religious festivals, street parades or to take part in the stick dances still often held in the Trás-os-Montes villages. Life in most rural towns revolves around the church and the local markets, but come alive for carnivals and *festas*.

SPECTATOR SPORTS
Football is the real passion for sport lovers in northern Portugal, as it is throughout the country. Porto has its own football team, FC Porto (www.fcporto.pt), who finished the 2003-4 season well placed in the top division, the SuperLiga. They play their matches at the *Antas Stadium* (avenida de Fernão de Magalhães; +351 225 570400; www.fcporto.pt), which they share with Porto's other team, Boavista. Braga and Guimarães also have teams in Portugal's first division, and all three towns will be hosting matches in next year's European Football championships.

Bullfighting is not as widespread in the north as it is in other areas of Portugal, and fights tend to only really take place at festival time, rather than monthly or weekly as in other towns.

For a guide to property prices in Costa Verde, turn to our Price Guide, starting on page 192

Madeira

MADEIRA

Madeira is renowned for its wine and its vibrantly colourful gardens, but it and the neighbouring island of Porto Santo offer a wealth of walking trails, much historic architecture and a wonderfully temperate climate all year round

PORTUGUESE TOURIST BOARD

Red-rooved houses, terraced hillsides and rocky coastline epitomise the island of Madeira

The Regions

Sheer cliffs and deserted inlets can be found all round the Madeiran coast

Madeira

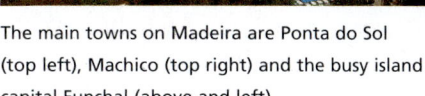

The main towns on Madeira are Ponta do Sol (top left), Machico (top right) and the busy island capital Funchal (above and left)

The islands of Madeira and Porto Santo, situated around 600km off the north African coast and 400km north of the Canary Islands, together make up one of Portugal's exotic outposts in the Atlantic. The islands are best known for their spectacular gardens, which remain an explosion of colour for most of the year, but they also boast spectacular volcanic rocky outcrops, sheer cliffs and craggy coastlines.

The islands were discovered in 1418 by two Portuguese sea captains on an expedition to explore the African coast. The larger island of Madeira became home to Portuguese entrepreneurs who established sugar plantations there, watered by a network of *levadas* or irrigation channels, dug out by slaves. Christopher Columbus was one such sugar trader who settled in Madeira, marrying the daughter of the governor of Porto Santo.

With an established sugar trade and a burgeoning wine industry, Madeira in the 16th century was caught up in pirate battles and invasions as trade between Europe and the Americas increased. In 1566, French invaders attacked Madeira's capital Funchal, killing many residents and looting homes and churches, and in 1580 Madeira passed into Spanish hands. It was won back for Portugal with the help of the British and, ever since, Madeira has had strong links to the UK, with English wine merchants settling on the island in the 17th century, British soldiers stationed there during the Napoleonic wars and thousands of Gibraltar residents housed on the island during World War Two.

It's no wonder that Madeira and Porto Santo are rising in popularity with foreign home-buyers, the British in particular. Its warm climate, interesting history and strong links with Britain make it ideal for retirees, as well as for those looking for a holiday home, and as its popularity rises as a weekend break option, travelling to Madeira has never been easier. If you are looking for an idyllic island in the sun, with all the benefits that being part of the European Union brings, Madeira is for you.

WORKING IN THE AREA

Madeira gives off an air of wealth, thanks mainly to the lush greenery and large, luxurious hotels in

The Regions

REGION INFORMATION

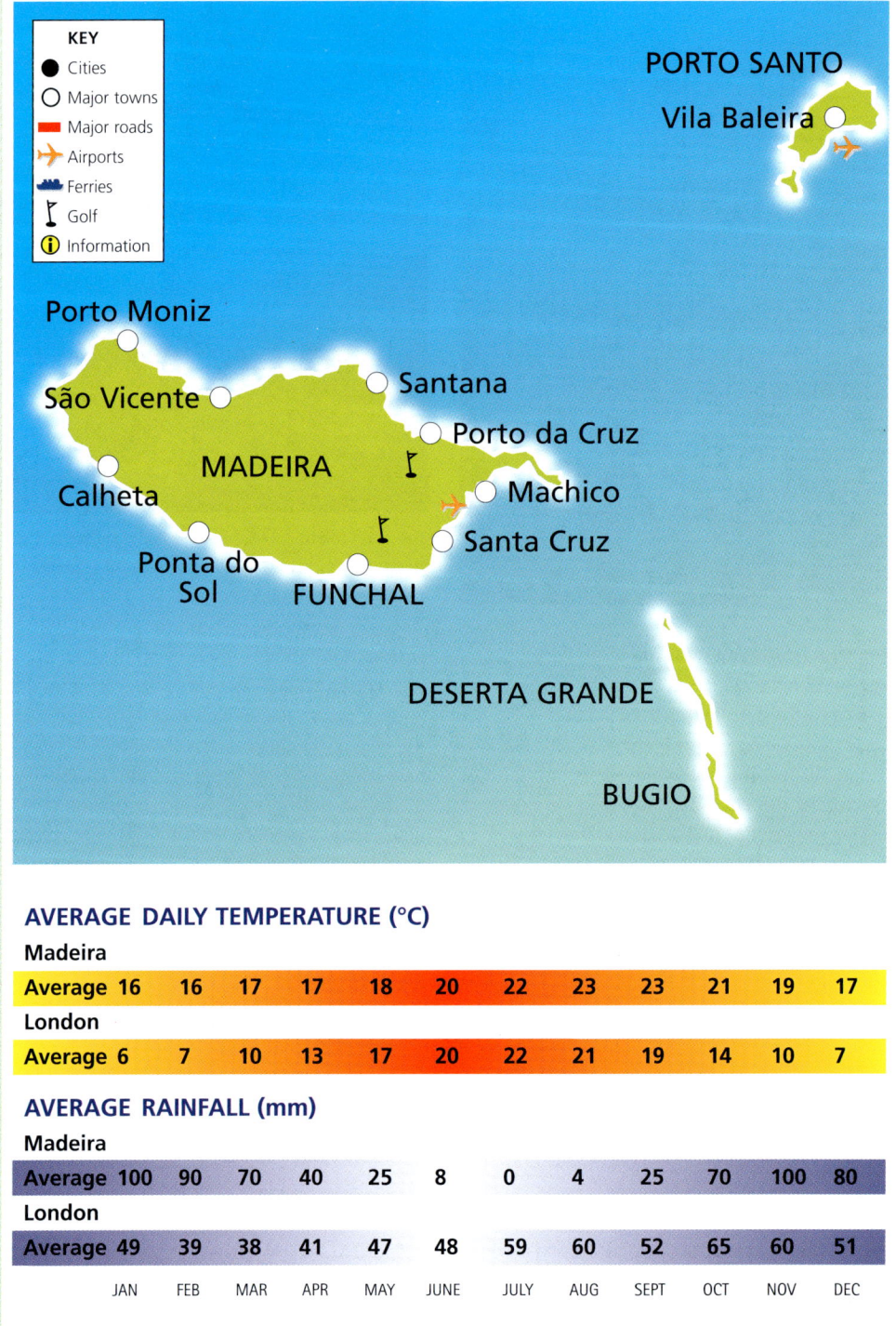

AVERAGE DAILY TEMPERATURE (°C)

Madeira
| Average | 16 | 16 | 17 | 17 | 18 | 20 | 22 | 23 | 23 | 21 | 19 | 17 |

London
| Average | 6 | 7 | 10 | 13 | 17 | 20 | 22 | 21 | 19 | 14 | 10 | 7 |

AVERAGE RAINFALL (mm)

Madeira
| Average | 100 | 90 | 70 | 40 | 25 | 8 | 0 | 4 | 25 | 70 | 100 | 80 |

London
| Average | 49 | 39 | 38 | 41 | 47 | 48 | 59 | 60 | 52 | 65 | 60 | 51 |
| | JAN | FEB | MAR | APR | MAY | JUNE | JULY | AUG | SEPT | OCT | NOV | DEC |

Madeira

GETTING THERE

AIR GB Airways (a subsidiary of **British Airways**: 0845 7733377; www.britishairways.co.uk) has regular flights to Funchal from London Heathrow. **TAP Air Portugal** (0845 601 0932; www.tap.pt) flies to Funchal from Gatwick, but also offers a wider choice of flights operating via Lisbon. Other charter and independent airlines offer various flights from UK regional airports to Funchal, mainly during the summer months. For details of these, it's worth checking with your travel agent.

SEA Madeira is a popular stop-off point for various Atlantic cruises, which often dock at Funchal harbour before pressing on to the Azores, South America and the Caribbean, or back to North Africa, the Canaries and the Mediterranean. Again, you should contact your travel agent for details of cruise operators.

Collecting canes to be made into the island's wickerwork, for which Madeira is well known

Funchal's Santa Cruz airport is busy all year

CLIMATE SUMMARY

Madeira has an ideal climate, its beautiful flowering gardens and verdant landscape testament to its mild winters, hot summers and warm springs. The average daytime temperature in December and January, for instance, hovers around the 18°C mark, while even the hottest summer days, when the temperature reaches around 30°C, are tempered by ocean winds. Most of Madeira's rain falls between October and March, with the least rain in July and August, the most popular time for holidaymakers to visit. Generally, it is warmer and drier in the south of the island, while the north and the more mountainous areas see more winds, slightly lower temperatures and more rain.

The island of Porto Santo has lower rainfall than Madeira, and temperatures can creep a couple of degrees higher, although again the sun is cooled by ocean winds and low cloud, which often descends at noon on summer days but clears within a couple of hours.

Funchal visited by the rich and famous, but there's no denying that there's an undercurrent of poverty, with many villagers only just managing to scrape a living through local crafts like wickerwork and embroidery. That said, however, there are openings for those moving to Madeira and to Porto Santo in terms of employment.

The most obvious avenue to consider is any job related to the tourist industry, especially as Madeira's climate makes it a popular destination all year round. And because of the popularity of the island with British tourists, many hotels, restaurants, shops and cafés look for English-speaking workers. There are also occasional vacancies in the various tourist offices around the island, although you will be expected to have a decent grasp of the Portuguese language in order to deal with tourists other than those from the UK.

If you're keen to run your own business, there are opportunities to open shops or hotels, although the geography, especially in Funchal, means the only space for new developments is usually in modern complexes. Over recent years, there has been a growth in rural tourism on Madeira, so there is scope to develop countryside properties, especially those near the popular towns of Santana and São Jorge, into hotels, restaurants or B&Bs.

Madeira's climate means it supports a wide variety of agriculture, so those with green fingers or an interest in the wine trade may be able to find jobs in

The Regions

EMPLOYMENT CONTACTS

Madeira Island Bulletin (English-language newspaper): Second Floor, rua 31 de Janeiro, Funchal; +351 291 231363

Madeira Life (English-language newspaper, with lively online ex-pat community and classified section): Quinta da Palmeira, São Caetano Terça, Ponta do Sol; +351 291 972779; www.madeiralife.com

The British School (opportunities for teachers): rua dos Iléus 85, Funchal; +351 291 773218; www.britishschoolmadeira.com

The International School (English-teaching posts): Calçada do Pico 5, Funchal; +351 291 225870; www.madeira-international-school.com)

Vinhos Justino Henriques (Madeira's largest employer in the wine trade): Parque Industrial da Cancela, Caniço; +351 291 934257; www.justinosmadeira.com

Portuguese Embassy: 11 Belgrave Square, London, SW1X 8PP; 020 7235 5331

British Embassy: rua de São Bernardo 33, 1249-082 Lisbon; +351 213 924000; www.ukembassy.pt

Portuguese Trade Office (for details about international companies with offices in Madeira): 2nd Floor, 21-25a Sackville Street, London W1X 2LY; 020 7494 1441

the huge number of vineyards, gardens and fruit plantations around the island, although much work is seasonal and generally low-paid. Those with experience, however, as well as a knowledge of Portuguese, should be able to find jobs in the related offices or managerial positions.

Anyone with teaching or TEFL qualifications should seek jobs with international schools or as private tutors, although most work will be centred around the main towns. And of course, if your Portuguese isn't perfect, it may be worth looking for a job linked to the expat community, whether it's in an English-run hairdresser or working in an Irish pub!

LEISURE TIME

Residents and visitors will all agree on the fact that there is no shortage of activities to fill your time on Madeira and Porto Santo, whether you're here for a week's holiday or for your retirement. On Madeira, in particular, there are countless gardens to visit and museums to potter around, while the more active visitors will no doubt seek out the walking and biking trails in the hills. Despite the lack of beaches, swimming is an extremely popular pastime, thanks mainly to a bearable sea temperature all year round, while less strenuous pursuits include bird-watching, whale-watching and horse-trekking.

Those after a bit of culture or nightlife can take advantage of Funchal's theatre and casino, as well as its many bars, restaurants and clubs, or perhaps take in a bit of daytime drinking at various Madeira wine lodges dotted around the island. And while you're travelling around the island, be sure to visit the quaint, typically Madeiran houses of Santana and São Jorge, with their steep thatched rooves and colourfully painted woodwork.

Despite its smaller size, Porto Santo has plenty to offer the visitor, too, with its Columbus Museum, walking trails, diving excursions and, of course, its

The verdant, if hilly, fields of Madeira sustain thriving agricultural and farming communities

BUYING IN MADEIRA

The ideal home to buy in Madeira is one of the quaint little cottages found mostly in the villages in the north of the island, with colourfully painted window- and doorframes and the traditional steeply-angled thatched rooves. The demand for these types of houses pushes their prices up beyond the imaginable, but if you can find one in less than tidy order, you may be able to afford it, albeit as a renovation project.

The most common property finds are apartments in the main towns of Funchal, Santa Cruz and Ponta do Sol, some in old townhouses, others within the modern tower blocks often just outside the main centre.

The apartments often come with strings attached (some bad, some good), whether it is complicated overseeing management companies or on-site swimming pools, so check exactly what the buying price includes.

Another popular option is the increasing number of purpose-built resorts and developments, many of which centre around golf or leisure complexes, with some being aimed entirely at the retirees who flock to Madeira and Porto Santo for the benevolent climate. These have the benefit of all amenities and leisure facilities being within easy reach, and are usually managed and tended by the complex staff, making them good for the security conscious whose homes may not be lived in for many months of the year.

With the tourism industry on Madeira and Porto Santo only recently starting to spread to the rural interior, it's still possible to find bargains in the countryside, although places for sale might be harder to find. Keep your eyes open for any bargains, though!

WHAT YOU GET FOR YOUR EUROS

PROPERTY 1

AREA: Funchal

DESCRIPTION: Once a monk's retreat, this 300-year-old property has been converted into a two-bedroom *quinta*. With views over the sea, it is only a short stroll from the traditional village square, and a short bus ride into the centre of Funchal. Close to all amenities and distractions the Madeiran capital has to offer, this property is blissfully secluded, and its verdant gardens and comfortable terrace, along with its stunning views, makes it highly attractive.

PRICE: 375,000 euros
UK EQUIVALENT: £250,000

PROPERTY 2

AREA: Funchal

DESCRIPTION: Located in a stunning development in the Balancal Golf Resort, these villas afford great views over Funchal bay. Surrounded by woodland and in an area of natural beauty, these properties are built to the highest standards. Offering three or four bedrooms, the villas and overlook Balancal's championship golf course. Located 500m above Funchal bay, in the foothills of the mountains, these are a great buy.

PRICE: 950,000 euros
UK EQUIVALENT: £633,335

For more properties in Madeira, turn to our Price Guide, starting on page 192

The Regions

Porto Santo's stretch of sandy beach never gets over-run with sunseekers

Madeira

Madeira and Porto Santo offer extravagantly beautiful gardens, intriguing diving excursions and lively celebrations for New Year in Funchal

beautiful stretch of beach. It also has a good selection of restaurants, where you can sample the local food and wine, with the fish often cooked fresh from the sea.

Madeira is famed for its walking trails, most of which follow the routes of the *levadas*, the oldest of which were carved out by slaves in the 15th century to irrigate the sugar plantations. The *levadas* cover almost a thousand miles, and their paths form a huge network of trails. They cover all kinds of terrain, so whether you're after a strenuous mountain hike or an undemanding stroll, there will be a *levada* to suit you. Cycling is also hugely popular on both Madeira and Porto Santo, although only the fittest should tackle the steep slopes and off-road unpaved trails. For a more relaxing way to see the island, take advantage of the guided jeep tours that take you up into the mountains for breathtaking views, such as that at Pico do Areiro.

The waters around the Madeiran islands are particularly temperate and, while there aren't many beaches (apart from the seven-kilometre sandy stretch on Porto Santo, and the rocky ones of Funchal and Prainha on Madeira), there are plenty of bathing platforms, diving boards and seawater pools dotted around the various towns along the coasts of

SNAPSHOTS

- The name Madeira comes from the Portuguese for wood, owing to the dense forests that covered the island when it was first discovered.
- In 1855, the Briton James Johnson discovered an impressive series of underground caves near São Vicente. The *grutas* are now one of the island's greatest attractions.
- Each year, on July 1, islanders commemorate the arrival of Portuguese explorers on the islands in 1418 with the Discovery of Madeira Day.
- In the 16th century, Porto Santo became home to a religious cult started by Fernando Nunes who, along with his niece, claimed God was speaking to him. The cult's followers, known as *profetas*, were eventually arrested and the cult stopped, but the *profeta* name lives on as a Madeiran nickname for residents of their neighbouring island!
- For those after a non-alcoholic alternative to the ubiquitous Madeira wine, try the *brisa maracujá*, a sparkling drink made from passion fruit.
- Indulge your passion for cars and speed by visiting one of Madeira's famous rallies: the Vintage Car Rally in June and the Wine Rally in August.

The Regions

RESTAURANTS

No visit to Funchal would be complete without a meal or snack on board the **Beatles Boat**, otherwise known as **The Vagrant** (avenida do Mar; no phone number available). This boat, now in dry dock on the harbourside, was originally owned by American millionaire Horace Vanderbilt and later owned by The Beatles. It's been a restaurant (albeit a kitsch one) since the 1980s, and is equally good for cheap pizza as it is for quality fish food. At the other end of the scale is the unsurpassed **Les Faunes** restaurant at **Reid's Palace Hotel** (estrada Monumental 139; +351 291 763001). Here you can taste high quality French food with Madeiran touches, surrounded by original Picassos and celebrity diners. For the best *espetada* kebabs on the island, try **A Seta** (estrada do Livramento 80; +351 291 743643) on a hill overlooking Funchal, where the skewered meats are cooked over coals then hung at the table. The restaurant holds regular dance and *fado* evenings too.

CLASSIC DISH
Espetada Madeira

The famed Madeiran skewered kebab is made using beef or lamb, fennel, onion, peppers and bay leaves.

both islands. Another coastal pastime is diving, particularly popular at Machico and Caniço de Baixo. Staying above the water, it's possible to hire and charter boats to visit Porto Santo and also the uninhabited Desertas and Selvagens islands, as well as for dolphin- and whale-watching tours, most of which depart from Funchal.

Back inland, visitors can play golf at one of the two main courses on Madeira. *Palheiro Golf Club* (+351 291 72116), just east of Funchal, is owned by the Blandy family, famous for Madeira wine production, while *Clube de Golf Santo da Serra* (+351 291 550100), in the east of the island, is famed for its amazing position and fantastic views.

EAT, DRINK AND BE MERRY

Madeiran cuisine is influenced by that of Portugal, and most food on Madeira and Porto Santo is relatively simple, with grilled fish and meat appearing on most menus. Unsurprisingly for an island, fish is a popular choice, and one particular speciality is the *espada*. Also known as cutlass fish, the unattractive *espada* (with their black skin and tiny sharp teeth) are caught in deep waters and, when grilled or fried, the white flesh tastes deliciously tender. Many Madeirans enjoy the fish baked in pastry with another island speciality: banana. Other local fish to look out for are *bodião* (parrot fish), *espadarte* (swordfish) and *atum* (tuna).

While meat stews often appear on inland menus, with *feijão guisado* (bacon, bean and tomato stew) being a particular favourite, another local speciality is the *espetada*. This skewered meat is usually cooked over a charcoal grill or on a hot griddle pan, and will either consist of large chunks of meat or meat with onions and peppers.

To finish a meal, it is worth taking advantage of some of the island's fruit, with bananas, guava, papaya, mango and starfruit featuring alongside melons from Porto Santo. Alternatively, try the traditional Madeiran *bolo de mel*, a cake made from honey and molasses.

Madeira produces various red and white wines, and of course you'll be able to try the ubiquitous Madeira fortified wine, usually served before or after a meal. Mellow in flavour, it comes in different varieties, depending on what grape it's made from: Tinta Negra Mole, Bual, Malvasia, Vedelho or Sercial.

FOR CULTURE VULTURES

Half of Madeira's population lives in or around Funchal, so obviously most cultural sites and events are centred in the capital. Funchal is home to many churches, from the small but peaceful chapel of Santa Catarina set in the lush park of the same

No visit to Madeira is complete without a taste of the Madeira wine, whatever vintage you choose

THE MADEIRA TOURIST BOARD

The island of Madeira is known for the abundance of beautifully vibrant flowers nearly all year round

name to the larger Sé cathedral with its imposing facade of contrasting dark stone and whitewashed plaster. Completed in 1514, its fairly plain interior is complemented by the brightly coloured stained glass windows and a beautiful wooden ceiling, inlaid with sections of ivory. A couple of streets away is the Palácio de São Lourenço, built for the first governors of Funchal in the 16th century. Its impressive state rooms, including the opulent ballroom and the impressive Portrait Gallery, are open to the public but you'll need to check with the tourist office for opening times.

Also in the old town is the *Teatro Municipal Baltazar Diaz* (avenida Arriaga; +351 291 233560), which hosts regular opera and musical performances, while at the east end of town, right on the seafront, is the imposing São Tiago fortress, which now houses a modern art gallery. There are plenty of other museums in the city (from the Museu de Arte Sacre exhibiting religious artworks to

WINE

Madeira is most famous for its wine, although many vineyards were devastated by the outbreak of phylloxera in the 18th century. The first vineyards were planted in the 15th century, and brought the island a large slice of income, eventually taking over from the sugar plantations in importance. Nowadays, the large majority of the island's grapes go towards making the fortified Madeira wine that comes in five varieties, depending on the grapes used. These are **Malvasia** (a sweet red or white), **Bual** (fruity warm white), **Tinta Negra Mole** (a red grape and the most common), **Vedelho** (dry white) and **Sercial** (citrussy white). The rarer unfortified wines are nowhere near as popular and not so commonly drunk, although they will appear on some restaurant menus, usually alongside a much wider selection of table wines from the mainland.

The Regions

MOST FAMOUS FESTIVALS

The most spectacular of Madeira's festivals is the **Festa da Flor**. In the week leading up to the festival in April, gardeners and shopkeepers, hoteliers and council workers in Funchal will begin decorating the houses, shops and street with garlands and window displays, filling the city with vibrant colour. The festival kicks off with the opening of the **Wall Of Hope**, where children bring bunches of flowers to the town hall square.

The celebrations continue for three days, involving competitions for best displays and the **Allegorical Parade**, where floats decorated with flowers process through the streets. The festival comes to an end with a firework display over Funchal harbour on the final night, when the waterfront is crowded with locals and visitors.

the Museu Franco, dedicated to the works of brothers and artists Henrique and Francisco Franco), and several merchants' houses, or *quintas,* are also open to the public, most having splendid gardens.

Other sights around the island worth a visit are the Amparo fort in Machico, the whale museum in Caniçal, the Ethnographical Museum in Ribeira Brava and the Christopher Columbus House museum in Vila Baleira on Porto Santo.

SHOPPING: GIFTS AND GROCERIES

The obvious souvenir to bring home from Madeira is the wine, which you can taste and buy from various lodges around the island. The most well known of these are the *Adegas de São Francisco* (avenida Arriaga 28, Funchal; +351 291 740110; www.madeirawinecompany.com) and the *Henriques & Henriques lodge* in Câmara de Lobos (Sitío de Belém; +351 291 941551). Other local crafts that you'll see for sale all over the island are embroidery and lacework, wickerwork (everything from furniture to life-size animals!) and inlaid woodwork.

For everyday shopping, Funchal has a large selection of shops and stores, with many of the larger ones being concentrated in the big modern complexes in the west of the city. For food and

From top: one of Madeira's bustling fruit markets, the famous wicker toboggan rides from Monte to Livramento and the new Funchal-Monte cable-car

Madeira

flowers, try the enormous *Mercado dos Lavradores* market (rua Brigadeiro Oudinot), set in a 1930s three-storey building, where you'll find a huge array of local produce, from fruit and vegetables to meat and fish, from plants and flowers to pets, household goods and wickerwork.

Madeira and Funchal also have a fair selection of supermarkets, the biggest being the main Pingo Doce store at the Anadia arcade, near the Lavradores market. There are also other Pingo Doce outlets around Funchal and in Machico. Meanwhile, on Porto Santo you'll find a Pingo Doce and a Super-Zarco supermarket in Vila Baleira.

GETTING AROUND
Various bus companies run services between Funchal and other towns on Madeira. These include *Horários do Funchal* (+351 291 705555) which operates in and around the city, *Rodoeste* (+351 291 220148) for the west of the island and *SAM* buses (+351 291 229144) for the east of the island. Porto Santo is served by a handful of routes, run by *Horários de Transportes* (+351 291 742444).

Many locals indulge in local crafts, either as a hobby or as their living. The most well known Madeiran crafts are embroidery, lace-making and wickerwork

FAMOUS RESIDENTS
If you're thinking of moving to Madeira to live, you'll be in fine company. One of the first names in history to make their home on the island was **Christopher Columbus**. In the years before his Atlantic explorations, he made his living as a sugar trader and was attracted to the plantations on Madeira. He was equally attracted to the daughter of Porto Santo's governor, Filipa Moniz, whom he married in 1479, settling on Porto Santo and later in Funchal. The house he lived in, in Vila Baleira, is now a museum. Also in the 15th century, the exiled king of Poland, **Wadislaw II**, was given land in Madeira by Portugal's king Dom João. He settled in Madalena do Mar, where the locals knew him as Henrique Alemão. In more recent times, in 1949, **Winston Churchill** spent almost a year on the island, taking a suite in the famous Reid's hotel. Here he relaxed, painted, sipped the Madeira wine and wrote an album of war memoirs.

The Regions

With beautiful villages, the quaint thatched houses of Santana, bathing beaches and twisty hillside roads, Madeira has something for everyone

Taxis and car hire on both Madeira and Porto Santo are affordable, and the roads are relatively quiet, although care should be taken when negotiating the tight mountain turns! Scooters and bikes are also available for hire on both islands, although they are more recommended on the less hilly island of Porto Santo.

There are various daily flights between Madeira and Porto Santo, as well as daily ferries between Funchal and Vila Baleira, run by *Porto Santo Line* (+351 291 210300). You can charter smaller boats to take you between the islands, although the journey can be rough and take up to two hours.

More unusual modes of transport are the *carriola* horse-drawn carriages in Vila Baleira and Funchal, the impressive cable-car linking Funchal and Monte and, of course, the *carros de cesto* wicker toboggans that are propelled on their metal runners down the steep hill from Monte to Livramento. It might be a bit of a tourist cliché, but it is definitely a Madeiran must-do and fantastic fun!

LOCAL LIFE

The pace of life on Madeira is relaxed, making it a perfect destination for retirees, but that doesn't mean the Madeirans don't know how to party, and in most towns there are lively bars and cafés that are well attended in the daytime and evening, particularly when hosting *fado* (a style of Portuguese song, with a vocalist accompanied by one or two guitars) or dance nights.

Nearly every home has a well tended garden, often terraced on the steeper slopes, and the island is characterised by a wealth of exotic flowers that

USEFUL CONTACTS:
EDUCATION, HOSPITALS, UTILITIES, TOURIST OFFICES

SCHOOLS
If you feel your child is young enough to be able to pick up the Portuguese language then it is often advised that they are enrolled in a local school. However, you may prefer to take advantage of a school that welcomes international pupils, such as **The British School** (rua dos Ilheus 85, Funchal; +351 291 773218) or **The International School** (Calçada do Pico 5, Funchal; +351 291 225870; www.madeira-international-school.com)

SERVICES
For electricity services, contact **EEM** (Empresa de Electricidade, avenida do Mar e das Comunidadas Madeirenses 32, Funchal; +351 291 221187). And to find out about phone services and telephone connections on Madeira and Porto Santo, contact the main office of **Portugal Telecom** (avenida Fontes Pereirade Melo 40, 1050 Lisbon; +351 213 540020). For water, gas and other electric and phone suppliers, contact your local town hall in Madeira.

HOSPITALS
Madeira has two main hospitals, both in Funchal: the main **Hospital Cruz Carvalho** (avenida Luís Camões; +351 291 705600) and the smaller **Hospital dos Marmeleiros** (estrada dos Marmeleiros; +351 291 705730). Many of the larger towns on Madeira and Porto Santo will have a health centre, called *centro de saúde*.

TOURIST OFFICES
The main tourist office on Madeira is in **Funchal** (avenida Arriaga 18; +351 291 211902). Other tourist offices on the island include those at **Machico** (Forte do Amparo, praça José António Almada; +351 291 962289), **Ribeira Brava** (Forte de São Bento; +351 291 951675) as well as those at Câmara de Lobos, Caniço de Baixa, Porto Moniz and Santana. The only tourist office on the island of Porto Santo is in the main town of **Vila Baleira** (avenida Henrique Vieira de Castro 5; +351 291 982361).

POLICE
The number for emergency services (police, fire brigade and ambulance) is **112**, as in the rest of Portugal. The main police station in Funchal is on largo de São João (+351 291 222022) while Porto Santo's police station is in **Vila Baleira** (Sítio das Matas; +351 291 982423).

ENGLISH NEWSPAPER
Madeira Island Bulletin Second Floor, rua 31 de Janeiro; +351 291 231363.

---

bloom from early spring to late autumn. To celebrate this is the annual *Flower Festival* (see *Most Famous Festivals* box on page 184) but Madeira also hosts many other festivals, including the Wine Festival in September, spectacular New Year celebrations and the Funchal Carnival at the end of February, when people dress in masks and costumes and parade through the streets with musicians, singers and dancers giving impromptu performances and stalls selling food, drink and balloons.

SPECTATOR SPORTS
With so many options for partaking in all kinds of sports, from golf and diving to walking and cycling, it's more usual to *do* rather than *watch* in Madeira. That, however, is before you take into account the island's passion for football. Madeira's main team, Marítimo, play in Portugal's SuperLiga, flying back and forth between the island and the mainland to play their matches. When at home, they play at Stadio Barreiros (rua do Dr Pita, Funchal; www.csmaritimo-madeira.pt), and it's easy to get hold of match tickets from the box office inside the stadium or from the club shop that doubles as Marítimo's museum (rua Dom Carlos 14). Funchal has a second team, Clube Desportivo Nacional, who have a club shop on rua do Esmeraldo, and most other towns on the island have teams that play in the lower divisions of the Portuguese Liga or the Madeiran football league.

Other spectator events include the PGA Madeira Golf Open, held at the Santo da Serra Golf Club in March, the World Surfing Championships in January and the Madeira World Tennis Tournament.

> For a guide to property prices in Madeira, turn to our Price Guide, starting on page 192

GLOSSARY

If you speak no Portuguese at all, there are a few key words which are well worth learning. **'Há'** (the H is silent), means 'there is' or 'is there', used, for example, in **'Há um quarto?'** (*Do you have a room?*). For more formal occasions, use **'Tem…?'**, meaning '*Do you have…?*', or **'Queria…'**, which means '*I would like…*'. Finally, there is the standard request **'Fala Inglês?'**, which means '*Do you speak English?*' and **'Não compreendo'**, meaning '*I don't understand*'.

ACCOMMODATION

a que horas é o pequeno almoço?
at what time is breakfast?

chave
key *nf*

com duche
with a shower

é caro, não o quero
it's expensive, I don't want it

é para uma noite (semana)
it's for one night (week)

é para uma pessoa (duas pessoas)
it's for one person (two people)

está bem, fico com ele
it's good, I'll take it

há quartos vagos?
do you have any rooms free?

há um quarto mais barato?
is there a cheaper room?

há uma pensão aqui perto?
is there a guesthouse near here?

o ar condicionado
air conditioning

o chuveiro/a luz não funciona
the shower/light doesn't work

pode darme mais um cobertor
may I have another blanket?

posso/podemos deixar os sacos aqui até…?
can I/we leave the bags here until…?

posso ver?
may I look round?

quanto custa?
how much is it?

queria um quarto simples/duplo
I would like a single/double room

tenho um quarto reservado em nome de…
I have a reservation in the name of…

AROUND THE TOWN

a central de telefones
telephone office

a embaixada de…
…embassy

a que horas abre/fecha?
what time does it open/close?

dinheiro
some money

onde é…?
where is…?

o banco (mais próximo)
(the nearest) bank *nm*

o centro da cidade/da baixa
the city centre

o hospital
hospital *nm*

o mercado
market *nm*

o posto da policia
police station *nf*

o posto de turismo
tourist office *nf*

os correios
post office *nf*

os sanitários
public toilets *nm*

os lavabos
toilet *nm*

o um posto de câmbio
exchange office *nm*

o um hotel
hotel *nm*

queria trocar…
I'd like to change…

quero usar o telefone
I'd like to make a telephone call

uns cheques de viagem
travellers' cheques

BASIC PHRASES

aberto
open

adeus
goodbye

agora/mais tarde
now/later

amanhã
tomorrow

até logo
see you soon

boa tarde/noite
good afternoon/night

bom dia
good morning

chamo…
my name is…

como
how

como está?
how are you

Glossary

encantado/a
pleased to meet you

desculpe, com fala inglês?
do you speak English?

fechado
closed

grande/pequeno
big/little

hoje
today

licença
sorry/excuse me

mais/menos
more/less

não compreendo
I don't understand

não sei
I don't know

obrigado/a
thank you

olá
hello

onde?
where?

ontem
yesterday

o quê?
what?

perto/longe
near/far

por favor/se faz favor
please

porquê?
why?

quando?
when?

quanto/quanto é?
how much is it?

sabe...?
do you know...?

senhoras/homens
ladies/gents

sim/não
yes/no

tem
do you have...?

DAYS & MONTHS

segunda feira
Monday

terça feira
Tuesday

quarta feira
Wednesday

quinta feira
Thursday

sextafeira
Friday

sábado
Saturday

domingo
Sunday

janeiro
January

fevereiro
February

março
March

abril
April

maio
May

junho
June

julho
July

agosto
August

setembro
September

outubro
October

novembro
November

dezembro
December

EATING/DRINKING

acepipes
hors d'oeuvres

a colher
spoon *nf*

a conta
bill *nf*

a conta se faz favor
the bill please

a ementa
menu *nm*

a entrada
starter *nf*

a faca
knife *nf*

o garfo
fork *nm*

o guardanapo
serviette *nm*

o jantar
dinner *nm*

a mesa
table *nf*

a lista de vinhos
wine list *nf*

a lista se faz favor
the menu please

a pimenta/o sal
pepper *nf*/salt *nm*

a sobremesa
dessert *nf*

o almoço
lunch *nm*

o pequeno almoço
breakfast *nm*

o prato do dia
today's special *nm*

o prato principal
main course *nm*

qual é a especialidade local?
what is the local speciality?

quero reservar uma mesa
I want to reserve a table

sou vegetariano/a
I am a vegetarian

tem uma mesa para seis?
do you have a table for six?

um copo
glass *nm*

uma garrafa
bottle *nf*

uma meia garrafa
half bottle *nf*

EMERGENCIES

chame a polícia!
call the police

Buying Guide

chame os bombeiros!
call the fire brigade!

chame um médico!
call a doctor!

chame uma ambulância!
call an ambulance!

estou perdido/a
I'm lost

fui roubado/a
I've been robbed

há um telefone aqui perto?
where is the nearest telephone?

onde é o hospital mais próximo?
where is the nearest hospital?

socorro!
help!

GETTING AROUND

a camioneta
the bus (intercity) *nf*

a que horas parte?
what time does it leave?

a que horas parte o comboio para…?
what time does the train leave for…?

bilhete (para)
ticket (to)

donde parte o autocarro para
where does the bus leave from?

esquerda/direita
left/right

está muito bem
that's great

é este o comboio para Coimbra?
is this the train for Coimbra?

ida e volta
round trip

o autocarro
bus (city) *nm*

o barco
boat *nm*

o comboio
train *nm*

o eléctrico
tram *nm*

o metro
metro *nm*

onde é a estação de camionetas?
where is the bus station?

onde é a estação de comboios?
where is the railway station?

onde é a paragem de autocarro para…?
where is the bus stop for…?

onde é a estação de metro?
where is the metro station?

onde e a paragem do eléctrico para…?
where is the tram stop for…?

onde é que se muda para…
where do you change for…?

pare aqui por favor
stop here please

para ir para…?
how do I get to…?

paramos em…
do we stop in…?

para onde vai?
where are you going?

quanto tempo leva?
how long does it take?

qual á a estrada para…?
which is the road to…?

sempre em frente
straight ahead

vou para…
I'm going to…

HEALTH

onde é um hospital/um centro de saúde?
where is a hospital/medical clinic?

preciso de um médico
I need a doctor

sou diabético/a, epiléptico/a, asmático/a
I'm diabetic/epileptic/asthmatic

sou alérgico/a a antibioticos/penicilina
I'm allergic to antibiotics/penicillin

LANGUAGE DIFFICULTIES

não percebo/entendo
I don't understand

percebo/entendo
I understand

pode escrever isso, por favor?
could you please write it down?

NUMBERS

1 ....um
2 ....dois
3 ....três
4 ....quatro
5 ....cinco
6 ....seis
7 ....sete
8 ....oito
9 ....nove
10 ....dez
11 ....onze
12 ....doze
13 ....treze
14 ....catorze
15 ....quinze
16 ....dezasseis
17 ....dezassete
18 ....dezoito
19 ....dezanove
20 ....vinte
21 ....vinte e um
30 ....trinta
40 ....quarenta
50 ....cinquenta
60 ....sessenta
70 ....setenta
80 ....oitenta
90 ....noventa
100 ....cem
101 ....cento e um
200 ....duzentos
500 ....quinhentos
1000 ....mil
2000 ....dois mil

PLACES TO EAT

a casa de pasto
a casual eatery with cheap, simple meals *nf*

a cervejaria
inn (literally meaning a beerhouse that also serves food) *nf*

a churrasqueira
a resturant serving grilled foods (meaning a BBQ or grill) *nf*

a marisqueira

Glossary

seafood restaurant *nf*

a pastelaria
pastry and cake shop *nf*

o salão de chá
teahouse *nm*

a tasca
simple tavern *nf*

SHOPPING

aberto/encerrado
open/closed (for a shop or office)

a loja de roupas
clothing store *nf*

é muito caro
it's too expensive

a farmácia
pharmacy/chemist *nf*

a lavandaria
laundry *nf*

a livraria
bookshop *nf*

o grande armazém
department store *nm*

o mercado
market *nm*

a papelaria
newsagents *nf*

posso ver?
Can I look at it?

quanta custa?
How much is it?

SIGHTSEEING

a biblioteca
library *nf*

a igreja
church *nf*

a Sé
cathedral *nf*

fechado para férias
closed for the holidays

o jardim
garden *nm*

o museu
museum *nm*

SIGNS

aberto
open

alfândega
customs

empurre/puxe
push/pull

entrada
entrance

entrada gratis
free entry

fechado/encerrado
closed

homens (H)
gents

informações
information

lavabos/WC
toilets

não fumadores
no smoking

perdidos e achados
lost property

proibido
prohibited

quartos livres
rooms avaliable

saida
exit

senhoras (S)
ladies

turismo
tourist office

THE TIME

á/ás…
at…

a que horas?
at what time?

dezanove
7pm

dez para as duas
ten to two

meio dia
midday/noon

meia noite
midnight

quando?
when?

que horas são?
what time is it?

quinze para as duas
quarter to two

sete da tarde
seven in the evening

uma da manhã
one in the morning (am)

uma e dez
ten past one

uma e meia
half past one

uma e quinze
quarter past one

uma da tarde
one in the afternoon (pm)

uma e vinte
twenty past one

USEFUL ADJECTIVES AND ADVERBS

belo
beautiful

bom/boa
good

casado/a
married

delicioso
delicious

doente
ill

excelente
excellent

faminto
hungry

feliz
happy

lindo
lovely

mais um(a)
one more/another

melhor
better

seguinte or próximo
next (in time)

zangado
angry

Berlitz Publishing produces a Portuguese Phrase Book (RRP £4.95), which is available in all good bookshops and contains a full glossary of useful lifestyle words and phrases to help those living and working in Portugal.
(ISBN 981-246-337-2)

The Price Guide

The Price Guide introduction

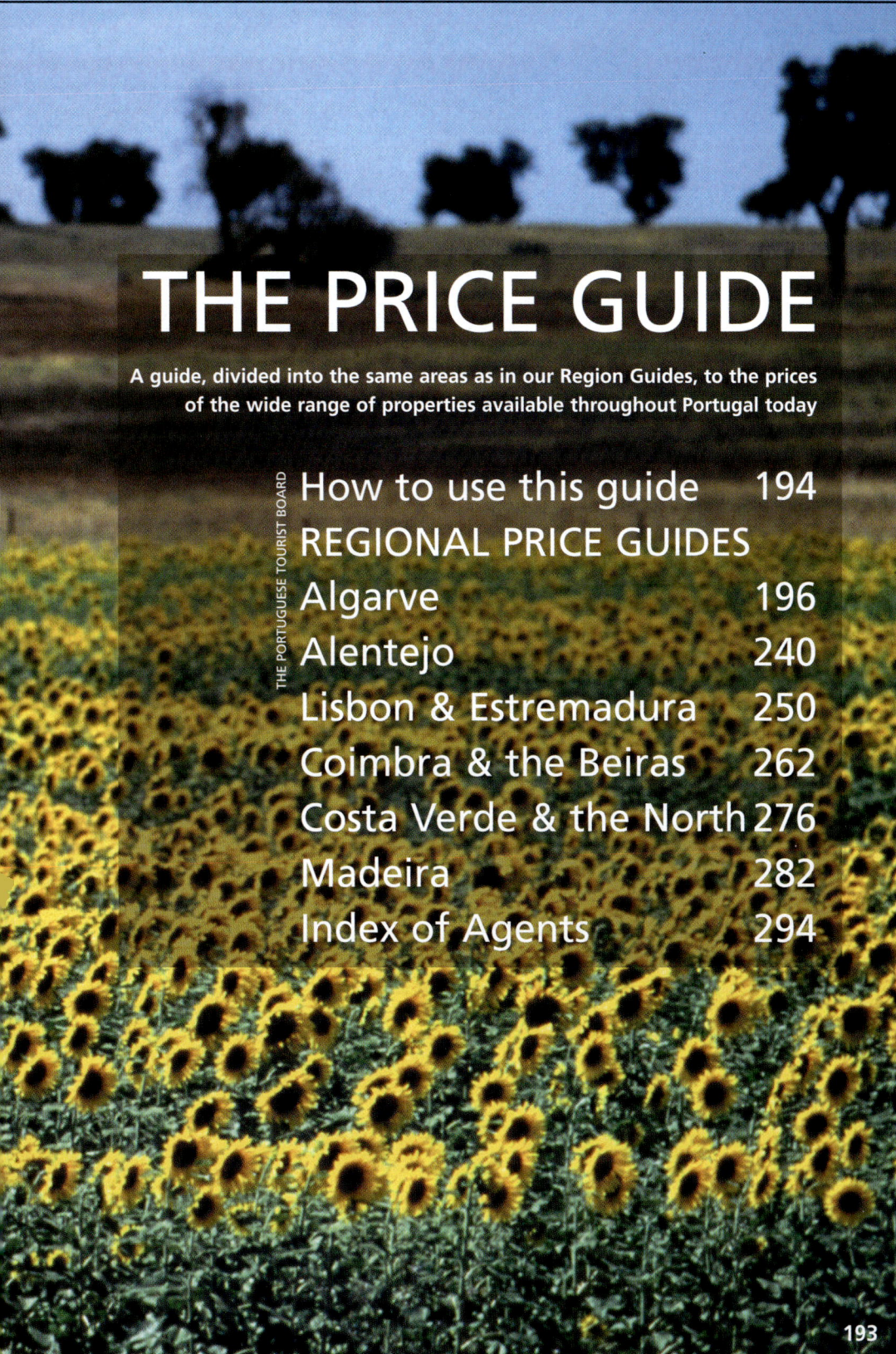

THE PRICE GUIDE

A guide, divided into the same areas as in our Region Guides, to the prices of the wide range of properties available throughout Portugal today

How to use this guide	194
REGIONAL PRICE GUIDES	
Algarve	196
Alentejo	240
Lisbon & Estremadura	250
Coimbra & the Beiras	262
Costa Verde & the North	276
Madeira	282
Index of Agents	294

THE PORTUGUESE TOURIST BOARD

■ Price Guide

USING THE PRICE GUIDE

How to Use the Price Guide

The Price Guide has been compiled to give you as much detail as possible to help make searching for your dream home in your ideal area – and within your budget – as easy as possible. Over the next 100 pages, you will find example properties throughout Portugal. These have been grouped into six sections to represent the regions into which we have divided Portugal (these appear in this Price Guide just as they do on the Regional Map on page 86).

The properties have all been on the market in the past six to 12 months. With prices given in euros and pounds sterling, they have been selected to suit all budgets, and have a detailed description showing you what to expect from a property at that price in the same region.

In some cases, the price given is the actual price the property was sold for (these are marked 'S'); in others, it was the guide price (these are marked 'GP'). To contact an agent whose properties appear in this section, turn to the Index of Agents starting on page 294, and check against the corresponding three-letter agent code.

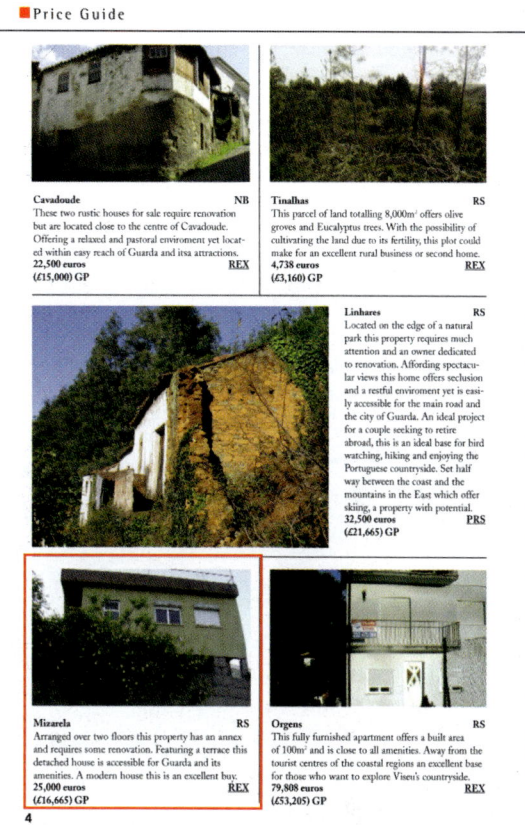

LOCATION
Each entry gives the name of the town or village in which the property is located, or is closest to

PRICE
The price, given in both euros and sterling, shows either the guide price **(GP)** at which the property was marketed or the price at which it was sold **(S)**

PARTICULARS
A description of the example property including information such as the number of bedrooms, plot size and whether the property is a new build **(NB)** or resale **(RS)**

AGENT CODE
With each listing there is a three-letter code that indicates the agent who marketed the property. This code can be cross-referenced against the list of agents that appears in the Index of Agents, on page 294

195

Price Guide

The Algarve Introduction

THE ALGARVE

As the most popular corner of Portugal for UK buyers, the sun-soaked Algarve has an abundance of properties for sale, ranging from studio apartments by the sea to village houses for restoration inland and luxury villas beside golf courses

Price Guide

Vilamoura   NB
Ideally located one- and two-bedroom apartments in the heart of this stylish resort. Just a short walk from the marina, these homes are extremely competitively priced. All amenities are conveniently located nearby.
140,000+ euros   MAC
(£93,330) GP

Almancil   RS
An elegant villa comprising five two-bedroom apartments and one further apartment with one bedroom in a stunning location. Surrounded by landscaped gardens, it is close to Quinta do Lago.
950,000 euros   MAC
(£633,330) GP

Vilamoura   RS
An exclusive four-bedroom holiday home overlooking the fairway of this resort's golf course. Affording three bathrooms, it offers extensive accommodation. With a large swimming pool and a lovely outlook.
1,600,000 euros   MAC
(£1,066,667) GP

Vilamoura   RS
A charming single-storey villa in a tranquil part of this busy town. With golfing facilities close by, it features three bedrooms, three bathrooms and a large swimming pool. This stylish home warrants a visit.
412,500 euros   MAC
(£275,000) GP

Cerro de Galo   NB
A fabulous plot overlooking the championship Vila Sol golf course. Within walking distance of the clubhouse, it offers a superb investment due to its prime location. Full of development potential.
730,894 euros   MAC
(£566,667) GP

Vilamoura   RS
A fabulously well designed villa perfectly located by one of the resort's older golf courses. Offering five bedrooms and three bathrooms arranged around a quadrangle, it has a big swimming pool. Plus views.
1,247,000 euros   MAC
(£831,330) GP

Vilamoura Marina

property that reflects prestige

Victoria Boulevard
Victoria Jardins Vilamoura

MACKENZIE GOLD

This luxury development consisting of 2 bedroom apartments plus 3 and 4 bedroom townhouses is located in the exclusive Victoria Jardins Vilamoura.

Victoria Boulevard has views over the prestigious Victoria Golf Course, designed by Arnold Palmer and is in close proximity to the lively marina, beach and sporting facilities.

An investment opportunity not to be missed

1st phase released - enquire now!

MACKENZIE
HOMES PORTUGAL

T. +351 289 328 368 · F. +351 289 328 268
UK: 0 207 107 9952 · info@mackenzie-homes.com

Denis Law
Former Manchester United & Scotland player

"I played with the best and now I've bought the best!"

In association with:

5657 ATELIER DO SUL

Price Guide

Albufeira NB
These stylish, modern three-bedroom townhouses feature two bathrooms and are conveniently placed just minutes from the beach in this much sought-after residential location. A great investment.
219,000 euros DHA
(£186,000) GP

Albufeira RS
This well located plot has planning permission for the development of 32 villas. Near to all amenities at this ever popular resort, this purchase has great business potential. A wonderful investment project.
1,600,000 euros AGI
(£1,066,000+) GP

Lagos NB
An elegant apartment development in the luxurious setting of the Lagos marina. Offering one and two bedrooms, these professionally finished properties enjoy fitted kitchens and terraces. They give stunning views over the marina, which is a popular site for water sports. Underground parking is optional and costs extra, but offers a secure option for vehicles. Just a 10-minute walk from the beach and amenities, these properties are competitively priced. Residents have free use of the shared swimming pool at the Marina Club.
133,880+ euros AQU
(£89,250+) GP

Silves NB
These apartments are situated in a beautifully landscaped area and offer a living space upwards of 316m². Well located in this historic town, all amenities are nearby. Making a great holiday base.
240,000+ euros ARY
(£160,000+) GP

Loulé RS
An attractive, four-bedroom villa that would make a lovely family home. Featuring three living rooms and a 3,100m² plot, it affords views of the Algarve mountains. Set in a peaceful and pretty, rural area.
344,200 euros AGI
(£229,466) GP

Living in Vila Sol with art and quality

Vila Sol Village launches 6th phase

Vila Sol Village
Apartments T2 & T3
5th phase now available

Villas do Golfe
Villas V3, V4 & V5
New plots

Sunset Villas
V2 & V3 Townhouses,
T1 & T2 Apartments

Find the home you've always dreamed of in Vila Sol Village, Villas do Golfe or very soon at Sunset Villas where stylish design is combined with high quality finishing. Every owner has access to Vila Sol - Beach, Golf & Country Club, with its magnificent golf courses and welcoming Members' Club. Vila Sol - the art of living.

UK only:
0800 962 147
Vila Sol, Morgadinhos,
8125-307 Vilamoura, Algarve, Portugal.
T: +351 289 300 502
F: +351 289 300 591
vendas@vilasol.pt · www.vilasol.pt

"I believe in Vila Sol"
Bobby Robson

Price Guide

Quinta do Mar   **NB**
A striking range of elegant and stylish three-, four- and five-bedroom homes situated in this thriving resort. Featuring up to 500m² of living space, each property includes a fitted kitchen, a jacuzzi, natural stone and ceramic tiles and a luxurious, heated swimming pool. These ultra modern homes afford ISDN telephone systems, under-floor heating and electric entrance gates and garage doors. Purchasers can have a high degree of input into the design of their homes' interiors and exterior.
975,000+ euros   **DHA**
(£650,000+) GP

Quinta do Lago   **NB**
A splendid five-bedroom, five-bathroom villa in an exclusive part of this resort. Built using the latest construction methods, it affords all mod cons and a true sense of luxurious living. A definite must view.
3,750,000 euros   **PRE**
(£2,500,000) GP

Albufeira   **RS**
Lovingly restored, this charming townhouse offers two bedrooms, one bathroom and a large living room with a fireplace, it is set in an established resort. A swimming pool is currently under construction.
164,500 euros   **NOV**
(£109,667) GP

Albufeira   **RS**
This magnificent villa affords direct access to the beach and lovely views of the Atlantic. An expansive and comfortable property, this home features five, spacious bedrooms that would easily house family or friends. Situated in the delightful Olhos de Água area, it enjoys privacy and convenient access to the thriving heart of this ever popular resort town. A fabulous property, it is well priced and has plenty of rental promise, as the golf courses of Vilamoura are easy to reach.
500,000 euros   **PRE**
(£330,330) GP

The first name in property...

premier
REAL ESTATE

For Luxury Villas, Town Houses & Apartments in Quinta Do Lago & surrounding areas

With four stunning golf courses to choose from, one of the finest beaches in Europe, superb restaurants and great shopping/leisure facilities, Quinta do Lago is truly an all-round paradise and the perfect location for a home in the sun.

The Premier team are on hand to help you with your property requirements.

Buganvilia Plaza, Loja 48/49, Quinta do Lago, 8135-013 Almancil, Algarve, PORTUGAL
Telephone +351 289 351170 **Facsimile** +351 289 351179
Visit our website **www.premreale.com**

Price Guide

Estoi   RS
An elegant three-bedroom villa with four bathrooms, (two en-suite) affording panoramic views to the countryside. Sold with furnishings, it has a laundry room, a BBQ, a large swimming pool and a garage.
273,595 euros   **EUV**
(£182,396) GP

Santa Barbara de Nexe   RS
A delightful property featuring a lovingly restored farmhouse with two bedrooms and a studio apartment. This expansive house would make an ideally placed B&B conversion. Competitively priced.
475,000 euros   **EUV**
(£316,667) GP

Quinta do Lago   NB
An elegant range of one- and two-bedroom townhouses in the select Vale dos Pinheiros area of this much-loved resort. Built to high standards, they include Technal lacquered aluminium doors and windows, oak-varnished interior doors, fitted kitchens with Bosch appliances and polished granite worktops. There is also a regional stone fireplace. In a peaceful location, these homes have traditional stone windows and door surrounds. They offer a great investment and rental potential.
585,000+ euros   **DHA**
(£390,000+) GP

Lagos   NB
These exclusive apartments in the fabulous resort marina, offer one, two or three bedrooms. With some properties sold already, they have a living area of 96m², air conditioning and large sun terraces.
136,500+ euros   **EUV**
(£91,000) GP

Luz de Tavira   RS
A charming four-bedroom villa with vineyards in a 1,000m² plot. With lovely views of the countryside and close to the beach, it is perfectly placed for nearby golf facilities and is well kept.
275,000 euros   **EUV**
(£183,330) GP

The Algarve

Lagos RS
Ideally positioned between the beach and the golf course, an elegant three-year-old house affording 13,750m² of land including a vineyard. It comprises five bedrooms, four bathrooms and a games room.
760,000 euros ARY
(£506,667) GP

Poço Mouro RS
A traditional four-bedroom, four-bathroom country house with a two-bedroom guest house. In a 20,000m² plot of orchards and botanical gardens, it has a swimming pool and lovely vaulted ceilings.
2,511,400 euros QUI
(£1,674,266) GP

Albufeira RS
This elegant, three-bedroom villa is set in the hillside of this charming village. An excellent and luxurious family home, it enjoys a heated swimming pool and a tennis court. On the outskirts of this very popular town, it affords easy access to several golf courses and wonderful beaches. Sold with furnishings, there are 10,000m² of attractive landscaped gardens to explore. With striking, panoramic views of the coast, this villa has a secluded feel to it. A unique and well maintained home.
560,000 euros ARY
(£373,335) GP

Vilamoura RS
A palatial five-bedroom villa affording three bathrooms located in a 3,600m² landscaped plot. Based in this ever popular and dynamic resort, it enjoys its own swimming pool and sun terraces.
1,250,000 euros DHA
(£833,330) GP

Lagos NB
A selection of beautifully designed three-bedroom villas with their own swimming pools. These spacious plots can be designed to suit the purchaser. Conveniently located near the town's amenities.
689,416 euros VGI
(£459,610) GP

Price Guide

Quinta do Lago   NB
An impressive five-bedroom villa with 450m² living space bordering the Norte golf course. In the popular Zona Noroeste area, it features a swimming pool, a BBQ area and uninterrupted views of the golf course.
1,950,000 euros   SOT
(£1,300,000) GP

Quinta do Lago   NB
A striking villa in a tranquil cul-de-sac near the São Lourenço golf course. Offering modern fittings, it has an airy AEG kitchen with a breakfast area and a large living room that offers a characterful fireplace.
2,100,000 euros   SOT
(£1,400,000) GP

Benagil   RS
This striking villa is set in a beautiful location in this traditional fishing village. Overlooking the Atlantic, with exceptional coastal views, it features covered sun terraces, an extremely well maintained garden and a luxurious salt-water swimming pool. It gives convenient access to the nearby popular town of Lagos and the breathtaking Praia a Marinha beach is closeby. Praia do Carvoeiro's three golf courses, the Vale de Milho, the Gramacho and the Pinta course are all nearby.
775,000 euros   FIS
(£516,667) GP

Carvoeiro   NB
A fashionable property built using the latest construction techniques that would make a luxurious family residence. Close to the beach and golf facilities, this lovely home has great rental promise.
1,163,600 euros   FIS
(£775,733) GP

Silves   RS
A beautifully restored country farmhouse situated by the river on the town's outskirts. Divided into individual apartments, it enjoys a picturesque outlook and offers good commercial possibility to an investor.
675,000 euros   FIS
(£450,000) GP

BUYING OR SELLING
WE WANT YOUR PROPERTY!

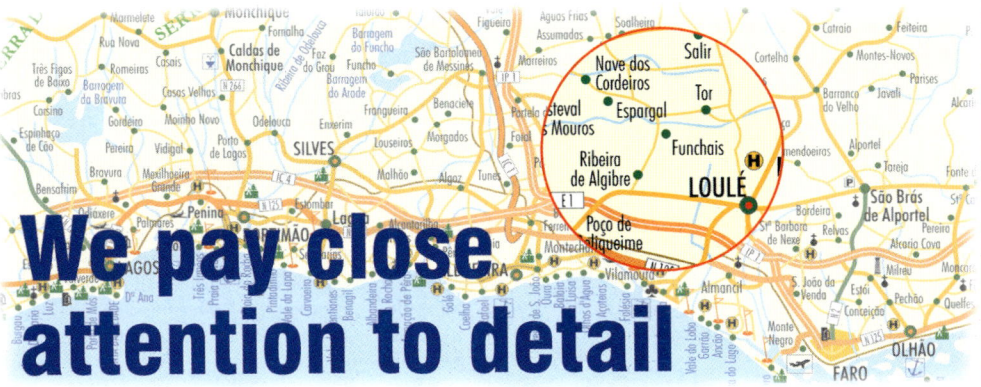

We pay close attention to detail

▲ Properties from 70 K to 2 million GBP
▲ Land, Ruins, Apartments, Villas, Commercial
▲ Interior Design and Furniture Packs
▲ Surveys, Planning and Project Development
- Bilingual Lawyers and Accountants
- Taxation - Tax Planning
- Mortgages - Commercial Funding
- Offshore Company Structures
- Buy to Let
- Residência - Wills
- Rates Exemption

The Complete Service
Allied to Buying and Selling

FINESPO ▲
INTERNATIONAL
Land and Real Estate Agents
Established 1990 - AMI Licença 5195

FINESCO
INTERNATIONAL
FINANCIAL

Tel: +351 289 560 261
Fax: +351 289 562 061
tim@finespo-algarve.com
www.finespo-algarve.com

Tel: +351 289 561 333
Fax: +351 289 562 061
finesco@mail.telepac.pt

Rua do Sol, 4 - 8200-448 Guia - Portugal

Price Guide

Pinheiros Altos   RS
An impressive and elegant four-bedroom villa that would make an idyllic golfer's home. Situated by the ninth fairway of one of the resort's fabulous golf courses, it has an air of exclusivity and privacy.
1,400,000 euros   VIL
(£933,330) GP

Quinta do Lago   RS
This stunning two-bedroom and two-bathroom villa is perfectly placed on the beautiful lake in this resort's Lakeside Village complex. With stunning views and a sun-terrace, it makes for a perfect holiday home.
517,500 euros   VIL
(£345,000) GP

Lagos   NB
A charming range of one-, two- and three-bedroom apartments based in the Rossio de São João district. With central heating and a secure entrance, each has a washing machine, fitted kitchen and double glazing.
105,400+ euros   IML
(£70,266+) GP

Lagos   NB
A beautiful three-bedroom villa in its own 750m² plot with panoramic views. In the peaceful Ameijeira Verde area, it has five bathrooms, a large swimming pool, a garage and expansive sun terraces to enjoy.
400,000 euros   IML
(£266,667) GP

Lagos   NB
These modern, semi-detached villas are very near to the beach. Each home features four bedrooms, three bathrooms and a fitted kitchen. There is ample space for a swimming pool to be installed in the grounds.
250,000+ euros   IML
(£166,667) GP

Albufeira   RS
An impressive and well appointed villa with four bedrooms and four bathrooms in the much admired location of Cerro de Aquia. Near to all golf facilities, this is a beautiful family home with rental potential.
688,000 euros   DHA
(£458,667) GP

Price Guide

Vilamoura   RS
A carefully renovated two-bedroom apartment just 20 metres from the marina. Offering fantastic views of the resort, it is furnished and its location renders it a fantastic investment. Competitively priced.
201,639 euros   FIL
(£134,426) GP

Vilamoura   NB
This ultra modern, three-bedroom townhouse is located a short walk from the resort's golf courses. Set in a plot of 450m², it enjoys a swimming pool and a garage, and affords easy access to the marina.
1,204,596 euros   FIL
(£803,064) GP

Vale do Lobo   RS
A delightful range of three-bedroom townhouses that have been successfully renovated to the highest standards. This prestigious and much admired resort has an abundance of facilities on its doorstep, including golf courses and tennis courts. Each home has a swimming pool and the living rooms afford stunning views across pine trees, undulating sand dunes and the Atlantic. These homes offer fabulous bases for a holiday and their exclusive address has rental potential. Very well priced.
685,850 euros   **DHA**
(£457,233) GP

Fonte Sante   NB
Ideally placed, a private complex comprising 12 stylish, semi-detached townhouses offering four bedrooms. These homes have an office, a garage, and each enjoys a shared swimming pool and garden area.
378,138 euros   FIL
(£252,092) GP

Loulé   NB
An exciting new development of four semi-detached houses that each feature three bedrooms, an office and a garage. On the town's outskirts, they afford striking country views and access to all amenities.
343,048 euros   FIL
(£228,698) GP

Price Guide

Albufeira   RS
An excellently placed, furnished apartment in this popular central Algarve town. A great holiday home, it affords two sun terraces and charming sea views. With a shared swimming pool and a garden.
92,500 euros   **AGI**
(£61,667) GP

Lagos   RS
A delightful villa located on a cliff-top overlooking this popular resort town. Set in well manicured gardens, it offers three bedrooms, each with a bathroom. With an attractive, separate guest cottage.
455,000 euros   **ARY**
(£303,330) GP

Azinheiro   RS
An elegant three-bedroom villa previously used as a popular rental property. Offering breathtaking views over a valley to the Atlantic. This lovely property has a sun terrace on its roof and has a secluded feel.
450,000 euros   **BOG**
(£300,000) GP

Pinheiros Altos   RS
A charming and well kept villa featuring three bedrooms and a separate one-bedroom apartment. Incorporating membership to the resort's golf course, it affords a jacuzzi, under-floor heating and views.
1,050,724 euros   **QUI**
(£700,482 GP

Marmelete   RS
A quaint, part-furnished cottage set in 10,000m² of grounds, residing in the beautiful Monchique hills. Enjoying extensive loft space and wonderful views towards the coastline, an extremely well kept home.
175,000 euros   **ARY**
(£116,667) GP

Vale St Antonio   RS
A charming apartment offering two en-suite bedrooms, situated in a resort near to Vale do Lobo. Equipped with all mod cons it offers a living room with a fireplace, plenty of storage and a sun terrace.
275,000 euros   **SOT**
(£183,330) GP

The Algarve

Quinta do Lago RS
A spectacular four-bedroom villa surrounded by beautifully landscaped gardens. With a salt-water swimming pool and several sun terraces, the accent is on relaxation. Plus a double garage and course views.
2,350,000 euros (offshore) SOT
(£1,566,667) GP

Quinta do Lago NB
This exceptional four-bedroom villa is located in a prime plot by the resort's golf courses. Its unique features include an overflow swimming pool and jacuzzi and a home cinema area. With a gym and a garage.
3,900,000 euros SEL
(£2,600,000) GP

Quinta do Lago RS
With four-bedrooms and four-bathrooms this striking villa gives views of the resort's North golf course and the Ria Formosa nature reserve. Plus air-conditioning, an irrigation system and a swimming pool.
2,242,500 euros (offshore) SEL
(£1,495,000) GP

Albufeira RS
This stylish and airy one-bedroom apartment covering 90m² has a modern design. A five minute walk from the beach it is extremely well situated and there is a closed balcony to the fitted kitchen. Plus storage.
99,760 euros NLI
(£66,506) GP

Almancil NB
This exclusive villa enjoys five bedrooms with en-suite bathrooms. Comprising high quality construction work, it has air-conditioning, an alarm system, a swimming pool and stylish landscaped gardens.
1,252,000 euros ROS
(£834,667) GP

Pinheiros Altos NB
An exclusive five-bedroom villa in this much sought-after location. With five en-suite bathrooms, a cinema, an entertainment room with a bar and a double garage. Furnished it has a well appointed kitchen.
4,425,000 euros SEL
(£2,950,000) GP

Price Guide

Quinta do Lago   NB
A luxurious range of two- and three-bedroom apartments in the Encosta do Lago development. With a huge swimming pool, tennis courts and the resort's golf club close by, this is a truly idyllic retreat.
595,000+ euros   AQU
(£396,667) GP

Quinta do Lago   RS
An exciting development of 55 freehold villas and 88, two- and three-bedroom apartments in an established resort. With shared tennis courts and a swimming pool, these homes will be three-storey constructions.
490,000+ euros   AQU
(£326,667) GP

Vale do Lobo   NB
A range of luxury, furnished, ground and upper floor apartments set in a prestigious development. Close to the local golf course, these homes are perfect for golfers. Conveniently placed, they are five minutes drive from the beach and 20 minutes from Faro airport. Offering all modern conviences, including satellite TV, air conditioning and shared swimming pools, golf rounds can be booked at special rates from this resort. Condominium charges are around 2,992 euros per annum.
160,000+ euros   AQU
(£106,667+) GP

Vila Albas   RS
Set in this fabulous resort, an exclusive one-bedroom apartment in a complex surrounded by a golf course. Facilities include several swimming pools, mature, well-tended gardens, a gym and a tennis centre.
185,000 euros   KGV
(£123,330) GP

Vale do Lobo   RS
A select five-bedroom villa in a 4,000m² plot in this desirable part of the Algarve. Recently renovated, it offers a large master suite and breathtaking views of the Atlantic and golf courses. Close to amenities.
1,350,000 euros   KGV
(£900,000) GP

KLAUS GRIGUTSCH, LDA.
KG VILLA SERVICE

EXPERIÊNCIA 30 anos

KG VILLA Service is the result of a family's long standing love affair with Portugal. Having started in property administration and sales as early as 1970 in one of the most well known developments in the Algarve, changes were brought about in 1974/5 which resulted in setting up a private company continuing in this field. The company was officially set up in 1983 and from the outset demonstrated a commitment and a reputation for quality service.

KG PROPERTIES

Quinta Córrego da Zorra Estrada de Vale do Lobo
Apartado 6 · 8135 Almancil Algarve · Portugal · Tel: +351 289 394 780 · Fax: +351 289 394 125
rentals@kgvillas.com · www.kgvillas-algarve.com · info@algarve-villa.com · www.algarve-villa.com
info@kg-properties.com · www.kg-properties.com

Price Guide

Albufeira NB
A shop premises set in a very busy thoroughfare. Easily accessible, it has its own garage and occupies a commercial part of the town. Purchasers seeking to run a business should definitely view this property.
190,000 euros **AGI**
(£126,667) GP

Quinta do Lago RS
A delightful and expansive villa in need of some renovation work. Featuring its own swimming pool and sun terraces and close to the Quinta do Lago golf course, it would make a fabulous base for golfers.
815,000 euros **DHA**
(£543,330) GP

Santa Barbara NB
A stylish and well constructed villa comprising four bedrooms with panoramic, breathtaking views of the coastline. Situated in a charming, well kept 2,400m^2 plot and garden, it enjoys a highly desirable location.
975,000 euros **DHA**
(£650,000) GP

Castro Marim NB
An exclusive complex of three-bedroom, terraced villas with their own plunge pools, close to the Spanish border, set in 206 hectares of land. Modern kitchens and plush bathrooms are being installed.
300,000 euros **DHA**
(£200,000) GP

São Brás RS
A charming, traditional country home with five bedrooms. Lovingly restored original features include high wooden celings, window shutters and skirting boards. Near Faro airport, golf courses and the beach.
930,000 euros **BOG**
(£620,000) GP

Vale Formoso RS
A fabulous four-bedroom, four-bathroom property in a much admired area. Just a short journey from surrounding beaches and golf facilities, this is truly a luxurious home that has been well maintained.
869,000 euros **KGV**
(£579,330) GP

The Algarve

Bouliqueime   RS
A beautiful house with four bedrooms and a converted windmill with two two-bedroom apartments. This unique property has room for expansion, a swimming pool, a BBQ and sea views.
640,000 euros   SUS
(£426,667) GP

São Brás   RS
An attractive and characterful farmhouse that has been converted into three studio apartments. Used for summer rentals, half the property is renovated and the roof, tiling and electrical supply are in good order.
341,251 euros   SUS
(£227,500) GP

Praia da Luz   RS
A characterful villa in an elevated position with four bedrooms and a studio apartment, plus a separate cottage and a heated swimming pool. With a roof terrace, gas central heating, a garage and a well.
585,000 euros   NON
(£390,000) GP

Albufeira   RS
A modern and stylish studio apartment with living space of 50m² and breathtaking views of the Atlantic. With a garage and a swimming pool. Set in a peaceful and well appointed part of Albufeira town.
77,350 euros   AGI
(£51,566) GP

Bordeira   RS
A traditional house affording splendid views of the west coast and the Monchique mountains on the village outskirts. With two bedrooms and bathrooms, a study, a fireplace and a servicable water well.
460,000 euros   NON
(£306,667) GP

Albufeira   NB
A very attractive shop premises situated in an excellent commercial part of the town. Close to other shops and amenities, this is very well priced and a must-view for anyone moving to start a business.
190,000 euros   AGI
(£126,667) GP

Price Guide

Estoi   **NB**
A breathtaking three-bedroom and three-bathroom villa featuring two separate apartments. Set in a 36,000m² plot, it is surrounded by peaceful countryside. Offering an impressive, large swimming pool.
1,650,000 euros   **DHA**
(£1,100,000) GP

Vilamoura   **NB**
A stylish development of two- and three-bedroom apartments in this cosmopolitan resort's marina, set to be completed in 2005. Competitively priced, these homes would make exclusive holiday properties.
225,000 euros   **PAR**
(£150,000) GP

Vale do Lobo   **NB**
A select one-bedroom apartment in the exclusive Barringtons Golf and Health Spa resort. With luxurious facilities on site, this property offers a perfect holiday home. It has obvious rental potential.
165,000 euros   **PAR**
(£110,000) GP

Quinta do Lago   **PLOT**
A competively priced plot of land in this thriving resort. In a prime location, there is an outstanding project to build a four-bedroom villa here, making this a fabulous investment. Close to all amenities.
1,250,000 euros   **PAR**
(£833,330) GP

Vale do Lobo   **RS**
A delightful, spacious two-bedroom apartment situated close to the prestigious David Lloyd Tennis Centre and the so-called 'Tennis Valley'. Close to all amenities and beaches, it is a fabulous property.
215,000 euros   **PAR**
(£390,000) GP

the Property Agency

Front-line Villa in Vale do Lobo

Offshore owned
Price on application

Just let us know the property you are looking for in Quinta do Lago, Vale do Lobo or surrounding areas.
WE MAKE IT EASY FOR YOU

Buganvilia Plaza, 1st floor, Shop 34, 8135-013 Quinta do Lago, Algarve, PORTUGAL
Tel.: (+351) 289 392 350　　　　　　　　　　　　Email: pa@mail.pt
Fax: (+351) 289 392 352　　　　　　　　　　　Web: www.PA-RealEstate.pt

Price Guide

Lagos NB
These luxurious three-bedroom villas offer purchasers an opportunity to have their say in the design process. Set in beautiful, landscaped plots, they each have a swimming pool and a feeling of seclusion.
763,145 euros VIG
(£508,763) GP

Lagos RS
This well maintained four-bedroom villa offers fabulous views to Monchique and the Atlantic. With an elegant design, it is furnished, has gas central heating and a heated swimming pool. Plus well kept gardens.
637,500 euros VIG
(£425,000) GP

Quinta do Lago NB
An exceptional range of two-bedroom apartments in the Encosta do Lago resort complex. With tennis, horse-riding and water sports on its doorstep, it is in close proximity to four famous golf courses. Full of luxurious touches and all mod cons, it includes Bosch equipped kitchens, en-suite bath and shower rooms, visitor's cloakrooms and essential air conditioning. There is satellite TV and a state-of-the-art security system. Ground floor properties have private gardens. Featuring views of a nearby lake.
595,000+ euros DHA
(£396,667+) GP

Vale de Lobo NB
A stunning new property featuring four bedrooms and four bathrooms in this extremely popular location. An impressive home, to be finished to a high standard using the latest construction methods.
1,100,000 euros SLV
(£733,335) GP

Vilamoura NB
A well located two-bedroom and two-bathroom apartment in a new complex at the Millennium Golf Course. Finished to a high specification, it is to be sold furnished and has a tidy garden to enjoy.
220,000 euros SLV
(£146,667) GP

PORTUGAL
ALGARVE - ALBUFEIRA
REAL ESTATE

www.novusmed.com

Licenced Governement AMI 4506
Av. da Liberdade, Ed. Linda Vista,
Nº 65 8200-003 Albufeira Portugal

Tel: **00 351 289 514 692**
Fax: **00 351 289 514 045**

Email: mail@novusmed.com

Artist's view from Townhouse

Vila Castelo
FERRAGUDO - ALGARVE
PHASE II
Luxury Three Bedroom Townhouses
Guaranteed Rental Returns
Direct from the developers
Contact:- Tel: 01604 584888   Fax: 01604 586444

www.vilacastelo.com

parque living

LUXURY GOLF VILLAS & BEACH VILLAS

Available for outright and fractional purchase

Tel: 00 44 (0) 1223 316820
www.parquedafloresta.com
e-mail: sales@vigiasa.com

PARQUE da FLORESTA
GOLF AND LEISURE RESORT

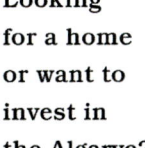

Looking for a home or want to invest in the Algarve?

Silver Holidays specialists in:

- Real Estate
- Construction
- Renovations
- Rentals

Near Vale de Lobo € 1,000,000

V4 in Porches € 450,000

Silver Holidays, Rua do Brasil, Loja 5 - 8125
Vilamoura, Algarve, Portugal
Tel : (+351) 289 314 312 silver.holidays@clix.pt
Fax: (+351) 289 314 260
- AMI NR. 4713 - www.silverholidays.com

DREAM HOUSES AND DREAM HOLIDAYS IN THE ALGARVE

Price Guide

Quinta do Lago   RS
A charming three-bedroom townhouse with a plunge pool in the famous Pinheros resort. Furnished, it is semi-detached and includes a pass for the Pinheiros Altos golf course. A great buy.
525,000 euros   SOT
(£350,000) GP

Santa Barbara de Nexe   RS
A striking three-bedroom house with a garage and a large swimming pool set in 10,125m² of land. Just 10 minutes from Faro and five minutes from the N2 motorway, it affords coastal views.
500,000 euros   HIL
(£333,335) GP

Quinta do Lago   RS
Offering four bedrooms with en-suite bathrooms, an impressive villa. With a swimming pool, a large living room and fireplace, a double garage, utility room, air conditioning and electric shutters.
2,775,000 euros   SEL
(£1,850,000) GP

Loulé   NB
An exclusive development of elegant townhouses on the highly desirable Vilasol golf complex. Situated in a vast landscaped plot, these homes are a blank canvas and purchasers are invited to specify any special touches that are required. Heated swimming pools are just one option for the discerning buyer. Each property comes with 2,700m² of attractive, landscaped garden. There is a cutting edge feel to the design of these homes and they have a great finish. Fabulous family properties.
1,125,000+ euros   HIL
(£750,000+) GP

Vale do Lobo   NB
A well located, three-bedroom apartment in this much appreciated area. Featuring an en-suite master bedroom with its own balcony, there is a partially covered sun terrace plus a luxurious plunge pool.
645,000 euros   SOT
(£430,000) GP

Quinta do Lago   RS
With three bedrooms this attractive villa affords wonderful views of the sea. Set in the Lakeside Village development, it offers easy access to the lake's watersports and has its own swimming pool. Furnished.
787,500 euros   SEL
(£525,000) GP

Albufeira   PLOT
This 627m² area of land has approved local authority permission for the construction of a two-storey villa with two bedrooms and a basement. In a prime location, this represents a superb investment.
124,700 euros   NLI
(£83,130) GP

Albufeira   RS
A spacious apartment in a fantastic, tranquil development. Located 1km from Forte São João beach, the complex has a shared swimming pool, a bar and restaurant. To be sold furnished.
76,504 euros   NLI
(£51,002) GP

The Algarve

Caldas de Monchique NB
An elegant villa enjoying four bedrooms, three bathrooms, a large living room and a designer kitchen. It features beautifully landscaped gardens, a swimming pool and panoramic views of the coastline.
693,000 euros **ARY**
(£462,000) GP

Tavira RS
An idyllyic 1,776m² valley plot with two ruins that could either be rebuilt or replaced with a new home. Surrounded by lush, verdant hills, whatever is built here will have a real sense of privacy and tranquillity.
105,000 euros **BOG**
(£70,000) GP

Quinta do Lago RS
An elegant, well appointed two-bedroom apartment in an established part of the Encosta do Lago development. Affording a spacious feel, it comprises two bathrooms, air conditioning and is alarmed.
495,000+ euros (offshore) **SEL**
(£160,000+) GP

Penina NB
A stunning four-bedroom villa situated near to the town's famous golf course. It has four bedrooms, three bathrooms, a large living room and several sun terraces. Set in an elevated position it has great views.
660,000 euros **ARY**
(£440,000) GP

Vilamoura NB
A stylish three-bedroom apartment in this select family, golf and marina resort. Built around a central shared swimming pool, this property has an attractive finish and has been very tastefully decorated.
295,000 euros **BOG**
(£196,667) GP

Vilamoura NB
Two- and three-bedroom apartments in one of the Algarve's most prestigious golf and beach resorts. Fashionably designed, these properties share a swimming pool and golf courses are very close by.
298,500+ euros **BOG**
(£199,000+) GP

Price Guide

Armação de Pêra RS
A modern villa with four bedrooms and three bathrooms. Situated in a well maintained residential complex with three swimming pools, three tennis courts, a shop, a restaurant and a poolside bar.
224,000 euros **ARY**
(£149,330) GP

Altura RS
A characterful, traditional country house with four bedrooms offering development potential. Well situated, it is just one km from several beaches and has stables, orchards, lawns and extensive gardens.
800,000 euros **BOG**
(£533,330) GP

Faro NB
Featuring three bedrooms and a study, a unique villa in the countryside outside the Algarve capital. It has a unique oval living room with a fountain, a swimming pool, under-floor heating and mod cons.
1,450,000 euros **SEL**
(£96,667) GP

Loulé RS
A carefully renovated farmhouse with a separate barn and a swimming pool. Offering four bedrooms, it is situated in a tranquil location on the outskirts of this historic market town. A great investment property.
435,000 euros **BOG**
(£290,000) GP

Loulé RS
A beautiful, six-bedroom farmhouse with bags of character and its own swimming pool. Divided into two self-contained areas, it has obvious rental potential, it is well maintained and in a great area.
430,000 euros **BOG**
(£286,667) GP

Tavira RS
A charming farmhouse plus two stone ruins in need of renovation. Located in a 1,500m² plot overlooking the meadow and a stream, it is just 10 minutes from the main village and offers a wealth of possibilities.
110,000 euros **BOG**
(£73,330) GP

The Algarve

Boliqueime   RS
Excellently restored, a delightful two-bedroom farmhouse in this rural location that is also not far from the western Algarve coastline. Modern facilities include under-floor heating, a sauna and garage.
225,000 euros   **HIL**
(£150,000) GP

Estoi   RS
A picturesque country house hotel with panoramic coastal views. With 13 spacious bedrooms (including five suites), it has a great reputation, its restaurant is reputed as one of the top five in the Algarve.
4,600,000 euros   **VSE**
(£3,066,667) GP

Vale do Lobo   NB
The two-bedroom 'Tulipa' apartment comprises 220m². Its features include a large master bedroom suite with a dressing area, a roof terrace with a BBQ and a jacuzzi. Plus sea views. Sold with furnishings.
595,000 euros (offshore)   **SOT**
(£396,667) GP

Caldas de Monchique   RS
A recently refurbished charming villa, featuring four bedrooms, three en-suite bathrooms and an expansive living area. It enjoys a swimming pool and lovely coastal views. A perfect permanent family home.
693,000 euros   **ARY**
(£462,000) GP

Quarteira   NB
An excellently priced one-bedroom apartment right in the heart of this town. Situated on the top floor, it has a balcony and a roof sun terrace. Just 200 metres from the seafront promenade, it is a fabulous buy.
99,500 euros   **HIL**
(£66,330) GP

Vilamoura   NB
A two-bedroom apartment on the Vila Sol Beach, Golf and Country Club in the heart of the Algarve. A golfer's paradise, there is a 27-hole golf course on site. The property has a high standard of finish.
375,000 euros   **SOT**
(£250,000) GP

Price Guide

Algoz RS
An attractive and cared-for three-bedroom house with three bathrooms (two en-suite). A 15-minute drive from Albufeira, it has a 10 x 5m² swimming pool, a separate annexe, a garage and a security gate.
525,000 euros NUB
(£350,000) GP

Vale de Judea NB
This characterful restored cottage covers 300m² and affords five bedrooms. Alarmed, it has an 8 x 4m² swimming pool, a garage and a carport for four cars. The water supply comes from an on-site borehole.
1,000,000 euros NUB
(£666,667) GP

Lagos NB
A range of highly desirable, elegant new apartments, built next to the town's marina. With stunning views right outside your window, these luxury homes are built using the latest cutting-edge construction techniques and enjoy a polished finish. These properties have the café culture and amenities of this popular location on their doorstep. A fabulous investment, they offer huge rental potential and enjoy a truly exclusive feel. Near the western peninsula of the Algarve, a great launch pad for yachts.
154,450+ euros FIS
(£102,966+) GP

Boliqueime NB
An elegant cottage comprising 235m² in the countryside near this town. Featuring four bedrooms, an automatic double garage and a laundry room, this exciting property is 20km from Faro airport.
600,000 euros NUB
(£400,000) GP

Vilamoura NB
Just a short journey from the marina, a stunning range of semi-detached houses. Offering four bedrooms, a swimming pool and a beautiful garden, each home is well designed, with ample living space.
837,980 euros FIL
(£558,653) GP

Algarvida

Your Estate Agent in the Algarve

Ihr Immobilienmakler an der Algarve

www.algarvida.com

Apartado 1260 . Rua do Barranco . Edifício Aurorasol . P 8401-911 Praia do Carvoeiro . Portugal
Tel: +351 282 356 577 . Fax: +351 282 356 994 . algarvidaimoliel@pac.pt

---

numero urbano
Mediação Imobiliária Unipessoal, Lda.

We do:

- ✓ **Holiday rentals in the Algarve**
  (over 120 beautiful properties)
- ✓ **Real Estate** (Apartments, Villas and Plots)
- ✓ Construction
- ✓ Administration
- ✓ Maintenance
- ✓ Decoration

Please contact us: Numero Urbano, Mediação Imobiliária Unipessoal lda, Edifº Portal de Vilamoura, Bloco A, Loja H – 8125-017 Vilamoura - PORTUGAL

Tel: +351 289 310260/2 Fax: +351 289 310262

Email: numerourbano@hotmail.com Email: numero.urbano@iol.pt

www.numerourbano.com

AQUARIUS
PROPERTIES ABROAD

We cover the whole coastline of the Algarve
Our Search facility can save you time and hassle!

We are multiple agency linked and can take away the hassle of you looking for your new home with several local agents. We can do all the searching and then make all the arrangements for you to view these properties, take you to meet a lawyer, management company, and fit out company. We have our own local representative who can deal with you personally during your viewing trip.

New & resale apartments, villas, plots, country properties commercial & Investment properties.

If you are interested in building a property investment portfolio talk to our Investment Division.

"Buying property abroad is no different to buying at home, its about Location, Location and Location." *Noreen Hynes B.COMM, FCA, AITI, Managing Director, Aquarius Properties Abroad*

You wont be one of a crowd with Aquarius Properties !

It costs you nothing to talk to Aquarius Properties !

Aquarius Properties also market properties in Spain, incl. The Canaries, Florida, and Cyprus

www.aquariusproperties.com
Email: info@aquariusproperties.com
Telephone: 00-353-1-2782900 for a free brochure

Members of FOPDAC

Price Guide

Pinheiros Altos RS
An impressive villa in an elevated spot with views of the golf development. Including golf membership, it features four bedrooms, four bathrooms (en-suite), a heated swimming pool and parking for two vehicles.
2,246,376 euros QUI
(£1,497,584) GP

Quinta do Lago RS
A delightful three-bedroom townhouse in a quiet part of the Lakeside Village resort. Well maintained, it affords two bathrooms, a modern kitchen, electric wall heaters and a swimming pool. In a 350m² plot.
717,391 euros QUI
(£478,260) GP

Encosta do Lago NB
This stylish three-bedroom apartment is ideally situated in a prestigious lake development. Enjoying access to a gym and on-site restaurant, it enjoys air conditioning, a fitted kitchen, and a swimming pool.
895,000 euros QUI
(£596,667) GP

Sao Lourenço RS
A spacious one-bedroom apartment close to the famous San Lorenzo golf course. Sold furnished, it offers air conditioning. Complex facilities include tennis courts and a large shared swimming pool.
427,536 euros QUI
(£285,024) GP

Pinheiros Altos RS
This cosy three-bedroom villa enjoys membership to the resort's prestigious course. Comprising 185m², it includes two bedrooms, a living room with a log-burning stove, a garage and panoramic views.
1,739,130 euros QUI
(£1,159,420) GP

Esplendor RS
Close to golf courses of Quinta do Lago and Vale do Lobo, a stunning five-bedroom villa. This immaculate home affords a floodlit tennis court, air conditioning, a heated swimming pool and satellite TV. Plus views.
1,956,521 euros (offshore) QUI
(£1,304,347) GP

The Algarve

Boliqueime　　　　　　　　　　RS
A characterful four-bedroom and four-bathroom single storey villa in the hills. Featuring antique doors and fireplaces, this cosy property would make an ideal family home. A short drive from all amenities.
2,300,000 euros　　　　　　　**DHA**
(£1,530,335) GP

Quinta do Lago　　　　　　　　NB
A spacious villa in the exclusive Parque Atlantico development, with four bedrooms and four bathrooms. Featuring a swimming pool, sea views, a BBQ and a large balcony, a truly luxurious home.
1,750,000 euros (offshore)　　**SOT**
(£1,166,667) GP

Armação de Pêra　　　　　　　RS
A recently renovated hotel with more than 30 rooms and breathtaking views over two beaches. With a bar, a games room and a well kept kitchen. An excellent business opportunity located in the central Algarve.
2,000,000 euros　　　　　　　**VSE**
(£1,330,335) GP

Quinta do Lago　　　　　　　　NB
Picturesque one- and two-bedroom townhouses in the exclusive condominium resort Pinheiros. Shared facilities include swimming pools, tennis courts, a gym with a sauna and a children's playground.
585,000 euros　　　　　　　　**SOT**
(£390,000) GP

Quinta do Lago　　　　　　　　NB
A golfer's dream, this one-bedroom apartment is located on the São Lourenço golf development by the same-named golf course. With views of the lake, it enjoys a shared swimming pool and tennis court.
270,000+ euros　　　　　　　**SEL**
(£180,000) GP

Price Guide

Vale da Lama   RS
An exclusive, well maintained villa affording three-bedrooms and two bathrooms with views of the Alvor lagoon. Just 10 minutes from the marina, it has a heated swimming pool, BBQ and spacious cellar.
577,500 euros   <u>NON</u>
(£385,000) GP

Lagos   RS
An attractive two-bedroom apartment ideally situated a short distance from the town centre and the beach. Well priced, it features a breakfast bar, gas central heating, a bathroom and a balcony with sunblind.
120,000 euros   <u>NON</u>
(£80,000) GP

Boliqueime   RS
A palatial and impressive family home based on the outskirts of this extremely attractive small town. It offers five large bedrooms, four en-suite bathrooms, three reception rooms and a spacious family room. Tastefully furnished, it is habitable from day one. With pretty gardens and a large heated swimming pool and tennis court, it is a luxurious home that could be changed to provide guest accommodation. Several terraces make this property a true sun-trap in the summer months. Well worth a viewing.
1,000,000 euros   <u>ARY</u>
(£666,667) GP

Praia da Luz   NB
A stunning range of three-bedroom cottages in the heart of this lovely resort. Located in the tasteful Luz complex, they enjoy a shared swimming pool and some seclusion. They afford wonderful sea views.
225,000 euros   <u>SUS</u>
(£150,000) GP

Carvoeiro   RS
An idyllically situated restaurant with an adjoining swimming pool. Seating 44, it has a well equipped kitchen and serves an international gourmet menu. Including an Indian kebab corner, a great investment.
301,000 euros   <u>SUS</u>
(£458,667) GP

SunSeaker Properties

Looking for a property in the Algarve?

We can help you

- We specialise in finding properties for sale in the Algarve.
- Luxury villas, apartments, townhouses, farmhouses, plots, ruins, commercial and first class golf resorts.
- Working through a network of reputable and licensed agents we a can offer one of the largest property portfolios covering the Algarve.
- FREE friendly, professional and personal English speaking service. Nothing is too much trouble and no question is too small to ask.
- Ring us now with your requirements and let us do the work for you.

Contact us now on:-
0871 733 1385 or +351 282 763 490
e-mail: info@sunseaker.com, www.sunseaker.com

Nonplusultra Lda.

Real Estate and Consultancy Agent in
Portugal/Algarve

Your professional partner by finding the house of your dreams in and around Lagos.

We advise and look after you!

Parque do Moinho, Lote 1B, Loja D,
8600-719 Lagos/Portugal,

Tel/Fax: **00351 282 764771**

Email: info@nonplusultra-lda.com

www.nonplusultra-lda.com

West Algarve Coast
LAGOS

Located in the West Algarve better known as the untouched Algarve, here is the spot where the world ends and the ocean begins. Lagos is surrounded by the most beautiful beaches of Europe and one of the greatest bay's in the world.

Among untouched nature you can relax and loose all the stress of your daily town rush. A life that you can easily get used to.

Lic. 2804/AMI

IMO LACCO
Soc. Med. Imob., Lda.

The best way to relax is owning a Property by the beach in one of the most beautiful Town of the Algarve.

LAGOS

For more info call us

Tel.: +351 282 760 691
Or : +351 919 006 722
Or : +351 919 404 891
Fax: +351 282 764 537
E-mail: imolacco@hotmail.com
Website: www.imolacco.com

SULGAR LDA.
PROPERTY SERVICES AND INVESTMENTS

Government Licensed Estate Agents · AMI N° 5013
Chartered Surveyors · Valuers

**Apartments · Villas
Building Land
Country Properties**

Established 1987
Over 40 years experience
English owned and run

Quinta da Praia, Lote 4, Loja 7
8500 Alvor · PORTUGAL
Tel: 00351 282 458 062 : Fax: 00351 282 458 063
Visit our web site **www.sulgar.com**
for a large range of properties
or e-mail: info@sulgar.com

Price Guide

Santa Barbara de Nexe RS
A fabulous, modernised farmhouse with two bedrooms and many authentic features. With a fitted kitchen, a separate one-bedroom guest house and an almond and olive orchard. Plus a swimming pool.
525,000 euros LAN
(£350,000) GP

Almancil NB
Three stylish townhouses affording two and three bedrooms near the town centre. With a shared garage for three vehicles, each home has luxurious extras including a jacuzzi bath and marble bathrooms.
237,000 euros LAN
(£158,000) GP

Lagos RS
This truely unique five-bedroom villa situated between Lagos and Carvoeiro, isloated only 1.5km from the beach and within easy reach of the Framacho Pinta golf course. A three-year-old villa set in 13,750m^2, this property has been constructed in a ranch style. Located close to all amenities and the main motorway, this villa offers spacious rooms, a wine cellar, games room and a small vineyard. The extensive, well appointed gardens include trees, shrubs and rockeries. With a large garage.
1,000,000 euros SCM
(£666,665) GP

Olhao RS
A delightful three-bedroom villa with a large swimming pool in a tranquil, rural location. Surrounded by nature, this really is an idyllic oasis with sweeping views of the Atlantic. Near the border.
350,000 euros CLA
(£233,330) GP

Tor RS
This lovingly rebuilt traditional townhouse is a home from home. Well located, it gives easy access to Loulé and features three bedrooms, a swimming pool, extensive sun terraces and a 300m^2 plot of land.
175,000 euros CLA
(£116,667) GP

SC Sociedade Mediação Imobiliária Lda.

is a Government licensed Real Estate Agency "Since 1996" at your service.

Fax: 00351 282 343 348
Tel: 00351 282 343 364
Mob: 00351 916 642 836
E-Mail: sc.imobiliaria@netvisao.pt

www.realestatealgarve.com

Landmark Sales & Project Development
Av. Duarte Pacheco, 226 8135-104 Almancil, Portugal

At Landmark Properties we are committed to simplifying the homeownership process:

We offer an integrated selection of services, which provide everything essential to buy or sell your home - all under one roof. It includes buying and selling services, mortgages, insurance, relocation and moving management, as well as a number of expanding e-services.

We have helped people achieve their dreams of home ownership. A single goal continues to drive us - making your transaction as easy and convenient as possible.

Tel: 00351 289 393848   Fax: 00351 289 395249
Email: landmarkproperty@mail.telepac.pt
www.landmarkpropertyalgarve.com

Classic & Antique
*Imobiliária*Immobilien*Real Estate*

Rua do Argel 10
P-8000 Faro
Tel 00351 289 825 272
Fax 00351 289 825 275
email: classic@mail.telepac.pt

**APARTMENTS / TOWNHOUSES / PLOTS / FARMHOUSES
GOLF PROPERTIES / VILLAS / QUINTAS
from €60.000 - €6.000.000**

please visit us on:
www.classic-antique.net
www.classic-antique.com

13569
Buying a home in Portugal?

Banco Totta & Açores

We're over here - and over there - for you!

YOUR HOME IS AT RISK IF YOU DO NOT KEEP UP REPAYMENTS ON A MORTGAGE OR OTHER LOANS SECURED ON IT.
Where a loan is arranged in a foreign currency the Sterling equivalent of your liability under a foreign currency mortgage may be increased by exchange rate movements.

For further information on our mortgage services, contact our UK branch.

The Mortgage Loan Department
Banco Totta & Açores
68 Cannon Street, London EC4N 6AQ
Telephone: 020 7651 0190
Facsimile: 020 7329 8207
Email: mortgage@btax.co.uk
Web: www.bancototta.co.uk

Price Guide

Faro   RS
An extravagantly decorated, unique castle property that could be turned into a small hotel. Close to Faro airport, this characterful property has bags of personality and represents an investment.
4,500,000 euros   HIL
(£3,000,000) GP

Quinta do Lago   RS
This impressive five-bedroom, five-bathroom home is a frontline golf development property. With attention to detail, it includes antique stone floors, a large swimming pool, air conditioning and central heating.
2,800,000 euros   KGV
(£1,866,667) GP

Alcalar   RS
A striking, well maintained villa offering four bedrooms, three bathrooms and two living rooms. Features include a wood-burning stove, a laundry, a pantry, a garage and a BBQ. With electric heaters.
400,000 euros   VER
(£266,667) GP

Vale Judeu   RS
A unique property set in 10,000m² of land, with a restored windmill as its focal point. This incredible home features a cascade swimming pool, a helipad and an unusual, characterful, circular dining room.
1,780,000 euros   EUV
(£1,186,667) GP

São Bartolomeu de Messines   RS
A delightful, furnished villa with three bedrooms and two bathrooms on the outskirts of this town. There is a split-level living area and a spacious living area, plus a 9 x 5m² swimming pool. It affords excellent views.
399,000 euros   ARY
(£266,000) GP

The Algarve

Alfanzina   RS
This charming, furnished cottage by the sea has four bedrooms and two bathrooms. Featuring a large plot and garden, a separate dining-room, kitchen, pantry, and electric wall heaters. Near town.
787,500 euros   VER
(£525,000) GP

Alcalar   RS
A characterful country villa with breathtaking mountain views. It offers three bedrooms, three bathrooms (two en-suite), garage, swimming pool, a living room, a wood-burning stove and a BBQ.
525,000 euros   VER
(£350,000) GP

Benagil   RS
Affording five bedrooms and three bathrooms, a well located country villa with a separate one-bedroom guest cottage. Enjoying a swimming pool, a BBQ and a garage, it has great rental potential.
1,000,000 euros   VER
(£666,667) GP

Quinta do Lago   NB
A stylish and tastefully decorated one-bedroom apartment in the much admired Pinheiros Altos golf and leisure resort. Beautifully furnished, it affords membership to the village's golf club and access to a shared swimming pool. With all mod cons, it has under-floor heating, air conditioning and will be sold furnished. There is an spacious, combined living and dining room and an modern fitted kitchen. Covering 82m², it has a secluded feel as the development has a snack bar and restaurant.
442,500 euros   SEL
(£295,000) GP

Porches   RS
A well maintained villa offering three bedrooms, this delightful property has three bathrooms, a living room and dining room with a wood-burning stove, swimming pool, gym and double garage.
466,667 euros   VER
(£700,000) GP

Alcantarilha   RS
Offering five bedrooms, this expansive country house is in a secluded, rural location. Set in seven hectares, it has three bathrooms and a fitted kitchen with a pantry. There is an office and BBQ.
773,780 euros   VER
(£515,850) GP

Carvoeiro   RS
This luxurious furnished villa enjoys three bedrooms and its own office. With three bathrooms (two en-suite), a living room with a wood-burning stove, this villa is close to the beach and amenities.
550,000 euros   VER
(£366,667) GP

Carvoeiro   RS
A single-storey, three-bedroom villa with stunning sea views. Offering a tennis court, a garage, a swimming pool, a living-room with a wood-burning stove, a BBQ and a well designed, modern kitchen.
600,000 euros   VER
(£400,000) GP

Price Guide

Vilamoura RS
An extremely well cared for, spacious five-bedroom villa with beautiful and expansive gardens. Overlooking a golf course, it has a tennis court and a great deal of privacy. All amenities are closeby.
1,600,000 euros *SLV*
(£1,066,667) GP

Santa Bárbara de Nexe RS
Comprising four bedrooms and a spacious lounge area, this villa has a living area of 400m^2. With grounds of 5,000m^2 which are fenced, this property allows the owner privacy and security. Well located.
310,000 euros REK
(£206,665) GP

Almancil RS
A recently refurbished family villa comprising three bedrooms (all with en-suite bathrooms) and a luxurious heated swimming pool. This lovely modern property affords a cloakroom, a combined living and dining room, a fitted kitchen, electric wall heaters and a beautifully landscaped garden. For assured security, the property has an alarm and is well situated for easy access to the beach and all surrounding amenities. A superb investment, it would make a good full-time home or holiday retreat.
712,500 euros ROS
(£475,000) GP

Loulé Hills RS
A magnificent villa with 20,000m^2 of grounds, this property offers spectacular ocean views. With four bedrooms and a splendid swimming pool and BBQ area, this villa has air conditioning. Close to the sea.
1,000,000 euros REK
(£666,665) GP

Vilamoura RS
This elegant and stylish villa is ideally placed near the marina and affords three bedrooms and two bathrooms. With room in the spacious basement for further development, this is a well maintained home.
350,000 euros *SLV*
(£233,330) GP

The Algarve

Mts de Alvor RS
A unique, partially restored townhouse with a separate studio apartment and separate entrances. This unusual home is open plan and comprises a 50m² walled plot. Ideal for complete renovation.
125,000 euros SUL
(£83,330) GP

Mont Judeu RS
An impressive villa in a much loved location. With four bedrooms, two bathrooms, a dining room, dressing room, guest suite, double garage, swimming pool and a 5,000m² plot, it is a fabulous home.
525,000euros SUL
(£350,000) GP

Alcalar RS
This splendid family villa affords three bedrooms and two bathrooms (one en-suite) in a much loved rural development. Plus a laundry room, swimming pool, garage, rustic fireplace and modern kitchen.
370,000 euros SUL
(£246,667) GP

Aldeia das Biscainhas RS
A characterful four-bedroom villa with a heated swimming pool in this picturesque location. With luxurious extras including solar panels and satellite TV. The villa is set in an attractive 1,320m² plot.
442,500 euros SUL
(£295,000) GP

Bemposta RS
A competitively priced one-bedroom apartment with 55m² living space in a popular holiday complex on the road to Portimão. Offering a balcony overlooking the shared swimming pool and spacious gardens.
110,000 euros SUL
(£73,330) GP

Quinta do Lago RS
An extensively renovated two-bedroom apartment in the popular Encosta do Lago area. Sold with furnishings, it comprises a swimming pool, a garden and access to shared tennis courts and restaurants.
580,000 euros SOT
(£386,667) GP

Price Guide

Vale do Lobo   RS
Close to the Royal Golf Course, a detached three-bedroom, 250m² villa. Right by the fairway, this golfer's dream is a short distance from the beach and restaurants, and has its own swimming pool.
1,012,500 euros   SOT
(£675,000) GP

Vale do Lobo   RS
Located on the resort's Ocean Golf Course, this three-bedroom, three-bathroom property enjoys luxurious facets including a basement with a bar and games room. With stunning views of the coast.
1,350,000 euros   SOT
(£900,000) GP

Quinta do Lago   NB
A beautifully designed five-bedroom villa with elegant en-suite bathrooms and golf rights to the resorts prestigious courses. Featuring luxurious extras including electric window shutters and under-floor heating, there is an airy living and dining room that give direct access to the sun terraces. To the front there is a large, heated swimming pool which can be enjoyed throughout the year. With a laundry and garage in the basement, a triple garage and south-facing garden.
2,775,000 euros (offshore)   SEL
(£1,850,000) GP

Quinta do Lago   RS
A grand four-bedroom villa situated on the resort's north golf course. It enjoys a beautiful, mature garden, a swimming pool and golf title for the resort. To be sold fully furnished. Ideal for golf lovers.
1,850,000 euros (offshore)   SOT
(£1,233,330) GP

Quinta do Lago   RS
A well maintained, second-floor one-bedroom apartment. A short walk from this popular resort's golden beaches and the Ria Formosa nature reserve, it is to be sold furnished. With electric wall heaters.
2,242,500 euros   SEL
(£1,495,000) GP

The Algarve

Quinta do Lago NB
A spacious modern apartment with three en-suite bedrooms set in a modern development. Air-conditioned, it enjoys access to a shared gym and a communal swimming pool. With coastal views.
895,000 euros SEL
(£596,667) GP

Almancil RS
A striking property comprising four bedrooms with en-suite bathrooms. Situated in a stylish and mature part of this well loved town, it has air conditioning, a swimming pool, garage and a landscaped garden.
1,300,000 euros ROS
(£866,667) GP

Almancil NB
Just a short walk from the beach and the Pinhal golf course, a prestigious property offering four bedrooms with en-suite bathrooms. With a swimming pool, air conditioning and a garage, it is a modern family base.
735,000 euros ROS
(£490,000) GP

Vila do Vispo NB
A fashionable range of two- and three-bedroom townhouses and villas sold on a part-ownership basis. Split between 12 owners, these affordable homes are in a modern and stylish golf and leisure complex.
32,000+ euros VIG
(£21,330) GP

Lagos RS
A golfer's delight, this attractive three-bedroom townhouse is perfectly situated at the heart of an exclusive golf village complex. Not offshore registered, it offers a spacious holiday home.
382,500 euros VIG
(£255,000) GP

Price Guide

Alentejo Introduction

ALENTEJO

If you love rolling countryside dotted with medieval hilltop villages, quaint white-washed houses with sea views and value for money, head north of the Algarve to the vast Alentejo region, home of farmhouses to renovate and plush villas

Price Guide

Portalegre   RS
A modern property with three bedrooms and three bathrooms, this home is set in the stunning São Mamede conservation area. With panoramic views over a freshwater lake, ideal for swimming and sailing.
258,000 euros   **BOG**
(£172,000) GP

Pavia   RS
An outstanding four-bedroom property built to very high standards on raised ground affording stunning views. Featuring a large swimming pool and planning permission for a stable block, a unique property.
580,000 euros   **PPI**
(£386,665) GP

Sta Clara   RS
A truely splendid property located in a mountian area, this dwelling offers four-bedrooms and stunning views over the nearby lake. With solar power, a well, and fully irrigated grounds of 14,000m², this supurb dwelling has a modern wood-panelled kitchen and a spacious living room. With a large garage and traditional fireplaces, this spacious property is arranged over two floors. This villa offers the owner complete peace and tranquility.
299,300 euros   **VER**
(£199,535) GP

Odemira   NB
This plot of 5,400m² is set within easy reach of the Algarve and close to the coast. With great views and planning permission already granted, this is an ideal location for the construction of a family holiday home.
57,000 euros   **PPI**
(£38,000) GP

Estremoz   RS
A historic 18th-century house, situated in the centre of Sousal village. With a total of 30 rooms and a small garden, this property offers itself as an excellent business opportunity. Easily accessible for town.
343,000 euros   **PPI**
(£228,665) GP

Premier bring you closer to the real Portugal

Examples of properties and land from our current brochures:

CENTRAL REGION

£103,500
€150,000

Murganheira 5-bedroom traditional Portuguese house: 2 living rooms, 2 bathrooms, kitchen, 2 garages; central heating; swimming pool; 3,000m² land with fruit trees

Ref: 3118

Ref: 3330

£27,600
€40,000

Anceriz Plot of land of 1,000m² with a small stone building; lovely views to the mountains; electricity some 400m away and telephone nearby, well needed for water

WESTERN REGION

£150,000
€217,500

Cortem House restored to a high standard; 3 bedrooms, living room with fireplace, cloakroom, bathroom, inner courtyard, fitted kitchen, BBQ area with terrace, land leads down to small river

Ref: 2451

Ref: 2464

£41,400
€60,000

Vale da Quinta 2400 sq m village plot with approved plans for a modern house and enjoying country views; approved plans available on request

NORTHERN & COASTAL ALENTEJO

£55,900
€81,000

Avis Building plot of 9,500m² with approved project for a house of 250 m², with panoramic views over Avis, the Maranhão dam and the Alentejo countryside; olive trees; water and electricity nearby

Ref: 3615

Ref: 3630

£142,800
€207,000

Mora Newly-built house of 180m² in beautiful village: living room, kitchen, 3 bedrooms, bathroom, storage space; garden, swimming pool; property fenced all around

The property prices shown here are shown in Euros – the Sterling comparisons have been based on an exchange rate of 1.45 and are subject to fluctuation

Please telephone 01935 881199 to receive our latest corporate brochure and price lists, featuring these and very many more properties.

Premier Properties International Group
Great Street,
Norton sub Hamdon
Somerset TA14 6SG

Telephone **+44(0)1935 881199 & 881992**
Facsimile **+44(0)1935 881762**
email: sales@premierpropertiesonline.com
www.premierpropertiesonline.com

Price Guide

Ourique   RS
This four-bedroom farmhouse nestles in 17,500m² of farmland and includes an established market garden. Located close to the motorway, this property is well situated for access to the Algarve and Lisbon.
210,000 euros   MAC
(£140,000+) GP

Redondo   NB
Situated on the shore of Lake Vigia, these villas offer spectacular views and access to an 18-hole golf course and swimming pool. Located only 5km from the nearest town, and only an hour from Lisbon.
295,000+ euros   FLO
(£196,665+) GP

Seixal   RS
The Orion Hotel and sports complex offers 34 rooms and has approval for development. Located near all local amenities, it offers living space of 1,356m² and grounds of 23,000m². An excellent business prospect.
4,380,000 euros   DOC
(£2,920,000) GP

Sines   NB
These newly built two- and three-bedroom apartments are located on the beachfront of this coastal town, not far from Lisbon. Just minutes from the town centre, the homes are also near the countryside.
150,000+ euros   BOG
(£100,000+) GP

Ourique   RS
Situated in a secluded location, this old watermill requires complete renovation. Only 15 minutes from the nearby village and amenities, this unique property is totally unspoilt and is surrounded by countryside.
118,000 euros   ESG
(£78,665) GP

Portalegre   RS
Requiring renovation, this traditional village house offers 23 rooms and features a courtyard and enormous garden. Located in a large town near the Spanish border, this property affords splendid views.
157,600 euros   BOG
(£105,065) GP

Alentejo

Ourique   NB
Located close to the coast and within easy reach of Lisbon, this luxurious property offers peace and tranquillity. With four bedrooms and a two-bedroom guest house, this villa nestles in 23 acres of well manicured gardens and stunning woodlands. Surrounded by glorious countryside, this home is an excellent base for excursions to the Algarve thanks to the new motorway link. Featuring a swimming pool and an attractive lake, this property is the epitome of style and luxury. A must-have villa.
550,000 euros   **BOG**
(£366,665) GP

Galveias   NB
A recently built house that offers the new owner the chance to finish it to their individual taste. With four en-suite bedrooms, large sitting room, dining area and modern kitchen, this is a high-standard home.
314,800 euros   **PPI**
(£209,865) GP

Grandola   RS
A ten-bedroom guest house located in peaceful pine woods and set only minutes from the nearby deserted beaches. Those who desire peace and tranquillity would find this peaceful property an ideal retreat.
723,000 euros   **BOG**
(£482,000) GP

Elvas   RS
A unique and characteristic property, this home is incredibly spacious and elegant. Offering seven bedrooms, this property features a historic bishop's bedroom, an old-fashioned bread oven, an ancient medieval wall and olive groves. The gardens are large and full of mature palm trees, while there are many stone outbuildings that could be renovated to form guest quarters. Stylish, chic and extremely comfortable, this villa is well located in the town of Elvas, and close to all amenities.
240,000+ euros   **BOG**
(£160,000+) GP

Price Guide

Ourique   RS

A superb old cottage with approximately 25 acres of land. A traditional Alentejan property, it is only a short walk from the main town. Featuring a private road that runs through the property, this home is easily accessible and has all utilities connected. This cottage requires renovation, but is an excellent prospect for development, ideal for those who seek a peaceful retirement or a spacious property for a business venture. Within easy access of Ourique and its amenities, this is a highly attractive property.
160,000 euros   ESG
(£106,665) GP

Santo Andre   RS

A three-bedroom property with living space of 200m², this house features a lounge, dining room and a spacious kitchen. With two bathrooms and a garage, this lovely property has a garden with two swimming pools and a well. Only 2km from the beach and coastline, this estate is well located for the nearest city of Sines. Affording excellent views and surrounded by stunning countryside, this lovely house is ideal for a family holiday home being situated close to all attractions. Certainly a must-see.
249,800 euros   PPI
(£166,535) GP

Ourique   NB

A newly built, modern property located on the outskirts of Ourique, this is an rare opportunity. Offering remarkable panoramic views, overlooking the countryside and distant Alentejan mountains. Fully air conditioned, with granite and marble floors, this villa is built to the highest standards. With a rustic style kitchen, attractive fireplace and spacious living area, the bathroom offers a sauna. The upper floor is open-plan, and there is a spacious three-car garage with a wine cellar.
239,000 euros   ESG
(£159,335) GP

Alentejo

Ourique RS
Requiring complete renovation and set within five acres of stunning countryside, this ruin resides in an area of outstanding natural and ecological beauty. It is situated only 5km away from all the amenities of Ourique, and only a 60-minute drive from Faro airport. Connected to all utilities, this property affords stunning views over the surrounding area. Ideal as a renovation project, and within easy reach of the coast, this dwelling would make a great project. A potentially lovely spot.
60,000 euros **ESG**
(£40,000) GP

Cercal RS
Requiring renovation, this property with 150m² of living space is set in 2,471 acres of farmland. Offering fantastic rural views, the estate is only 20km from the nearest beach and only 500m from the main road network. Easily accessible for the Algarve, Lisbon and their attractions, this property is surrounded by countryside and is extremely peaceful, suiting an owner who is seeking a relaxing retreat. Ideal as a renovation project in a highly agricultural area that offers great prospects.
125,000 euros **PPI**
(£83,335) GP

Ourique RS
Located in the south of Alentejo, this plot of 15,000m² of land comes with planning permission to build a dwelling of 250m². Just a few minutes' walk from the local village, the plot is only 12km from the main town and set close to a nature reserve. With spectacular views across to the mountains, this would be a perfect spot to build a rural retreat as the location is superbly secluded. Fully fenced and planted with fruit trees, the land also offers opportunities for a rural business. Plenty of potential.
85,000 euros **ESG**
(£56,665) GP

Price Guide

Cercal   **RS**
An old detached house with a stable, residing in 26,250m² of arable land. This property requires either renovation of the existing house or a rebuild, but offers great potential, especially being situated just three minutes from the bustling, small town of Cercal near Alentejo's western coast. The grounds of the property are well looked after, with mature bamboo, walnut and pear trees, as well as an apple orchard. The land also has a stream. With some work, this could become a dream holiday home.
110,000 euros   **ESG**
(£73,335) GP

Ourique   **RS**
Requiring renovation, including a new kitchen and bathroom, this property has large, airy rooms and an attractive interior. The views offered by this property are breathtaking and the generous 20,000m² grounds include a courtyard, an orchard, olive grove and eucalyptus trees as well as outbuildings ideal for conversion. Located near the main road, this property is only five minutes' drive from nearby Barragem da Rocha lake with its fishing and sailing opportunities. Worth consideration.
294,000 euros   **ESG**
(£196,000) GP

Ourique   **RS**
This old Alentejan stone farmhouse is set in 90,000m² of land including a river. The house is set in an elevated position overlooking the grounds and the river with its small beach areas. Situated in an area of archeological and ecological interest, the house requires renovation but offers enormous potential, especially as it is only 10 minutes from the nearest village and all its amenities, and just 15 minutes from the town of Ourique. A desirable dwelling, though requiring some hard work.
160,000 euros   **ESG**
(£106,665) GP

Alentejo

Garvão   **RS**
This old cottage is ripe for renovation and is situated only a short walk from the stunning lake of Monte da Roche, offering an abundance of watersports. Surrounded by cork and olive trees, this property has grounds of 50,000m². Only five minutes walk from the traditional and pretty village of Garvão, and within easy reach of Ourique, this home is only 15 minutes drive from the Algarve. With all amenities close by and easy access to the main road, this cottage is well located.
165,000 euros   **ESG**
(110,000) GP

Pavia   **RS**
An excellent opportunity for a development or business venture, this plot of 240,000m² includes some ruined buildings that could be renovated to create a holiday home. Only 15 minutes from the motorway and 40 minutes from Albufeira, this plot rests in beautiful and unspoilt countryside. Ideal for those who want proximity to the Algarve, but desire a more refined and peaceful atmosphere, access routes are accessible. A must for the keen developer and perfect for those who love the countryside.
200,000 euros   **FIN**
(£133,335) GP

Santana da Serra   **RS**
A secluded but highly comfortable home, this house has been recently rebuilt and is extremely well maintained. With three bedrooms and an attractive lounge, this house has been decorated in a traditional Alentejan style. With terracotta tiled floors throughout, the home also features a patio with BBQ area. Included with the property is a private jetty for fishing and sailing on the impressive lake, and beautiful ornamental gardens, featuring numerous fruit trees. Ten minutes from the nearest village.
415,000 euros   **ESG**
(£276,665) GP

Price Guide

LISBON & ESTREMADURA

From cosy city centre apartments or renovated townhouses in the bustling Portuguese capital, to stunning villas in the pretty seaside resorts to the north and south, you are spoiled for choice in Lisbon and the surrounding areas

Price Guide

Óbidos   NB
A beautiful five-bedroom villa situated in a secluded area of this prestigious development. Offering a large heated swimming pool and a garage, this property is sold fully furnished and features on-site facilities.
950,000 euros   <u>SOT</u>
(£633,335) GP

Sintra   NB
This country estate rests in 12,000m² of land. With five bedrooms, all en-suite, this property also boasts a library, tennis court and swimming pool. Featuring wooden ceilings and traditional tiling throughout.
1,600,000 euros   <u>SOT</u>
(£1,066,665) GP

Obidos   NB
Located in the Praia d'El Rey Golf & Country club, these exclusive villas offer stunning views and luxurious surroundings. With beautifully manicured gardens, these developments reside in 500 acres of unspoilt countryside in the peaceful Estremadura region. With sporting and leisure facilities available, these properties are the perfect location for a family home. An ideal purchase for those seeking peace and quiet away from the Algarve, this development is the epitome of elegance and luxury.
825,000+ euros   <u>WCH</u>
(£550,000+) GP

Obidos   NB
Overlooking the Praia d'El Rey golf course, this beautiful villa offers stunning views and its own swimming pool. Close to Lisbon and offering various leisure facilities, this home is very well located.
825,000 euros   <u>WCH</u>
(£550,000) GP

Obidos   NB
This new four-bedroom villa with en-suite facilities has a living space of 750m² and offers grounds of 3,200m². The villa also features a heated swimming pool, games room, basement and a double garage.
1,650,000 euros   <u>SOT</u>
(£1,100,000) GP

PRAIA D'EL REY

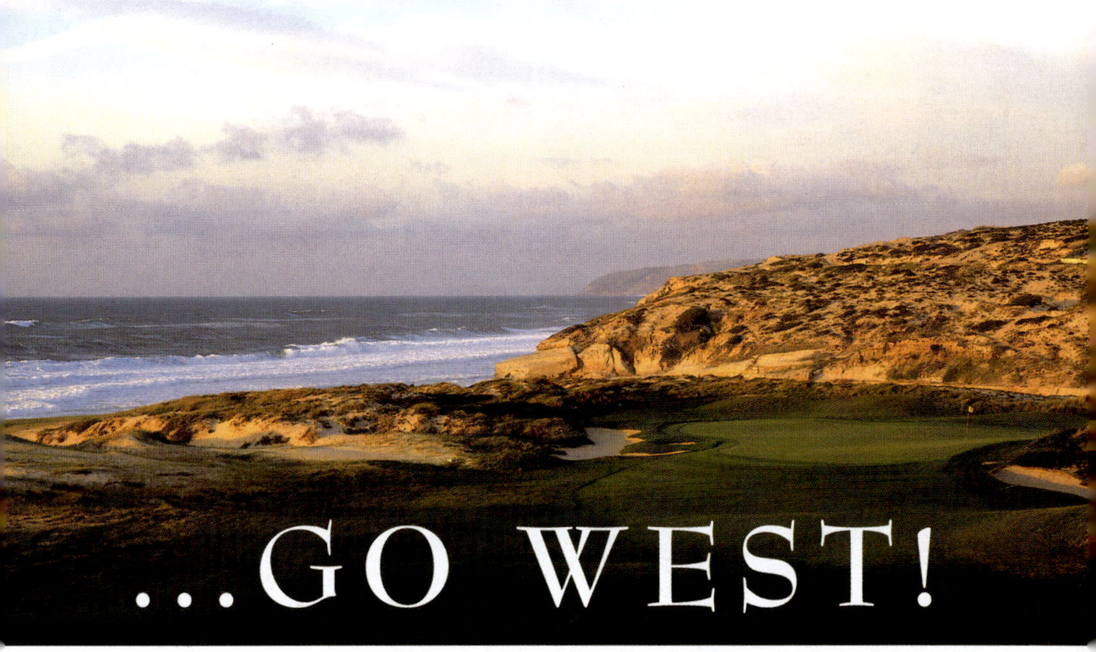

...GO WEST!

To the fabulous Praia D'El Rey course, situated on the West Coast, and rated nº 1 in Portugal by Peugeot Golf Guide. Just 45 minutes from Lisbon airport and close to the medieval town of Óbidos, Praia D'El Rey has all the facilities of a first class resort with a 5 star Marriott resort hotel on site.

VILLAS, TOWNHOUSES AND APARTMENTS FOR SALE AND RENT

Nearby attractions

- Medieval town of Óbidos - a Unesco world heritage site • Port town of Peniche famous for its seafood restaurants • Berlengas Islands nature reserve • Local "quintas" for wine tasting visits • More than 10 championship golf courses within 1 hour drive • Lisbon for museums, sightseeing and shopping.

Opening late 2003

TOP 100 EUROPEAN COURSES
RANKED 13

PRAIA D'EL REY
Golf & Country Club
ÓBIDOS - PORTUGAL

Tel. +351 262 905 000   Fax +351 262 905 003   sales@praia-del-rey.com
rentals@praia-del-rey.com • golf@praia-del-rey.com
World Class Homes - Freefone - **UK** 0800 731 4713

www.praia-del-rey.com

Price Guide

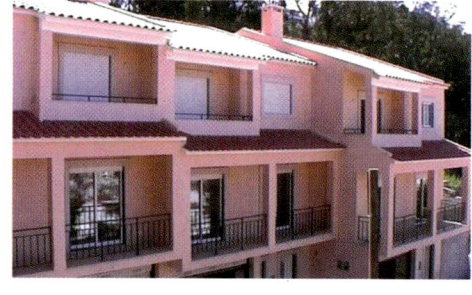

Sintra   NB
This new five-bedroom villa is located on Sintra's golf course and is built in the style of a traditional Portuguese manor house. A high quality home, it is easily accessible for both Lisbon and Sintra.
905,000 euros   **BOG**
(£603,335) GP

Nazaré   NB
These townhouses currently under construction are being built to the highest quality and offer a living space of between 150 and 208m². Each home offers four bedrooms, a garden and views over the Atlantic.
250,000+ euros   **IMA**
(£166,665+) GP

Penha Longa   NB
Located in a sought-after area on the outskirts of Lisbon, this beautiful villa offers five bedrooms, the master bedroom having a walk-in closet and fireplace. It also boasts a large living/dining area with an open fireplace, a separate study and a modern kitchen. With a large garage, this home boasts stunning, mature gardens and glorious views. Easily accessible for Lisbon centre, this property affords peace and quiet in this relaxing, residential area. A stylish house, perfect for a family home.
1,800,000 euros   **SOT**
(£1,200,000) GP

Nazaré   RS
An ancient mansion, this impressive home was once the property of the late French ambassador. Located high up on the mountainside with spectacular views over the ocean and the red rooves of the nearby town, the local facilities are within easy reach. Offering bright spacious rooms and a lovely, well tended garden full of mature trees and shrubs, it offers grounds of 2,000m² with outbuildings and a studio. Requiring some renovation.
680,000 euros   **IMA**
(£453,335) GP

GEORGE KNIGHT
Soc. de Mediação Imobiliária, Lda.
AMI 1592

Looking for a property to buy or to rent in Portugal?

Look no further! We will help you find your property in Portugal!
We have a wide range of villas, apartments, land, traditional houses, from North to South of Portugal.

Founded in Great Britain, with more than 20 years of experience in the Portuguese market, GEORGE KNIGHT is the real estate agent that will provide for a friendly and professional service that you need.

CONTACT US!

Edifício Avis - Av. Fontes Pereira de Melo, 35 - 18º B -1050 LISBOA
tel: (351) 213 540 001 / fax: (351) 213 541 914
email: gknet@esoterica.pt   site: www.georgeknight.pt

Price Guide

Obidos NB
These three- and four-bedroom properties are set in a wooded valley on the Praia d'El Rey golfing development. With a secluded setting and a relaxing, uncommercialised atmosphere, a peaceful home.
825,000+ euros WCH
(£550,000+) GP

Obidos NB
Set in grounds of 2,128m², this four-bedroom villa offers an indoor pool, spacious basement, bar and wine cellar. Affording sea views, this home is a must for golfing enthusiasts and second home seekers.
1,675,000 euros SOT
(£1,116,675) GP

Casal da Silveira RS
An old village property requiring an owner willing to renovate and refurbish, this 2,300m² plot offers enormous potential with ample room for a swimming pool. The one-storey home boasts two bedrooms and a separate annexe, allowing plenty of space for families. The grounds feature a well and the home offers spectacular views of the surrounding villages and beautiful countryside. A very peaceful and relaxing area, ideal as a rural retreat yet still within reach of amenities.
108,000 euros PPI
(£72,000) GP

Cascais NB
Resting in grounds of 10,000m², this property comprises a main house, guest quarters and a poolside building. With a swimming pool, total privacy and panoramic views over the ocean, a luxurious home.
2,200,000 euros SOT
(£1,466,665) GP

Obidos RS
Situated in a protected area and offering stunning sea views, this plot includes a ruin and is a superb project for renovation or a new-build. Within easy reach of Obidos and Caldas da Rainha, a great prospect.
80,000 euros BOG
(£53,335) GP

Lisbon & Estremadura

Peniche RS
With a living space of 120m², this home has no garden but is only nine minutes from the beach, the nearby golf course and Peniche's marina. A well located property with plenty of potential.
150,000 euros IMA
(£100,000) GP

Obidos RS
Arranged over three floors, this impressive property close to Lisbon has three bedrooms and a pretty garden. Ready for habitation this house is built to the highest standards and has wonderful views.
185,000 euros IMA
(£123,335) GP

Sintra RS
This estate consisting of five villas would make for an excellent business venture, with the whole development offering up to 14 bedrooms. Allowing the owner the luxury of a second home while generating rental income from the other four villas, this estate resides in a quiet, tree-lined plot. Only five minutes from the beach and 30 minutes from Lisbon, this property is well located and offers good access routes. An excellent opportunity, this offers good potential for a business venture.
960,000 euros BOG
(£640,000) GP

Nazaré RS
Only 5km from Nazaré, this large plot of land is directly located on the Atlantic coast, offering immediate access to the kilometre-long sandy beach. Situated in a protected area and offering grounds of 1,650m², this plot has an authorised building licence to allow the construction of one or two houses. This plot has enormous potential for those willing to put in the investment and time needed for a property development project.
130,000 euros IMA
(£86,665) GP

Price Guide

Mafra   **RS**
A spacious four-bedroom villa, this property is modern in construction and is situated in the countryside surrounding Lisbon. Affording a swimming pool and a large garage, this home has a newly fitted kitchen offering all modern conveniences. With central heating and a well designed interior, the garden totals one acre and includes a stretch of attractive stream. Located in a peaceful, rural area and with stunning views, this is an excellent and desirable location with easy access to the Lisbon area.
700,000 euros   **BOG**
(£466,665) GP

Nazaré   **NB**
This beautiful new property is located only 1km from Nazaré's stunning sandy beaches. With living space of 300m², this property boasts four bedrooms with balconies, an office and a lovely garden with BBQ.
274,500 euros   **IMA**
(£183,000) GP

Casa da Boa Vista   **RS**
A stunning, detached property with a summer house, swimming pool and BBQ, this home is located in a typical Portuguese village affording panoramic views and close to all facilities. Featuring a snooker room.
374,000 euros   **IMA**
(£249,335) GP

Mafra   **RS**
This three-bedroom house offers wooden beamed ceilings, a traditional stone fireplace, two bathrooms and dramatic views through its large windows. Combined with this are modern luxuries such as central heating and a fully fitted kitchen. With beautiful, mature gardens, this home is situated in the village of Mafra, on Lisbon's outskirts. Easily accessible for the capital and the coast, this excellent property exudes comfort and luxury. An excellent purchase for those seeking peace and rural surroundings.
250,000 euros   **BOG**
(£166,665) GP

Lisbon & Estremadura

Valado dos Frades   RS
Located in a tranquil area, yet only minutes away from the A8 highway and the beaches of Nazaré, this property has two bedrooms, a fireplace and garden with BBQ area. Close to tennis courts and a park.
109,800 euros   **IMA**
(£73,200) GP

Cabaços   RS
An unique property, this old granite house was once an olive oil mill but now requires complete renovation. Set in peaceful rural surroundings, the property offers a garden of 1,000m^2 and a stream.
42,500 euros   **RUT**
(£28,335) GP

Foz do Arelho   RS
Located in a village near Columbeira, this old stone watermill requires an owner willing to renovate and restore. The property comes with a small area of land featuring a beautiful stream, and is set in peaceful area surrounded by countryside. Close to the beach and the attractions of Foz do Arelho, it is only a short distance to Lisbon itself. Ideal for restoration as a family holiday home, this water mill offers good access routes and many attractions in the area. A great opportunity.
47,500 euros   **PPI**
(£31,665) GP

Pombal   RS
This recently renovated country home is situated halfway between Lisbon and Porto. With splendid views and a swimming pool, this rural retreat offers six bedrooms, a jacuzzi and a spacious patio area.
220,000 euros   **RUT**
(£146,665) GP

Salir do Porto   RS
A very attractive single-storey beach house, this property requires renovation although is perfectly habitable. With three bedrooms and wooden floors, there are three annexes within the spacious grounds.
207,000 euros   **PPI**
(£138,000) GP

Price Guide

Columbeira   RS
This two-bedroom country property is arranged over one storey and comes with 3,600m² of land. The front garden offers roses and eucalyptus trees while the spacious back garden offers stunning views.
130,000 euros   **PPI**
(£86,665) GP

Foz do Arelho   NB
Arranged over two floors, this attached villa is located in a beach town and offers balconies overlooking the Obidos lagoon. With three bedrooms, this property has a fitted beech kitchen featuring all appliances.
192,000 euros   **PPI**
(£128,000) GP

Ansião   RS
Newly renovated, this cottage is located on the edge of a pine forest with stunning views overlooking a small valley. This property has been restored to the highest standards and features three bedrooms, three bathrooms, a spacious kitchen and dining area. Outside is a garden of 800m² comprising a covered eating area and BBQ, a swimming pool and land planted with fruit trees. The flooring throughout is of handmade terracotta tiles. An extremely pleasant home, only 8km from the market town of Ansião.
270,000 euros   **RUT**
(£180,000) GP

Nazaré   RS
Located in a beautiful, authentic Portuguese fishing village this one-year-old apartment is fully furnished with four bedrooms. The apartment's two terraces offer magnificent views of the harbour and coastline.
165,000 euros   **IMA**
(£110,000) GP

Foz do Arelho   NB
Located in the centre of a seaside town, this house offers five bedrooms and a separate annexe with two bedrooms and two bathrooms. This property, ideal for a family holiday home, has a large walled garden.
259,000 euros   **PPI**
(£172,665) GP

Lisbon & Estremadura

Mafra   RS
This plot of land has been granted building permission and is ideally located for a newly built villa. Only 20 minutes from Lisbon airport, this plot of 2,020m² offers great views over the rural area.
200,000 euros   BOG
(£133,335) GP

Caldas da Rainha   RS
A large and spacious villa located on the outskirts of Caldas da Rainha, featuring a pool and mature gardens and grounds totalling 3,030m². Centrally heated and offering a garage, workshop and shed.
500,000 euros   BOG
(£333,335) GP

Estoril   RS
A luxurious property set in one of Lisbon's most sought-after areas, this villa has a stunning garden and is adjacent to a golf course.
3,750,000 euros   REN
(£2,500,000) GP

Caldas da Rainha   RS
Within walking distance of the centre of Caldas da Rainha, this modern house offers tidy gardens and a high quality finish. Within easy reach of Lisbon, this property would make a great holiday home.
300,000 euros   BOG
(£200,000) GP

Obidos   RS
A recently renovated three-bedroom farmhouse, this property is located in the beach resort of Obidos, and is close to all amenities and the beach. Affording stunning views, an extremely comfortable villa.
210,000 euros   BOG
(£140,000) GP

Price Guide

COIMBRA & THE BEIRAS

For lovers of the great outdoors, buying a home in the rugged, unspoiled Beiras regions of Portugal, with their forests, sandy coastlines, and ancient towns, is ideal. From small rural cottages to large modern homes, all tastes and budgets are catered for

THE PORTUGUESE TOURIST BOARD

WORLD PICTURES

THE PORTUGUESE TOURIST BOARD

Price Guide

Gonçalo   RS
Located close to the town of Guarda and its amenities, this farm property is set in idyllic rustic surroundings. Ideal for a possible tourist business or as a working farm, well located for the motorway.
14,000 euros   **REX**
(£9,335) GP

Pereiro Além   RS
This house has been superbly renovated, making it a stunning home. Built from stone, this spacious house affords fantastic views over its manicured gardens and includes a swimming pool. Close to amenities.
300,000 euros   **PRS**
(£200,000) GP

Penela   NB
This newly built, detached property is located in the town of Penela near Coimbra. Within easy reach of either stunning countryside or the coastline, this is an ideal location for a peacefl family holiday home.
130,000 euros   **PRS**
(£86,665) GP

Meãs   NB
A luxury detached property located in this stunning area near the city of Coimbra, this home offers four bedrooms. From the well manicured, mature gardens the marvellous views of the area can be enjoyed.
22,500 euros   **REX**
(£15,000) GP

Pereiro Além   RS
This unique old mill requires renovation but offers 2.5 acres of stunning grounds and 120 metres of trout-filled river. Affording stunning views over its own lake, this property features a swimming pool.
160,000 euros   **PRS**
(£106,665) GP

Fruimes   RS
This large colonial house comprises 21 rooms and has been partially restored to its former glory. With exposed timber beams, two new shower rooms and a new kitchen, this property offers extensive gardens.
761,500 euros   **PPT**
(£507,665) GP

Price Guide

Caseiros RS
A modern detached property located near the town of Miranda de Corvo and only a 15-minute drive from Coimbra. Located in a secluded and peaceful area, this home offers three spacious bedrooms.
137,500 euros PRS
(£91,665) GP

Turgal RS
This two-bedroom stone cottage, located in a picturesque area, offers views over a stream, is in need of renovation. Set in a rustic environment yet within reach of Coimbra, this is in an idyllic location.
40,000 euros PRS
(£26,665) GP

Bodiosa RS
This detached property requires a little renovation and an owner willing to modify. Located near the main road and within easy reach of Viseu, this property is ideally located for those seeking a quiet and peaceful lifestyle. The surrounding region features many historic attractions and is far removed from the hustle and bustle of other, busier parts of Portugal. Combining historic interest with beautiful countryside, this property offers huge potential and is an ideal base for a family holiday home.
30,000 euros REX
(£20,000) GP

Urjariça RS
This three-bedroom property is set in a rural location offering stunning countryside views and a restful atmosphere. Featuring a mature garden, this country home is well located, being easily accessible to main roads, the coast and the town and its local amenities.
55,000 euros PRS
(£36,665) GP

Chá RS
This spacious, rural, detached house is surrounded by lush gardens and features a stream. Built in the style of a country manor, this home is in rural isolation but isn't far from a motorway. Offering peace and tranquillity for those seeking a pastoral retreat.
90,000 euros PRS
(£60,000) GP

Coimbra & the Beiras

Pombalinho NB
Two rural cottages requiring renovation, located in a small village close to the town of Penela. An excellent renovation project, this property is ideally located in one of Portugal's quieter areas, yet close to amenities.
50,000 euros PRS
(£33,335) GP

Vale Maceira RS
Set close to town, this three-bedroom semi-detached house is habitable and requires little work. Well located for local attractions and shops, this property offers the owner quiet yet modern surroundings.
60,000 euros PRS
(£40,000) GP

Esphinal RS
A small cottage ideal as a renovation project, this property would be an great holiday home. Set in an area with access to skiing in the mountains and the warm beaches of the western coast, a perfect location.
32,500 euros PRS
(£21,665) GP

Casa Novas RS
A small ruin on the edge of a village, this property is an ideal renovation project. Near the city of Elvas and close to all amenities, this area offers lush countryside and beautiful views. A lovely holiday environment.
25,000 euros PRS
(£16,665) GP

Peniche RS
This tastefully renovated property has two bedrooms and affords views over the sea. With a rustic interior of tiled floors and exposed stone walls, this characterful cottage is well located for access to town.
140,000 euros BOG
(£93,335) GP

Coimbra NB
A two-bedroom property located in a traditional Portuguese village near Coimbra, this home is a relaxing retreat. Set in quiet, well tended grounds, this home is equally handy for the nearby beaches.
250,000 euros BOG
(£166,665) GP

Price Guide

Coja   RS
Arranged over four floors, each with a living area of 180m², this property is extremely spacious. Requiring redecoration, this dwelling is located in the centre of the village and only ten minutes from Coja town.
160,000 euros   PPT
(£106,665) GP

Gonçalo   RS
A rustic stone farmhouse nestled in 2,300m² of land with a living space of 60m². Requiring maintenance work, this property is ideal for a holiday home, affording the owner a restful escape from urban life.
35,000 euros   REX
(£23,335) GP

São Martinho do Porto   RS
This two-bedroom property is situated in delightful countryside with wonderful views across an expansive valley to the distant hills. With a mature, well manicured garden, surrounded by shady pine trees and featuring flagstoned paths, this property's grounds offer seclusion and privacy as well as a welcome escape from the afternoon heat! Within easy reach of the local sandy beach in a quiet, sheltered bay, this home is a delightful prospect. This town is located right on the seafront and within easy reach of the motorway and Lisbon.
195,000 euros   BOG
(£130,000) GP

Pombal   RS
Located above the beach and the ocean, this property offers stunning views and consists of six bedrooms, a heated swimming pool and a landscaped garden with waterfalls. A beautifully constructed, idyllic home.
780,000 euros   BOG
(£520,000) GP

Anceriz   RS
A stone house requiring renovation with two stone barns. Standing in 60,000m² of woodland and farmland, this property is secluded, ideal for someone seeking peace and quiet. Offering stunning views.
399,000 euros   CPP
(£266,000) GP

Coimbra & the Beiras

Arganil RS
With a stable block, swimming pool and 20,000m² of grounds, this luxury three-bedroom home offers two separate cottages and views.
450,000 euros   **CPP**
(£300,000) GP

Arganil RS
A large modern house comprising of a small office, this property is very stylish. The generous 2,000m² of land includes immaculate lawns, mature shrubs, a garage and dog kennels. The house consists of an entrance hall with a spacious dining room and a large lounge with a wood-burning fireplace and patio doors. The basement offers a bar area while the kitchen is fully fitted with all modern conveniences. There is a large bathroom with a corner bath plus four bedrooms that each open out on to a pleasant terrace with views.
225,000 euros   **CPP**
(£150,000) GP

Arganil RS
A small house located in a quiet area, this three-bedroom property has a spacious garden and lovely views. A very comfortable home.
50,000 euros   **CPP**
(£33,335) GP

Price Guide

Tomdela   RS
This traditional village house is located in a quiet village near the town of Tomdela. Offering two bedrooms, a bathroom, dining room and kitchen, this property also offers storage areas under the house and a traditional veranda. It does require some renovation work, in particular on the kitchen and bathroom, but utilities are already connected. This home would provide an excellent prospect for a buyer seeking to develop a property as it offers an ideal location for those seeking refuge from the hustle and bustle of urban life.
14,000 euros   CPP
(£9,335) GP

Tabua   RS
With grounds of 15,000m², these two ruins are ideal for any potential developer. Located close to the river, on sloping ground, this plot is only ten minutes from town and offers superb views over the countryside.
69,000 euros   PPT
(£46,000) GP

Tabua   RS
This plot of farmland includes four buildings requiring renovation standing in 40,000m². Although nearly ruined, this purchase would offer a fantastic renovation project for an attractive second home.
160,000 euros   CPP
(£106,665) GP

Tomdela   RS
A large property with barns and outbuildings, set in 40,000m² of grounds planted with fruit trees. This house requires renovation and has been neglected in recent years, therefore it requires an owner willing to develop and modernise the property. With a spacious lounge and a equally large dining room, this home has five bedrooms and a small study, which features a balcony. With a kitchen and separate scullery, this house offers spacious rooms and extensive grounds. A home full of potential.
175,000 euros   CPP
(£116,665) GP

SUBSCRIBE TO french magazine

For only £17.00 for six issues*
Over 200 pages in every issue packed with inspirational editorial and properties to buy and let

NEW! 6 ISSUE SUBSCRIPTION ONLY £17

Thinking about buying a property abroad? Not sure how to go about it or what's available in your price range? Look no further than the *mGuides* series of property buying guides; with annual updates, these are the ultimate guidebooks for the serious overseas homebuyer.

Available now: ■ France ■ Spain ■ Portugal
Coming soon: ■ Italy ■ North America ■ Greece, Turkey, Cyprus and the eastern Mediterranean

CALL THE ORDER HOTLINE: 01225 786844
*(UK price)

Want to live at a slower pace of life?

Everything from land to a Mansion.

Over 100 properties on our list.

Let us help you find your dream in

CENTRAL PORTUGAL

For more information, contact us on:

Tel: **00 351 235 728924**
or
Email: **c.portugal.p.f@clix.pt**

Price Guide

Arganil RS
A stone building requiring conversion and renovation, this property sits in 15,000m² of cultivated land and woods with its own well. Situated in a quiet area, this home is close to all amenities.
50,000 euros CPP
(£33,335) GP

Arganil RS
Close to the centre of Arganil, this townhouse offers a spacious lounge and terrace area as well as four bedrooms. With a patio and small store room, utilities are connected. Requiring some renovation.
50,000 euros CPP
(£33,335) GP

Mortagua RS
A large village property with five bedrooms, this home offers various outbuildings and a storage area under the house. With spacious grounds and on the edge of a village, this property boasts fantastic views.
125,000 euros CPP
(£83,335) GP

Nelas RS
A three-storey manor property, this home offers 15 room, a tenants' house and outbuildings. With mature gardens full of rose bushes and fruit trees, this property requires repairs, but enjoys peace and views.
330,500 euros CPP
(£220,335) GP

Arganil RS
A disused watermill ready for conversion, this property is set in 10,000m² of grounds and includes a two-storey barn ready for renovation. Requiring modernisation, this property is set in a peaceful valley.
60,000 euros CPP
(£40,000) GP

Penalva de Alva RS
Arranged over two storeys, this property requires an owner willing to renovate. Situated in a stunning position offering picturesque views over the tranquil valley, this home is an ideal, secluded rural retreat.
32,250 euros CPP
(£21,500) GP

Coimbra & the Beiras

Cavadoude   NB
These two rustic houses located close to the centre of Cavadoude require renovation. They are based in a relaxed and pastoral environment yet still within easy reach of Guarda's amenities, and its attractions.
22,500 euros   **REX**
(£15,000) GP

Linhares   RS
Located on the edge of a natural park, this property requires much attention and an owner dedicated to renovation and restoration. Affording spectacular views, this house offers its owner seclusion and peace.
4,738 euros   **REX**
(£3,160) GP

Arganil   RS
A semi-detached property located on the edge of the village, this home is well situated. Only 12 minutes from Arganil and Gois, this dwelling is set in a traditional valley village. With living space of 200m².
35,000 euros   **PPT**
(£23,335) GP

Pinheiro   NB
Newly completed, this detached property is built to a very high standard. Consisting of two bedrooms, with an open-plan lounge, diner and kitchen, this dwelling is located in a remote area, set in woodlands.
100,000 euros   **PPT**
(£66,665) GP

Mizarela   RS
Arranged over two floors, this detached property comes with an annexe but requires some renovation. Also featuring a terrace, this modern home is easily accessible for the town of Guarda and all services.
25,000 euros   **REX**
(£16,665) GP

Orgens   RS
This fully furnished apartment is situated away from the main tourist centres of the coastal regions yet is close to all local amenities. An excellent base for those who want to explore the Viseu countryside.
79,808 euros   **REX**
(£53,205) GP

Price Guide

Sarzedo   RS
An unfurnished family house located in picturesque rural surroundings, this property offers an outbuilding and three bedrooms. With a garage and storage space, this home is set in easy reach of amenities.
105,000 euros   **BAR**
(£70,000) GP

Lousã   RS
This three-bedroom cottage offers annexes and is situated in spacious, fertile grounds surrounded by countryside. Located within easy reach of Lousã's amenities and Coimbra, set close to the motorway.
80,000 euros   **PRS**
(£53,335) GP

Penacova   RS
Close to the Mondego river, these two houses are set in 5,000m² of grounds planted with fruit trees. The first house features three bedrooms while the second is smaller. Also offering a shed and storage space.
198,000 euros   **PPT**
(£132,000) GP

Tabua   RS
A modern property, this home offers three bedrooms and two bathrooms. With a large garden, the house has a dining room and well equipped, modern kitchen. The gardens are mature and well kept.
165,000 euros   **PPI**
(£110,000) GP

Santa Comba Dão   RS
This modern style house, located just off the main road, resides in spacious gardens of 10,000m². Arranged over three floors, this luxurious dwelling is secluded from views by large hedges and a fence.
220,000 euros   **PPT**
(£146,665) GP

Couto de Cima   RS
A plot of land for sale totalling 500m² near to local amenities and the motorways. Located in a tranquil area, this plot would be ideal for a new-build holiday home, away from the bustle of urban Portugal.
27,434 euros   **REX**
(£18,290) GP

Coimbra & the Beiras

Tres Postos   RS
An excellent potential renovation project, this small rustic cottage, set on a picturesque river, features two acres of land. Affording lovely views, it's an ideal location for a rural retreat while still near a town.
30,000 euros   PRS
(£20,000) GP

Vale Maceira   RS
This modern detached property has four bedrooms, two sitting rooms and two kitchens. Located near the town, this home is close to all amenities while allowing the owner to enjoy peace and quiet.
140,000 euros   PRS
(£93,335) GP

Penela   RS
Modern and stylish, this detached property boasts a generous four bedrooms and an acre of well manicured, spacious gardens leading down to a river. Located in the large town of Penela, which offers all necessary amenities, this home is easily accessible for the city of Coimbra and its many attractions, as well as for the coast and all local sports and culture facilities. Surrounded by stunning countryside and affording lovely views, this property still retains a sense of seclusion and quiet privacy, thanks to its spacious grounds.
240,000+ euros   PIR
(£160,000+) GP

Pinheiro Bordalo   RS
This rustic farmhouse is habitable but requires some renovation. Offering enormous potential as a second home, this property is well located for access to all amenities and the surrounding cultural attractions.
100,000 euros   PRS
(£66,665) GP

Ansião   NB
A luxurious five-bedroom house located on the edge of town, this property is elegant and stylish. With lovely views and a stunning garden, this home is well located for all local amenities. An excellent buy.
180,000 euros   PRS
(£120,000) GP

Price Guide

COSTA VERDE & THE NORTH

From ancient townhouses in the historic second city of Porto, to modern developments in its large towns and colonial-style villas by the coast, the Costa Verde offers buyers a clear choice between the old and the new

Price Guide

Quinta do Crasto RS

This is a unique opportunity to purchase a vineyard established in the 18th century and situated in the well known Vinho Verde wine region of the Minho. This 10-hectare vineyard is surrounded by spectacular scenery and includes a seven-bedroom villa and various outbuildings. Only 37km from Porto, approximately a 40-minute drive, this property is well located for access to amenities. An excellent proposition for the discerning buyer.
960,000 euros QUA
(£640,000) GP

Monção RS

A stunning cottage located in a rustic market town, this granite-built property is located in the foothills of a pine forest. The 600m² grounds contain fruit trees and a stream, making it ideal for nature lovers.
115,000 euros CFS
(£76,665) GP

Porto RS

This riverside mansion located in the centre of Porto is arranged over three floors with a living space of 1,000m². A unique historic property that requires interior renovation behind its protected façade.
1,600,000 euros BOG
(£1,066,665) GP

Caminha RS

A luxurious South African-style villa, Casa Olivos is perfectly located in the beautiful countryside just outside Caminha and only 6km from the beaches. It offers a peaceful environment with fantastic views and a delightful garden. Set in one hectare of grounds, this modern property has five bedrooms, two bathrooms and an office, and features a second house with a garage and one bedroom. A stunning and unique property, and a must buy.
598,000 euros IMA
(£398,665) GP

Costa Verde & the North

Monção RS
This period, granite cottage, dating from 1734, features a cobbled courtyard, orchard and BBQ area. Set in beautiful grounds of 2,000m², the gardens are completely enclosed by a stone wall. With stunning views over the surrounding countryside, this property is located only 10 minutes outside of a rural village and offers the potential owner plenty of space and an abundance of fruit trees. With one bedroom and one bathroom, this is an ideal home for those seeking retirement.
200,000 euros **CFS**
(£133,335) GP

Monção NB
A superb example of one of Portugal's prestigious manor houses, this property has been externally restored to its former glory. Requiring an owner with a passion for interior design and renovation, this unique home offers grounds of 150,000m², which include stable blocks and various outbuildings. This is a property for the more discerning owner, and an ideal property for a family holiday home. Located in the beautiful and peaceful surroundings of the Minho, an ideal rural retreat.
700,000 euros **CFS**
(£466,665) GP

Monção NB
This large bungalow with four-bedrooms offers a swimming pool and 1,450m² of ornamental gardens. With a pristine lawn and beautiful old willow tree, the gardens include electric lights and a pool changing area complete with shower cubicle. The gardens are incredibly private, surrounded by thick hedging and fencing, with a variety of bushes, shrubs and fruit trees, including apple and orange. With a garage and front sun veranda, this bungalow affords great views over the Minho valley.
290,000 euros **CFS**
(£193,335) GP

Price Guide

Monção   **RS**
A granite-built house offering plenty of living space, this property is set in grounds of 15,000m² that include a variety of outbuildings. This villa offers views over the rolling countryside, beyond its walled grounds, that are planted with chestnut trees. This is an excellent opportunity for someone seeking a property to house family and friends, or for a budding developer. This impressive home also features terraces and space for a swimming pool. and is just a ten-minute drive from Porto airport.
225,000 euros   **CFS**
(£150,000) GP

Monção   **RS**
Set in an elevated position above a small Portuguese hamlet, this granite-built cottage offers superb views over the surrounding hills. Set in a very tranquil location, this secluded property offers plenty of space to keep livestock and horses. Only 20 minutes from Porto airport, the house is set in 15,000m² of grounds featuring various outbuildings, ideal for renovation as holiday homes. An excellent rural retreat, this cottage does require renovation but would be perfect for a keen developer.
125,000 euros   **CFS**
(£83,335) GP

Monção   **NB**
Set in 6,000m² of terraced pasture land, this elevated property is built from granite and is located only ten minutes from a superb river beach. Affording fantastic views over the verdant countryside, it is in an extremely tranquil location, with only two other inhabited cottages in the area. With a cobbled driveway and terraces, the grounds also feature two barns and an old wine press. With two bedrooms and a separate basement, this spacious cottage needs some work to make it fit for habitation.
110,000 euros   **CFS**
(£73,335) GP

Costa Verde & the North

Monção   RS
This riverside property has 9,000m² of gardens that lead down towards the private slipway. The well manicured gardens are all walled or fenced, offering the property plenty of seclusion and privacy. This incredibly luxurious five-bedroom villa is just three minutes' drive from town and features patio areas and enough room to allow the installation of a tennis court and swimming pool. The three garages have ample room for several cars and a speed boat. An incredible property with great potential.
410,000 euros   **CFS**
(£273,335) GP

Monção   RS
Situated on the edge of a small rural village, this part-granite dwelling has very good access to the road network, and is only ten minutes' drive from the motorway. The property comprises a small cottage, a large garage and two outbuildings. Surrounded by terraced grounds of 5,000m², there are numerous fruit trees and field areas. Featuring a wine press and a farmhouse-style kitchen, this property affords panoramic views over the distant hills and countryside from its balcony.
185,000 euros   **CFS**
(£123,335) GP

Monção   RS
This tourism complex property is a must for the budding developer or entrepreneur. Tucked away in the corner of Portugal's 'Garden of Eden', this superb property is highly impressive. Offering quality accommodation and luxurious furnishings, this complex affords great views over the surrounding countryside. Operating throughout the year, this tourist complex has huge potential, located as it is in the stunning area of the Minho. A hugely unique opportunity and excellent prospect. A must-see.
850,000 euros   **CFS**
(£566,665) GP

Price Guide

Madeira Introduction

MADEIRA

Anyone looking for an true island paradise with a year-round temperate climate will find Madeira irresistible. There is a wide variety of property to buy here, from quaint cottages in fishing villages to upmarket apartments in purpose-built resorts

283

Price Guide

Funchal   **NB**
A four-bedroom manor house located on high ground offering stunning views over the bay and coastline of Madeira. Resting in a plot of 2,862m², this home is surrounded by beautiful woodlands.
950,000 euros   **MRS**
(£633,335) GP

Funchal   **NB**
These plots of land overlook the entrance to the Balancal Palheiro golf course. With spectacular views of the surrounding woodlands and coastline, this is an ideal location for a peaceful and tranquil home.
165,000-385,000 euros   **MRS**
(£110,000-256,665) GP

Funchal   **NB**
Located in the Balancal Golf Resort, these villas afford spectacular views over Funchal bay. Surrounded by tranquil woodland and in an area of outstanding natural beauty, these properties are built to the highest standards. These exclusive villas offer three or four bedrooms and overlook Balancal's championship golf course. Located 500m above Funchal bay, in the foothills of the mountains, these exquisite homes offer a swimming pool and 2,000m² of manicured gardens.
950,000 euros   **MRS**
(£633,335) GP

Palheiro   **NB**
Offering spectacular views over the Atlantic and the capital Funchal, these Portuguese manor houses have three or four bedrooms and boast a living area of 450m². Built using traditional methods and materials.
1,900,000 euros   **MRS**
(£1,266,665) GP

Funchal   **NB**
Set in a spacious, tranquil and wooded environment, this property offers stunning views over the coastline and the nearby area. Built in a typical Madeiran style, they have luscious surroundings.
750,000 euros   **MRS**
(£500,000) GP

MADEIRA ISLAND

Palheiro Golf

Estalagem Casa Velha do Palheiro

Balancal Palheiro Golf

A golfer's paradise high above the Bay of Funchal, truly one of Europe's most spectacular courses.

The country house hotel set within the famous original Gardens of Palheiro - a haven of peace for those who appreciate a privileged way of life.

Exclusive real estate bordering the Palheiro Golf course with stunning views of Funchal and the Atlantic.

Sociedade Turística Palheiro Golfe, S.A

Tel: + 351 291 792 116
Fax: + 351 291 792 456
www.palheirogolf.com
email: info@palheirogolf.com

Sociedade Turística Palheiro Ferreiro, S.A

Tel: + 351 291 790 350
Fax: + 351 291 794 925
www.casa-velha.com
email: info@casa-velha.com

Sociedade Imobiliária Balancal, S.A

Tel: + 351 291 795 161
Fax: + 351 291 795 150
www.madeira-real-estate.com
email: balancal@mail.telepac.pt

Price Guide

Canico   NB
This private condominium with sea views is currently under construction. Easily accessible for the airport, two golf courses and all the amenities of Funchal, this is an ideal property for a holiday or permanent home.
105,000+ euros   <u>QUA</u>
(£70,000+) GP

Funchal   NB
This unique residential complex is under construction and offers three-bedroom apartments in one of Funchal's most prestigious developments. With a high quality finish, this is ideal for a second home.
165,000+ euros   <u>QUA</u>
(£110,000+) GP

Funchal   RS
Once a monk's retreat, this 300-year-old property has been traditionally converted into a two-bedroom *quinta*. Commanding panoramic views over the sea, it is only a short stroll from the traditional village square and just a short bus ride into Funchal centre. Close to all the amenities and distractions Funchal has to offer, this property is blissfully secluded and its verdant gardens and comfortable terrace along with its stunning views make it a highly attractive potential purchase.
375,000 euros   <u>BOG</u>
(£250,000) GP

Arco da Calheta   NB
A two-bedroom country villa, this property is located at the top of the Arco da Calheta valley offering incredible views over the entire district and the sea. Perfect as a low-maintenance, rural holiday home.
109,500 euros   <u>QUA</u>
(£73,000) GP

Santa Cruz   NB
These three-bedroom apartments offer attractive surroundings, a small garden and a balcony affording stunning views. This large town is located on Madeira's east coast and offers all amenities.
225,000 euros   <u>VIR</u>
(£150,000) GP

Madeira

Prazeres   RS
Located in Calheta, near the coastline, with easy access to the main road networks, this villa is close to all amenities. The property offers a living space of 140m^2 and is set in 750m^2 of stunning grounds. With well manicured and mature gardens, this modern property has potential to be an ideal holiday home. Set on the edge of the Parque Natural, this home is extremely welcoming and perfect for those who desire a more relaxing atmosphere, close to nature and Madeira's sandy coastline.
235,000 euros   CNS
(£156,665) GP

Garajāu   RS
This modern home offers four bedrooms, in a hillside situation, on the coastline close to Funchal. Offering a living space of 400m^2, this comfortable villa is situated in 700m^2 of mature gardens and would make an ideal holiday home. With stunning views, which can be enjoyed from the balcony and large patio doors, it is perfect for those who seek a restful environment. With a generously spacious interior, the rooms are light and airy. This home is fully fit for habitation. An excellent site.
749,000 euros   CNS
(£499,335) GP

Reis Magos   RS
This pretty two-bedroom villa is close to the beach and not far from all the amenities that Funchal offers. With a splendid outlook, this property is set in 950m^2 of well manicured, mature gardens, offering great potential to keen green-fingered buyers. The property benefits from 180m^2 of living space and a terrace, and as it is situated only 15 minutes from two golf courses and seven minutes from the airport, it is easily accessible. The villa also boasts a second property within the grounds
526,000 euros   CNS
(£350,665) GP

Price Guide

Funchal   RS

Located in the Funchal area of Madeira, in the small suburb of Monte, this modern property with a futuristic design offers the buyer spacious rooms and a light and airy environment. With a living space of 300m^2 and residing in mature, neat gardens of 350m^2, this home enjoys attractive views and features a patio. With a generously sized garage and the benefit of private parking, this property offers three bedrooms and a roomy living area. Ideal for a permanent property and located in an ideal situation.
325,000 euros   <u>CNS</u>
(£216,665) GP

Funchal   RS

A four-bedroom villa located in São Goncalo. Offering a living space of 470m^2, this is a spacious property with well tended gardens.
576,000 euros   <u>CNS</u>
(£384,000) GP

Calheta   RS

Located on the west coast of Madeira, this renovated country cottage is built from stone and features attractive wooden shutters. Sold fully furnished, this property has one bedroom and would be ideal for a retirement home or a couple's holiday home. This cosy cottage has a traditional interior and is accessible for the motorway network. Tucked away in one of Madeira's quieter areas, this is a truly excellent opportunity set on the edge of the Parque Natural. A tranquil and beautiful spot.
115,000 euros   <u>CNS</u>
(£76,665) GP

Purchasing a home in Madeira is a lot easier when you know how...

...and we do!

CALDEIRA & STEVENSON

With 15 years' experience as agents on the Island, we have assisted literally hundreds of people in realizing their dream of having a Place in the Sun.

We will find you your dream property in Madeira, from our listings and in conjunction with the network of agents that we work with.

Should you choose to build your own home, we can assist you in all stages of design, planning permissions, project management, as well as decorating.

CALDEIRA & STEVENSON REAL ESTATE

Rua da Carreira 92, 9000-042 Funchal Madeira, PORTUGAL

Tel: **00351 291 228435** Fax: **00351 291 220206**

Email: **mp11c@mail.telepac.pt**

www.caldeirastevenson.com

Price Guide

Funchal   **RS**
A stunning, modern villa located in the environs of Funchal and close to all attractions and amenities. Affording lovely sea views and offering three bedrooms, this property has lovely, mature gardens of 800m² planted with exotic flora. The home offers a living space of 250m² with spacious and well designed rooms. Although positioned on the outskirts of the city, this is an ideal property for those seeking a quiet, relaxed environment for their second home, as it has a tranquil feel.
570,000 euros   **PIR**
(£380,000) GP

Funchal   **RS**
This luxurious four-bedroom villa has fantastic views and is set in manicured grounds of 1,180m² featuring a swimming pool.
1,250,000 euros   **CNS**
(£833,335) GP

Funchal   **RS**
Located in the suburb of Boeiro, this property is extremely well located for Funchal's services and diversions. With a living space of 200m², this villa has extensive, well maintained gardens. It also boasts a collection of covered and open terraces where the owner can enjoy open-air meals and barbecues, and experience the wonderful panoramic views. With four bedrooms and a host of spacious rooms, this property also has a garage and is ideal as a permanent property or holiday home.
300,000 euros   **CNS**
(£200,000) GP

Madeira

Funchal   **RS**
Located in Chao da Loba, this stylish and modern villa offers well manicured, spacious and mature gardens of 2,115m². With a large terrace affording splendid views over Funchal and the sea, this property has plenty of living space. Truly luxurious and featuring four bedrooms, this is a residence for the more discerning buyer. Excellent for those seeking a retirement home in the sun, this beautifully appointed house is also well located for all the capital's amenities and the sandy coastline.
998,000 euros   **CNS**
(£665,335) GP

Funchal   **NB**
In the suburb of Pilar, this four-bedroom villa has a living space of 460m². With a large tidy garden and with great access to amenities.
575,000 euros   **CNS**
(£383,335) GP

Ribeira Brava   **RS**
Located in the well developed town of Ribeira Brava, this two-bedroom villa affords fantastic views over the coastline and is close to all services and the main road network. With balconies on each floor, this is an ideal coastal property from which the whole family can enjoy the dynamic island of Madeira and all its attractions. With a built area of 190m², the rooms are spacious and light. The property enjoys a neat garden of 210m² and private parking with a garage available. A stylish and modern residence
210,000 euros   **CNS**
(£140,000) GP

Price Guide

Funchal   RS
With extensive gardens of 1,300m², this recently built villa property has a living space of 360m² and is surrounded by greenery. Offering three bedrooms, this property has good access to all main roads and is close to all the necessary amenities. Within easy reach of Funchal and its beaches and attractions, this is an excellent location for a holiday home, being extremely spacious and comfortable. A fairly new and modern property, it enjoys all utilities and modern conveniences. With impressive views of the area.
325,000 euros   CNS
(£216,665) GP

Estreito da Calheta   RS
With a living area of 380m², this modern and chic villa is built on high ground and enjoys stunning views across the surrounding countryside. Located on the island's west coast, this home is set in something of a secluded area but is close to most main access routes and has amenities nearby. With three bedrooms and set in pleasant, well manicured grounds of 570m², this property enjoys day-round sunshine, thanks to its lofty position. With a terrace area and a balcony, it is a perfect home.
275,000 euros   CNS
(£183,335) GP

Arco da Calheta   RS
Offering a swimming pool and gardens of 620m², this two-bedroom property has a living space of 120m². Situated on the west coast and beautifully located on the edge of the Parque Natural, this is a must for those who love being in the countryside. Near the sea and close to all services, this area has a good road network. With splendid views due to its elevated situation, this villa features a terrace area where the owner can enjoy outdoor meals and peaceful evenings. A comfortable home.
160,000 euros   CNS
(£106,665) GP

NO.1 FOR SPANISH LIFESTYLE AND PROPERTY

TURN YOUR SPANISH DREAM INTO REALITY

If you're thinking about buying property in Spain and need extra help in deciding where or how to get started, and a guiding hand through the whole process, you'll be keen to check out our sister publications

SPANISH PROPERTY BUYING GUIDE 2004

Over 350 pages, this is the definitive guide to all aspects of buying property in Spain. It includes:

- Price Guide to more than 1400 properties
- New builds
- Re-sales
- Businesses
- Profiles of the history, culture, cuisine and idiosyncrasies of each region of Spain
- Glossary of terms
- Index of agents specialising in the Spanish market
- Real world case studies – learn from other people's experiences
- Extensive listing of regional and national contacts, from estate agents to solicitors, tradesmen and property managers
- Practical expert advice

SPANISH MAGAZINE

Available at all leading newsagents, Spanish magazine is the leading magazine for anyone interested in Spain and owning property in Spain. As well as travel and cultural features, Spanish Magazine will offer:

- Regional guides
- City guides
- Real life stories of people like you who are already living their dream of owning a home in Spain
- Expert legal advice
- Expert financial advice
- A massive selection of dream homes for sale

REAL LIVES ■ REAL HOMES ■ REAL SPAIN

CALL: 01225 786850

Merricks Media

Subscriptions Department, Merricks Media Ltd, Charlotte House, Charlotte Street, Bath BA1 2NE Tel. 01225 786 800 Email: info@merricksmedia.co.uk

INDEX OF AGENTS

Key to the three-letter codes identifying the agents, based both in Britain and Portugal, whose properties are featured in the Price Guide

Index of Agents

CODE	NAME & ADDRESS	CONTACT DETAILS
AGI	**Agimoura Imobiliaria LDA** Rua Dunfermline Edificio Mar do Sul, Loja T Valmangude Areias São João 8200 Albufeira Portugal	Tel: +351 289 592609 Fax:+351 289 572659
AQU	**Aquarius Properties.** Somerton Cross Avenue Blackrock Co Dublin Ireland	Tel: +353 127 82900 Fax:+353 170 60414
ARY	**Algarve Realty** Rua 25 de Abril 7 R/C 8300 - 184 Silves Portugal	Tel: +351 952 502445 Fax: +351 282 442471
BAR	**Bart Binnema Projectos** Rua Oliveira Matos 16 1º 3300-062 Arganil Portugal	Tel: +351 235 205245
BOG	**Bougainvillea Properties** Barreiras Brancas, 8100-227 Loulé Portugal	Tel: 351 289 413199
CFS	**North Portugal Estate Sales** Quinta do Regueiro Bogadela Barbeita 4950-044 Moncao Alto Minho Portugal	Tel: +351 251 531251
CLA	**Classic & Antique** Rua do Argel 10 8000-215 Faro Portugal	Tel: +351 289 825272 Fax: +351 289 825275
CNS	**Caldeira and Stevenson** Rua da Carreira 92 9000-042 Funchal Madeira Portugal	Tel: +351 291 228435
CPP	**Central Portugal Property Finders** Salguerial 3305-189 Coja Portugal	Tel: +351 235 728924

Price Guide

CODE	NAME & ADDRESS	CONTACT DETAILS
DHA	**David Headland Associates** 67 Wellingborough Road Rushden Northants NN10 9YG.	Tel: 01933 353333
ESG	**Esaguy Propriesdades Lda** Avenida 25 de Abril, N°.6 7670-250 Ourique Alentejo Portugal	Tel: +351 286 516124 Fax: +351 286 516185
EUV	**European Villa Solutions** 618 New Market Road Cambridge CB5 8LP	Tel: 01223 514241
FIS	**Finespo** Rua do Sol 4 8200-448 Guia Albufeira Portugal	Tel: +351 289 560261 Fax: +351 289 560261
FLO	**Parque da Floresta** Vale du Poco Budens Portugal	Tel: +351 282 690000 Fax: +351 282 690011
HIL	**John Hill** Av 5 de Outubro 20 8135 - 101 Almancil Portugal	Tel: +351 289 395735 Fax: +351 289 397212
IMA	**Imatico LDA** Av. Manuel Remigio Ed. Palmar 2450-160 Nazaré Portugal	Tel: +351 262 551552 Fax: +351 262 551501
JOS	**Jose Rogado** Passeio das Garças Lote 2BR/C B 1990-395 Moscavise Portugal	Tel: +351 967 014786
KGV	**KG Villas** Apartado 3006 8135-901 Almancil Portugal	Tel: +351 289 394780 Fax: +351 289 394125
LAN	**Landmark** Avenida Duarte Pacheco 226 8135-104 Almancil Portugal	Tel:+351 289 393848 Fax: +351 289 395249

Index of Agents

CODE	NAME & ADDRESS	CONTACT DETAILS
MAC	**MacKenzie Real Estate** Loja 1B, Bloco B Marina Plaza 8135 Vilamoura Algarve Portugal	Tel: +351 289 315784 Mobile: +351 289 395249
MRS	**Sociedade Imobiliária Balancal** Sitio du Balancal São Gonçalo P9050-296 Funchal Maderia Portugal	Tel: +351 291 795161 Fax: +351 289 395249
NLI	**Nulita da Quinta** Rua de Dunfermiline Poenta Comercial Loja 4 Areias São João 8200 Albufeira Portugal	Tel: +351 289 586540 Fax: +351 289 587374
NON	**Sociedade de Mediaçao Imobiliária LDA** Parque de Moinho Lote 1B Loja D 8600-719 Lagos Portugal	Tel: +351 282 764771
NUB	**Numero Urbano** Portal de Vilamoura 8125-017 Vilamoura Portugal	Tel: +351 289 310260
PAR	**Paula Aco Real Estate LDA** Bourganvila Plaza 34, 1 Quinta du Lago 8135-013 Almancil Portugal	Tel: +351 289 392350
PPI	**Premier Properties International** Great Street Norton sub Hamdon Somerset TA14 6SG	Tel: 01935 881199
PPT	**Properties of Portugal Ltd** Quinta das Latas Fruimes 3360 Penacova Portugal	Tel: 01373 469955 Tel: +351 239 476344

Price Guide

CODE	NAME & ADDRESS	CONTACT DETAILS
QUA	**Quadrant Overseas Property Services** 50 Brackendale Road Camberley Surrey GU15 2JR	Tel: 01276 507513
QUI	**Quinta Property** Apartado 3730 8135-909 Almancil Portugal	Tel: +351 289 396073
RAI	**Rainbow Estates** 45 Gower Street London WC1E 6NA	Tel: 0207 637 4805 Fax: 0207 580 2067
REK	**ReKantu's ao Sol** Av. 5 de Outubro, 278 8135-103 Almancil Algarve Portugal	Tel: +351 289 393960 Fax: +351 289 292987
REN	**Rentavila** Rua Marques Leal Pancada 24 2750-430 Cascais Portugal	Tel: +351 214 827075 Fax: +351 917 327188
REX	**Remax** Rua do Miradouro 6 2720-376 Alfragide Portugal	Tel: +351 214 702200 Fax: +351 214 702200
ROS	**Rosario Busch** Bouganvilia Plaza 46 Quinta da Lago 8135-013 Almancil Portugal	Tel: +351 289 392065
RUT	**Country Homes Portugal** Alisabethgaarde 52 1403 KB Bussum Netherlands	Tel: +351 356 918418
SCM	**S C Med** Rua Alfredo Keil Edificio 5, Loja 3 8400-328 Lagos Portugal	Tel: +351 282 343348

Index of Agents

CODE	NAME & ADDRESS	CONTACT DETAILS
SEL	**Select Resorts** 2nd Floor Old Generator House Bourne Valley Road Poole Dorset BH12 1DZ	Tel: 01202 786490 Fax: 01202 763615
SLV	**Silver Holidays** Rua do Brazil Casa Italiana, Loja 5 8125-079 Vilamoura Portugal	Tel: +351 289 314312 Fax: +351 289 314260
SOT	**Sotheby's International Realty** Apartado 2116 Quinta da Lago 8135-024 Almancil Algarve Portugal	Tel: +351 289 392780 Fax: +351 289 392047
SUL	**Sulgar Lda** Quinta da Praia Lote 4 Loja 7 8500 Alvor Portima Portugal	Tel: +351 282 458062 Fax: +351 282 458063
SUS	**Sunseaker** Rua Castelo dos Governadores 66 8600-563 Lagos Portugal	Tel: 0871 733 1385 Tel: +351 282 763490
VER	**Vernon** Rua Porodobarro 1 Praiado Carvodeiro 8400 Lagos Portugal	Tel: +351 282 357109
VIR	**Vieiranima Ltd** Centro Comercial Monumental Lido 1o, Loja 17 9000-101 Funchal	Tel: +351 291 765023 Mobile: +351 967 052977
VSE	**Villa Search Lda** Vale da Azinheira, Lote 58a, Loja G Albufeira 8200 Algarve	Tel: +351 289 508073
WCH	**World Class Homes** 22 High Street Wheathampstead Herts AL4 8AA	Tel: 01582 832001 Fax: 01582 831071

■ The Price Guide

DIRECTORY

Listings of businesses offering services to both the buyers and owners of property in Portugal

Accountants	302
Air Conditioning	302
Architects	302
Banks and Building Societies	302
Builders and Decorators	303
Building Supplies	304
Business Advice	304
Car Care	304
Car Hire	304
Car Sales	305
Carpenters	305
Computer Care	305
Currency Converters	305
Electricians	306
Financial Services	306
Funeral Services	307
Gardeners	307
Insurance	308

The Directory

Interior Decorators	308
Language Services	308
Legal Services	308
Maids and Domestic Services	310
Medical Services	310
Opticians	310
Pet Transportation	310
Plumbing and Central Heating	311
Property Management	311
Removals	311
Supervisory Bodies	312
Swimming Pools	312
Tax Specialists	312
Telephone Services	313
Travel	313
TV and Satellite	313
Utilities	314
Vets	314

Directory

Accountants

AJL
Praceta Simoes Almeida
Junior 6-r/c
Dt° Abraao
2745-332 Quelez
+351 214 377112

Artur Lino Silva
Rua St Luzia 58
1-C Pompal
3100-483 Pompal
+351 236 216702
linosilva@mail.telepac.pt

Carlos Jose PA Sousa
Avenida Sao Pedro lote A-3
1 Pontinha
1675-169 Pontinha
+351 214 790772

Carlos Seabra
Rua Serpa Pinto 127
9 Paredes
4580 Parades
+351 255 785474

Contita
Avenida 24 1019
2-s G Espinho
4500-201 Espinho
+351 227 319808
contita@netcabo.pt

Daniela MLF Pinho Teles
Avenida Franca 72
2-s C Porto
4050-275 Porto
+351 226 000153
info@danielateles.com.pt

Eurovia
Avenida Almirante Gago
Coutinho 87
1700 Lisbon
+351 218 429 480

Air Conditioning

Afonso Sergio
Rua Edith Cavell 12-A
1900 Lisbon
+351 218 149435

Arsado Lda
Rua Mouzinho Albuquerque
3-loja C
2910 719 Setubal
+351 265 708130
arsado@sapo.pt

Coolair International Lda
Beloura Office Park
Rua Centro Empresarial
Edificio 6
Piso 1
2170-444 Sintra
+351 210 029241
c.I@netcabo.pt

Efcis
Rua Enrique Paeva Couaero
15-17
Vanda Nova
2700 Amadora
+351 214 999000

Electrofrio
Zona Urbanizacoa 3 lote 8-3-r/c-E
7050-275 Montemor o Novo
+351 266 893498

Frifafe
Av Brasil R/C 47 Bl B
4820 Fafe
+351 253 598685
frifafe@mail.telepac.pt

Frigicoll
Rua Nova S. Crispim 2471 Dt°
4000 Porto
+351 228 300394

Mister Cool
Rua Mouzzimbo de
Albufuertue, 49
Mato Serrao
Praia do Carvoeiro
Lagos
+351 282 357292
Mobile: +351 917 175818
mistercool_telmorodrigues@hotmail.com

Oliveira e Ribeiro Lda
Rua Eca de Queiros
6 Serra da Silveira
2605-135 Belas
+351 214 367262
orl_@hotmail.com

Pinto and Cruz Lda
Rua Eng Ferreiras Dias 469
4100 Porto
+351 226 100901

SACL
Vale de Lousas EN 125
8365-027 Alcantarilha
+351 282 314190
sacl@telepac.pt

Sistavac Sistemas Acquecimento
Rua Monte dos Pipos
Armazem 7
4460 Guifoes
+351 229 533202

Techniclima
Avenida Duque de Loule 28
2795 Linda a Velha
+351 214 147360
techniclima@mail.telepac.pt

Ventilarco
Avenida Almirante Gago
Coutinho126
1749-043 Lisbon
+351 218 436630

Architects

Aida Goncalves Pen
Rua D. Manuel I
Predio Pena-r/c
D Pontinha
1675-230 Pontinha
+351 962 515106
aidagoncalves@vizzavi.pt

Alexandra Schiappa
Rua Filipe Folque 33
1 Lisbon
1050-111 Lisbon
+351 213 158843
alex.schiappa@mail.telepac.pt

Algarlinea
Rua D. Dingo de Sousa
lote 20
cv-D Lagos
8600-571 Lagos
+351 282 768025

Aloteico
Rua Paio Galvao 1
2-s-A Guimaraes
+351 253 512540
atico.lda@clix.pt

Antonio M Latino Tavares
Travessa Joao Deus 10
1200-235 Lisbon
+351 213 421835

Arquitraco
Calcada Tapada 143
1300-541 Lisbon
+351 213 610250
arquitraco@arquitraco.pt

Atelier Oscar Santos
Avenida Conde Valbom 71
1050-207 Lisbon
+351 217 934825
aos.atelier@netcabo.pt

Carlos Alberto Gomes
Rua Ramiro Ferrao 26 r/c
Cova de Predade
2800-503 Almada
+351 212 748073
carlos.a.gomas@netcabo.pt

GIAD Gabriela Iglesias
AP Pinhal da Falesia
Pinhal do Concelho
8200-380 Albufeira
+352 289 502408
giad.arge.des@mail.telepac.pt

Goncalo Byrne
Rua Escola Politecnica 285
1250-101 Lisbon
+351 213 883119
gbyrne@mail.telepac.pt

Machado Perry and Braganca
Rua Embaixador 119
1600-216 Lisbon
+351 213 617910
mpb.arq@netcabo.pt

Ponto
Travessa Fiuza 39 - pt 5
1300-249 Lisbon
+351 213 660912
pontoi@mail.telepac.pt

Risco
Travessa Conde Ponte 16-A
1300-141 Lisbon
+351 213 610420
risco@risco.org

Sua Kay Arquitectos
Rua D. Luis 13 5 D
1200-149 Lisbon
+351 213 931960

Banks and Building Societies

Abbey National
Edificio Co de Rosa r/c Esq.
EN 125 Quatro Estrades
8125 Quarteira
Portugal
+351 289 393481

Directory

ABN Amro Bank
Avenida Da Liberdade
131 –5°
1269-036 Lisbon
+351 213 211800

Banco Alves Ribeiro S.A.
Avenida Eng. Duarte Pacheco
Torre 1, 11°
1070-101 Lisbon
+351 213 821700

Banco Atlantico S.A.
Avenida Dusque de Avila 185 A
1050-082 Lisbon
+351 213 170150

Banco Bilbao Vizcaya
Avenida Da Liberdade 222
1250 Lisbon
+351 213 117200

Banco Cetelem
Sa Sucursal
Avenida Dos Combatentes
43-12
Lisbon
+351 217 215800

Banco Chemical Finance S.A.
Rua Barata Salgueiro 33
Lisbon
+351 213 137300

Banco Comercial Dos Acores S.A.
Rua Doctor Jose Bruno
Tararros Carrero
9500-119 Panta Delegada
+351 296 629070
www.bca.pt

Banco de Investimento Global S.A.
Praca Duque de Saldanha
N. 1-8
Lisbon
+351 213 305300

Banco de Investimento Imobiliario
Rua Augusta 62/74
Lisbon
+351 213 211000

Banco de Negocios Argentaria S.A.
Rua Soeiro Pereira Gomes
lote 1-2
1600 - 198 Lisbon
+351 21 792 5300

Banco de Portugal
Rua do Ouro 27
1110-150 Lisbon
+351 213 130000

Banco Espirito Santo de Investimento
Rua Alexandre Herculano 38
1269-161 Lisbon
+351 213 196900

Banco Finantia S.A.
Rua General Firmino
Miguel 5, 1°
1600 Lisbon
+351 217 202000

Banco Internacional de Credito
Avenida Fontes Pereira de
Melo 27
1000 Tras
1050 Lisbon
+351 213 157135

Banco Madesant - Sociedad Unipessoal
Avenida Arriaga 73, 2°
Sala 211
9000-070 Funchal
+351 291 203110

Banco Mello de Investimentos
Rua Alexandre Herculano 50
4/5
Lisbon
+351 213 125000

Banco Nacional Uloteramarino S.A.
Avenida 5 de Outubro 175
Lisbon
+351 217 930112

Banco Pinto & Sotto Mayor S.A.
Rua do Ouro 28
Lisbon
+351 217 991300

Banco Portugeus Do Atlantico
Praca D. Joao 1 28
4000 Porto
+351 222 072000

Banco Portugues de Investimento
Rua Tenente Valadim 2-4
Porto
+351 226 073100

Banco Privado Portugues S.A.
Rua Mouzinho da Silveira 12
Lisbon
+351 213 137000

Banco Trotta & Acores S.A.
Rua do Ouro 88
1100-03 Lisbon
+351 213 211500

Banco Internacional do Funchal S.A.
Rua de Joao Tavira 30
5004 - 509 Funchal
+351 291 2077000

Banque PSA Finance Holding
Rua General Firmino Miguel
3-8
Lisbon
+351 217 200219

Barclays Bank Plc
Avenida Da Republica 50-2
1050 Lisbon
+351 217 911100

BPI
Centro EmpRua
Torres de Lisbon
Torre E - 14°B
+351 226 088438

BPN - Banco Portugues de Negocios S.A.
Avenida Da Franca 680/708
4200 Porto
+351 228 341900

Caixo Geral De Depositos
Rua Laura Alves 7, 1°
1050-053 Lisbon
+351 217 927555

CENTRAL - Banco de Investimento S.A.
Rua Castilho 233
1050-185 Lisbon
+351 213 197600

Citibank Portugal S.A.
Rua Barata Salgueiro 30-4
6056 Lisbon
+351 213 116300

Credifin - Banco de Credito ao Consumo
Rua do Pinheiro Manso
N.662
4000 Porto
+351 226 150121

Credito Lyonnais Portugal S.A.
Avenida Duque Avila
1050 Lisbon
+351 213 190010

Credito Predial Portugues S.A.
Rua Augusta 237
Avenida Duque Avila
Lisbon
+351 213 123600

Deutsche Bank (Portugal) S.A.
Rua Castilho 20
Lisbon
+351 213 111200

FCE Bank plc
Rua Araugo 2, 6°
1250-195 Lisbon
+351 213 182100

Finibanco S.A.
Rua Julio Dinis 157
4050-323 Porto
+351 226 000725

Generale Bank
Rua Alexandre Herculano 50,
6°
1250-011 Lisbon
+351 213 139300

Interbanco S.A
Rua Castilho 2,
1250 073 Lisbon
+351 213 176500

Builders and Decorators

German Master-Mason
Urbanisation Quinta Santo
Antonio
lote B-21
loja 2
8600-315 Lagos
+351 964 891267

Directory

Matas Decoracoes Lda
188-B-r/c loja A Estrada
Monumental
Funchal
+351 291 763117

Never paint again
Avenida De Outobro 100-1
Dt° B
Apartado 3089
8135 Almancil
+351 289 397632

New Houses and Renovations
Vale da Igreja
Odaira
8600-257 Lagos
+351 282 798995

Builders Supplies

JAntonio Teixeira
Avenida Fernao Magalhaes 1122
4300 Porto
Portugal
+351 225 104728

Canalcentro
Parque Industrial Charneca do Bailadouro
Pousos
2410-211 Leira
+351 244 800160

Desibanho Com. Materiais Construcao
Est.Velha de Talaide
2775 Parede
Portugal
+351 214 210634

Drogaria Padinho Lda
Rua Jose Martins Maia 45
4480-854 Vilar de Pinheiro
Portugal
+351 229 272370

Ferraz ans Marques Lda
Rua Dalgreja Velha 400
4465 Sao Mamede de Infesta
Portugal
+351 229 412174

Heideiros Jorge Augusto Luz Lda
Avenida5 de Outubro 59 -R/C
2900 Setubal
Portugal
+351 265 524259

Jose Manuel Santos and Filhos Lda
largo Do Bom Retiro 17
4730 Vila Verde
Portugal
+351 253 311138

Jose Oliveira Nogueira and Filhos Lda
Rua Gil.Vicente 2
4800 Guimaraes
Portugal
+351 253 512545

Largiro
Rua de Trigueiros Martel lote 1 E 2 - Cave
2685 Sacavem
Portugal
+351 219 409950

Lugarde
Sitio do Carmo
8400-405 Lagos
Portugal
+351 968 924158
ip226536@ip.pt

Navalho
Avenida Eng. Arantesde Oliveira1-1 Esq
1900 Lisbon
Portugal
+351 218 08619

Pichelaria Mouzinho Lda
Praca D, Mana 1524
4760-111 V.N. Famalicao
Portugal
+351 252 501550
Fax +351 252 312907

Porfite
Rua do Outeiro 280 lote 3
4470 Moreira Mai
Portugal
+351 229 410583

Tergom
Avenida Do Brasil 149 A/C
Apartado 50213
1706 Lisbon
Portugal
+351 218 431400

Business Advice

Associacao Comercial de Lisbon
Camara de Comercio
Rua das Portas de Santo Antao 89
1194 Lisbon Codex
+351 213 427179
Fax: +351 213 424304

Atlelier do Sul
Esplanada da Sta.Maria
8100-070 Boliqueime
+351 289 363340
Mob; 07941 534697
Fax: +351 289 366439
fred.phillips@atelierdosul.com

Cat Video Systems
Fir Tree House
40 Maloteings Road
Brightlingsea
Colchester
CO7 0RG
01206 305018
Fax: 01206 307098
info@cat-video.co.uk

ICEP Portuguese Trade and Tourism Office
2nd Floor
22-25a Sackville Street
London
W1S 3LY
0207 4941517
Fax: 0207 4941868
tourism@portugaloffice.org.uk

Portuguese Chamber of Commerce
1st Floor
22/25a Sackville Street
London
W1S 3DR
0207 4941844
Fax: 0207 4941822

Car Care

Auto Ourique
Rua Sao Goncalo de Lagos 15-8000 Faro
+351 289 898890
autoorique@mail.telepac.pt

AV Rent a car
8365 Armacao
Lagos de Pria 13
8365 Amacáode Bera
+351 282 315700
avrentacar@netvisao.pt

Escola de Conducao Tome
Pedrode Santarem 130 E
2000 -Santarem
+351 243 332936
ccatome@mail.telepac.pt

Grancoop
Avenida Joao Crisostomo 66 - 1D
1000- Lisbon
Portugal
+351 213 535263

Ensino conducao Moderna
Rua Marquesa Alorna 26 -1D
1700- Lisbon
+351 218 472105

Car Hire

Auto Europe
Kings Court
Earl Grey Way
Royal Quays
North Shields
Tyne and Wear
NE29 6AR
0800 1696414

Alamo II
Edificio Atlantico
Avenida Infante D. Henrique
8900 Monte Gordo
Algarve
+351 281 513960
alamo@alamo-rentacaRuapt

Alamo-Rent a car
Miraparque
Acoteis
8200 Albufeira
+35 289 502052
alamo.rentacar@mail.telepac.pt

Avis Rent-a-car
08700 100287

Bolicar
8125 Vilamoura
Algarve
+351 289 322948

Directory

Bravotur
Mercado de Areias de
Sao Joao
Bloco M 1° P/7
8200 Albufeira
+351 289 542410
info@bravotuRuacom

Easy Autos
1 High Street
Twyford
Reading
RG10 9AB
08700 540203

Holiday Autos
Holiday Autos House
Pembroke Broadway
Camberley
Surrey
GU15 3XD
0870 400441

Mudarent
Rua da Silva 18D
8800-331 Tavira
+351 281 321599

Pandacar
Edificio Oura Village
loja 3
Areias de Sao Joao
8200 Albufeira
+351 289 513057

Rentauto
Edifcio Francisco
8125 Quarteria
Faro
+351 289 310100
headoffice@rentauto.pt

Scooterrent
Rua do Bocage126A
8000-297 Faro
+351 289 818530

**Skycars International
loted**
Monument House
215 Marsh Lane
Pinner
Middlesex
HA5 5NE
02084 296460

World Algarve Rent-a-car
Parque de Campismo de
Albufeira
8200-555 Albufeira
0800 3896623
worldalgarverentacar@clix.pt

Car Sales

Auto Zarco
Rua Nova do Pico de Sao
Joao
2004-501 Funchal
+351 291 743421

C.I.A.M
Ruados Ferreiros 154
9000 Funchal
+351 291 230519
Fax: +351 291 221277

Carpenters

Quimar
Avenida Elias Garcias 20 C e
48 - B
1000 Lisbon
+351 217 970832

Computer Care

Betalogica
Leite de Vasconcelos 1A
1170 - Lisbon
+351 218 152410
betalogica@mail.telepac.pt

BZI
Rua Dr Alberto Souto N46
3800 Aveiro
+351 234 378940
biz'mail.telepac.pt

Cimsoft
Rua Constituicao 656
Sala 202
4100-194-Porto
+351 225 550962
geral@cimsoft.pt
www.cimsoft.pt

Dualinfor
Rua Major Joao Gomes
lote 32, R/c - C
2640-491 Mafra
+351 261 814043
dualinfor@mail.pt

Folio
Rua TomasRibeiro 510
4- Sala 42
4450-295 Matosinhos
+351 229 385206
folio.david@mail.telepac.pt

Ifhenelse Lda
Avenida 25 de Abril
25- C.C.Pindo-Douce loja 14
2795 Linda-a-Velha
+351 214 155128
info@ite.pt

Inforarte
Rua Padre David Neto N3
Alvor
8500 - Portimão
+351 282 458194
estudio@inforarte.pt

Lusorede
Avenida Republica 90
Galeria 1
1600 -200 Lisbon
+351 217 991060
geral@lusorede.pt

Microjovem
Rua de Alpiarca 27-29
2080-Almeirim
+351 243 593867
microjovem@mail.telepact.pt

Micro Computer World
Est. Circunvalacao Armz.
A/B/C
2795 Linda a Velha
+351 214 246868

Muloteimix
RuaMaria Lamas 275
2720 - Damaia Amadora
+351 214 905610
muloteimix.ac@netc.pt

RFB Microelectronica Lda
Rua da Liberdade
lote 3 - 1 Dt°
Vale Pequeno
1675-293-Pontinha
+351 214 784206
rfb@mail.telepac.pt

Sisinfo
Rua Entra Venidas, 848
4535-312 Pacos de Brandao
+351 227 470450
sisinfo@yahoo.com

SPR
Urb.Massama Norte
lote 151- 5 Esq
2745 Quelu Massama
+351 214 382227
spRuainfor@mail.telepac.pt

Sufico Lda
Rua Jose Branquinho 183 R/C
Esq
3510 Viseu
+351 232 415445
info@sufico.pt

T.I. Tecnologia Informatica
Praceta das Descobertas 8
1675 Potinha
+351 214 781590
tecnologia@mail.telepac.pt

TMS
Rua dos Bragas 300, 1 Dt°
4050 Porto
+351 223 389605
jcfidalgo@mail.telepac.pt

Viseusoft
Rua Candido dos Reis 15
3510 - Viseu
+351 232 422394
geral@viseusoft.pt

X64 Lda
Rua Pedro Homen de
Melo 55
4100-Porto
+351 226 169632
info@x64.com
http://x64.com

Currency Converters

**ACV Agencia de Cambios
de Vilamoura Lda**
Avenida Tivoli Ed Algamar
loja 11
Vilamoura
8125-410 Quarteira
+351 289 312049

**Agencia de Cambios
Central Lda**
Avenida Luisa Todi 226-r/c
2900-452 Setubal
+351 265 548040
agicentral@vizzavi.pt

Directory

Areanet
Torre Medronheira loja 3
8200-370 Albufeira
+351 289 502277

Comturis-Comunicacoes Turisticas Lda
Rua Silva Lopes 26-r/c
8600-623 Lagos
+351 282 767951

Cotacambios-Agendia de Cambios SA
Rua Madalena 36
1100-321 Lisbon
+351 218 824740
geral@novacambios.com

DBL
Avenida Almirante Gago Coutinho 128
1700-033 Lisbon
+351 218 454200

Frederico Agencia de Cambios Lda
C Com Vila Nv-loja 37
Areias S.Joao-Albufeira
8200-285 Albufeira
+351 289 589291

Halewood International Foreign Exchange
59-60 Thames Street
Windsor
Berkshire
SL4 1TX
01753 859159

Mundial-Agencia de Cambios Lda
Rua Augusta 151
1100-049 Lisbon
+351 213 225498

Foreign Currencies Direct
The Old Malotehouse
Currrencies Court
5 The Broadway
Amershaw
Bucks
HP7 0HL
01494 725353

Novacambios
Calcada Carmo 61 D
1200-091 Lisbon
+351 213 242550
geral@novacambios.com

Sarmento e Castro and C LDA
Rua Sa Bandeira 772
4000-432 Porto
+351 222 085600
turicambio@mail.telepac.pt

TTT Moneycorp
2 Sloane Street
Knightsbridge
London
SW1X 9LA
0207 8237800

Unicambio
Rua Silva Lopes 26-loja C-r/c
8600-623 Lagos
+351 282 767950

Electricians

Aginaldo Rosa Luz
Rua 22, 6
7565-035 Alvalade
+351 269 590002

Anibal Palma Lda
Largo Sao Francisco 46
8000-142 Faro
+351 289 812485
anibal.palma.lda@mail.telepac.pt

Augusto Magalhaes Lda
Rua Padre Maia 24-r/c-D Vilar Andorinho
4430-479 Vila Nova De Gaia
+351 227 823697
www.am-lda.planetaclix.pt

Electricista Botho Bartell Lda
Abertas-Odiaxere
8600 Lagos
+351 282 799362

Electrificadora Gomes Pereira
Avenida Gomes Pereira 54-B
1500-331 Lisbon
+351 217 154431
adafonso@netcabo.pt

Electro Tadeus
Estrada de Men Martins 249-B
2725-391 Mem Martins
+351 219 216880

Electrofortios Lda
Rua Escola Primaria lote 27
7300-663 Fortios
+351 245 399252

Helder H Ramos Losna
Urbanizacao Palmeiras Bl 3-loja
8400 Parchal
+351 282 412854

Montalux
Rua Comandante Joaquin Sagurada lote 11
loja directa
Cascais
+351 214 831129

Pardal and Lamuria Lda
Rua Douter Eduardo F Oliveira 3
7830-457 Serpa
+351 284 459658

Pascoal Luz e Som Lda
Rua do Comercio N 100
3500 Viseu
+351 232 424314

Resistividade-Estudo e Montagens Electricas Lda
Urbanizacao Vila D'Este lote 54
1 D Vilar Andorinho
4430-569 Vila Nova De Gaia
+351 227 829143
resistividade@sapo.pt

Financial Services

Ana Maria Silvestre
1°C Beco dos Caldeireros
8500 Portimão
+351 282 415672
ams@ip.pt

Bennett & Co
144 Knutsford Road
Wilmslow
Cheshire
SK9 6JP
01625 586937

Continental Financial Services
204 Church Road
Hove
East Sussex
BN3 2DJ
01273 772811
enquiries@contifs.com

Currencies4Less
Bakery Place
Altenburg Gardens
London
SW11 1JQ
0207 2287667

Expat Financial
c/o TFG Global Insurance
216-2438 Marin
West Vancouver
CV V7V 1 L
+16 043 515278

Finance Assured Financial Services
1 Halifax Road
Godmorden
OL14 5AG
0800 0858950

FX Solutions
FX Solutions House
86 High Street
Orpington
Kent
BR6 0JZ
0870 9007007

Henley and Partners AG
Haus zum Engel
Kirchgasse 24
8001 Zurich
+41 126 76090
zurich@henleyglobal.com

Lloyds TSB
Serrano no. 90
28006 Madrid
0034 915 209980

PropertyFinance4Less
Bakery Place
Altenburg Gardens
London
SW11 1JQ
0207 9247314
info@propertyfinance4less.com

Directory

SJS Mortgages
93 Chatterton Road
Bromley
Kent
BR2 9QQ
0208 4647444
info@sjsmortgages.co.uk

The Mortgage Exchange loted
86 Glenthorne Road
Hammersmith
London
W6 0LP
0208 5637575
enquiry@4mortgageadvice.co.uk

TTT Moneycorp
2 Sloane Street
Knightsbridge
London
SW1X 9LA
0207 8237800

Funeral Services

Agencia Fueraria Familia Monteiro
Rua Penha Franca 81-r/c
1170-300 Lisbon
+351 218 135010
Fax: +351 218 147454

Agencia Funeraria das Condominhas
Rua Condominhas 521
4150-223 Porto
+351 226 178833
Fax: +351 226 109236
fune.condominhas@mail.telepac.pt

Agencia Funeraria Gil Lda
Rua Limoeiro 19
1100-308 Lisbon
+351 218 863449
Fax: +351 218 885427

Agencia Funeraria Guerreiro
Rua Jose Paletti 14
8600-746 Lagos
+351 282 769827

Agencia Funeraria Tavares
Estrada Benfica 315-A
1500-074 Lisbon
+351 217 780065
Fax: +351 217 743009
agenciatavares@hotmail.com

AgenciaFuneraria Rosarro and Rosa Lda
Praca D. Alfonso III 21
8100-666 Loule
+351 289 462271

Anselmo Lages and Filhos Lda
Rua Paraiso Foz 3
4150-566 Porto
+351 226 180835
Fax: +351 226 105208
armador-foz@mail.softema.pt

Gardens

Adubopor
Sitio da Boavista
Portimão
+351 282 422929/ 282 415900
adubopor@mail.telepac.pt

AKI
Avenida Cavaleiros 70
2794-059 Carnaxide
+351 214 164000

Cando Jardins
Rua Francisco Xavier Ataide de Oliveira
lote 33
Escritorios D, E, F
Lagos
+351 282 792160
candojardins@mail.telepac.pt

Centro Bonsai de Campolide
Rua Campolide 270-A
1070-039 Lisbon
+351 213 827450
info@luso-bonsai.com

Dècor
Zona Industrial
4520-409 Mosteiro
+351 256 802552

Espacos Verdes Projectos e Construcao Lda
Bairro Alvito lote AF
1300 Lisbon
+351 213 632233

Forcalis
Arruamento Mainha lote C-Nave C-2
1900-649 Lisbon
+351 218 610480
forcalis@mail.telepac.pt

Hammers and Blades
+351 918 328666
hammersnblades@mail.telepac.pt

Horto do Campo Grande Lda
Campo Grande 171
1700-090 Lisbon
+351 217 826660
info@hortodocampogrande.com

Jardim Mundo
Urbanizacao Marrocos
8500-332 Portimão
+351 282 471041
jardin.mundo@clix.pt

Jardins da Arrabida Lda
Casal de Ft'e-Aldeia Irmaos
2925 Azeitao
+351 212 190776
lobomartins@mail.telepac.pt

Jardinsol
Qt Valverde
8135-037 Almancil
+351 289 394473
jardinsol@mail.telepac.pt

Jovefijar
Rua Carvalheiras 101
4000-159 Porto
+351 222 087333
jovefijar@aloteavista.net

Lugarde Iberia
Sitio do carmo
EN 125
Lagos
+351 282 342370
contact@lugarde-iberia.com

Pixley
Valenca Bx
8500 Portimão
+351 282 471347

Plantagri
Avenida Joao XXI 47 1 E
1000-299 Lisbon
+351 218 461308
plantagri@clix.pt

Sofemel
Rua Boavista 96/100
1200-069 Lisbon
+351 213 467146

Directory

TAF-Terrace Arte Floral
Rua Comt'e Fragoso 21
7050-163 Montemor-o-Novo
+351 266 891795

Zonda
Sitio Pereiras Cima
Cx Postal 562A
Sitio da Casca Cheira
Quatro Estradas
8125 Quarteira
+351 289 356233
zonda@vizzavi.pt

Insurance

Andrew Copeland International loted
230 Portland Road
London
SE25 4SL
0208 6568435
roy@andrewcopeland.co.uk

John Wallis
Apartado 138
8501-906 Albor
Portugal
+351 282 457835
+351 282 457865

Medal
Apartado 948
8501-919 Portimão
+351 282 430800

Interior Decorators

Antonio Bacalhau Lda
Urb. Da Passagem
lote 3
Parchal
8400 Lagos
+351 282 417144/5

Daphane Cooper Interiors
Apartado 3088
Estrada Vale de Lobo
8135 Almancil
Algarve
+351 289 393028
daphane@clix.pt

Finca d'Ideias
Rua dos Pescadores
113 A/B
Praia do Carvoeiro
8400 Lagos
+351 282 081141

Kitchens and Bathrooms

A S Veiga Lda
Rua Reinaldo Ferreira
31- C Lisbon
+351 218 472265
asveiga.lda@onninet.pt

Art'Gois
Rua Damiao Gois
107 Porto
+351 225 098410
artgois@clix.pt

Brooks Kitchens
Rua Jose Ventura Neto Cabrita
lote. 3-loja B
Lagos
+351 282 798966

Carpimonta
Rua D.Pedro V Armz
Pirescoxe
2695-373 Santa Iria de Azoia
+351 219 562518

Catering assiste
Rua Eduardo Bairrada 41
1300-212 Lisbon
+351 213 619570
cateringassiste@mail.telepac.pt

Cem Papas
Elplanada Castelo 41 Porto
4150-202 Porto
+351 226 169424

Dulbor
Rua Emigrante 259 Canelas
4405-234 Canelas Vng
+351 227 533456
dulboRualda@clix.pt

Eurocozinhas
Rua Nv-Casal Azenha
3- A Pt'e Bica
+351 219 804666

Ferlac
Rua Lugar 8 Fermentelos
3750-454 Fermentelos
+351 234 720283
ferlac@clix.pt

Furur Casa Lda
Sitio das Escahxinas
8135-016 Almancil
+351 289 393238
futureasa_design@iol.pt

Ibercozi
S. Goncalo
4600-013 Amarante
+351 255 432888

Importeco
Complexo Industrial do Camo
lote 13
8400-405 Lagos
Algarve
+351 282343645

J Ramos and Cruz
Zona Industrial 13
7860-076 Moura
+351 285 250280

Moveis Rosinhas Lda
Rua Vera Cruz 92 loja 1
4400-332 Vila Nova De Gaia
+351 223 750445
moveisrosinhas@oninet.pt

Movicol
Rua Doutor Diogo
P A Santos 260 Alfaiatas
2420-192 Colmeias
+351 244 720310
movicol@clix.pt

Movicozinha
Casal Popa
A - dos- Cunhados
+351 261 981200
movicozinha@clix.pt

Movoeste
Rua Doutor Jose Bastos
11-C-loja Torres Vedras
2560-332 Torres Vedras
+351 261 330200
movoeste@movoeste.pt

Mucofran 2
Avenida Nacoes Unidas
1-A Lisbon
+351 217 164490
mucofran2@vizzavi.pt

Sol Ambiente
Apartado 1009
P-8400
Praia do Carvoeiro
+351 282 341272

Language Services

Sintgma
Rua Jose Regio, 9 r/c Dt°
Quinta das Palmeiras
2780-129 Oeiras
+351 214 674383
info@sintagma.net

Triplicardo
Avenida 25 Abril, lote 83
Vila Fria
2780 Porto Salvo
+351 142 10932

Legal Services

Advogados International Law Office
Est Rua Nac. 125/10
Est Rua do Aeroporto
Edificio Celfil, 4
Montenegro
8000-124 Faro
+351 289 887440

John Howell & Co Solicitors
The Old Glass Works 22
Endell Street
Covent Garden
London
WC2H 9AD
0207 4200400
info@europelaw.com

Lita Gale Solicitors
43 - 45 Gower Street
London
WC1E 6NA
0207 5802066
info@litagale.com

Luso Real Estate loted
52 Hayes Road
Bromley
Kent
BR22 9AA
0208 4645170
hallgente@aol.com

Lusojurist
Rua Almeida Brandao 19
1200-602 Lisbon
+351 213 975180
info@lusojurist.pt

IT IS NOT ALL SUN, SEA AND SAND!

THERE ARE IMPORTANT DECISIONS TO BE MADE IF YOU PLAN TO BUY PROPERTY IN PORTUGAL TO RENT AND EVEN MORE IF YOU PLAN TO BECOME A PERMANENT RESIDENT.

SOME DECISIONS MUST BE MADE BEFORE YOU LEAVE HOME.

AFTER 22 YEARS OF LIVING HERE, I MAY NOT BE ABLE TO DO EVERYTHING FOR YOU, BUT I DO KNOW WHO IS RELIABLE AND HONEST TO DO THOSE THINGS THAT I CANNOT.

A RECENT ARTICLE IN THE "ECONOMIST" FOUND PORTUGAL TO BE 100% WORSE THAN FRANCE FOR EFFICIENCY AND BUREAUCRACY! SO IT IS IMPORTANT THAT YOU CHOOSE THE RIGHT PARTNERS WHEN MAKING LIFE CHANGING DECISIONS.

I CAN HELP WITH:
- HEALTH INSURANCE • TRAVEL INSURANCE • BUILDINGS AND CONTENTS INSURANCE • MOTOR INSURANCE FOR UK REGISTERED VEHICLES • LIFE AND CRITICAL ILLNESS COVER

ALL PRODUCTS ARE UNDERWRITTEN BY LEADING UK INSURERS

FOR FURTHER INFORMATION WITHOUT OBLIGATION:

JOHN WALLIS

APARTADO 138 8501-906 ALVOR PORTUGAL
TEL: 351-282-457835 FAX: 351-282-457865 MOB: 919630276
E-MAIL: john.wallis@mail.telepac.pt

Directory

Maids and Domestic Services

Europ Assistance
Avenida Alvares Cabral 41-3
1200-Lisbon
+351 213 886282

Fernanduslimpa-Limpezas Industriais Lda
Rua Jose Estevao 12
Apartado 2263
4701-903
Braga
+351 253 277908
fernanduslimpa@sapo.pt

S.O.S Canguru
Rua Sacadura Cabral
Shopping Grande Galiza
loja.61
2765 Estoril
+351 214 660888

Medical Services

Bupa International
Apartado de Correos 16
29120 Alhaurin El Grande
Malaga
+34 952 491115

Clinica da Face
Complexo Hospitalar das Torres de Lisbon Rua Tomas da Fonseca-Torre F
1600-209 Lisbon
+351 214 424065
Fax: +351 214 460834
faceclinic@mail.telepac.pt

Clinica Dentaria da Barroca
Rua da Barroca 48
Lagos
+351 282 763496

Clinica Medicina Dentaria
Rua Joao Anes 3-3° Dt
8500 Portimão
Algarve
+351 282 425053
+351 282 425053

Clinica Todos Os Santos Lda
Rua Goncalves Crespo 39 - 39A
1690-084 Lisbon
+351 213 520200
+351 213 545710

Clinic de San Antonio
Avenida dos Hospitals cvs 8
Reboleira
2720-275 Amadora
+351 252 615111
+351 252 615353

Dmi
Praceta Henrique Moreira, 150
4400 Vila Nova de Gaia
+351 223 776800
+351 223 776899
dmi@mail.telepac.pt

International Healoteh Centre
Largo Luis Camoes
Rua do Regimento
Dezanoeve, 67, 2°
2750-474 Cascais
+351 214 845317

Morgan Price International Healotehcare
2nd Floor
Bush House
Queens Square
Attleborough
NR17 2AF
01953 458040

Servicos de Urgencia de Centro de Saude
Avenida Linhas Torres 243
1750 Lisbon
+351 217 573121

Socifar
Largo. De Camoes 11
8000 Faro
+351 289 802106

Opticians

Adao Oculista
Rua St Catarina 287
4000-451 Porto
+351 222 073710
adaooculista@mail.telepac.pt

Centro Ocular Iberlente Lda
Rua Passos Manuel 4-C
1150-260 Lisbon
+351 213 520649

Centro Optico Pai and Filhos Lda
Avenida Chaby Pinheiro 15-loja
2725-265 Men Martins
+351 219 211563

Mario Oculista Lda
Largo D. Nuno A Pereira 5
7800-018 Beja
+351 284 324040
mariooculistalda@clix.pt

Ocullista das Avenidas
Avenida 5 Outubro 122-B
1050-061 Lisbon
+351 217 999060
ocav@visus.pt

Optica Elsa Lda
Avenida Mnuel Fonseca 21-loja A
7540-105 Santigo do Cacem
+351 269 829381
opticaelsa@mail.telepac.pt

Optica Miopia
Rua Miguel Bombarda 173-B
2830-089 Barreiro
+351 212 169143
geral@opticamiopa.com.pt

Optica Morais
Praca 8 Maio 11 Fig Foz
3080-054 Figuera Da Foz
+351 233 402660
opticamorais@hotmail.com

Visao Plus
Edificio Panorama-lote 4 loja A/C
Avenida Sa Carneiro
8125-120 Quarteria
+351 289 301786

Pet Transportation

Airpets Oceanic
Willowslea Farm
Spout Lane
Stanwell Moor
Staines
Middlesex
TW19 6BW
01753 685571

Animal Airlines
35 Beatrice Avenue
Manchester
Lancashire
M18 7JU
0161 2234035

Directory

Animal Inn
Dover Road
Ringwould
Deal
Kent
CT14 8HH
01304 373597

Chilworth Pet Exports/Chilworth Kennels
Lordswood Lane
Chilworth
Southampton
SO16 7JG
02380 766876

Pet Travel Services
168 Appin Crescent
Dunfermline
Fife
KY12 7TX
01383 722818

Skymaster Air Cargo
Room 15
Building 305
Cargo Terminal
Manchester Airport
M90 5PY
0161 4362190

The Dog House International Kennels and Cattery
Camino De La Sabatera 5
Teulada/Moraira
Alicante
Spain
+34 965 741302

Transfur
19 Dean Close
Salisbury Green
Southampton
SO31 7TT
01489 588072

Plumbing and Central Heating

Afonso Sergio
Rua Edith Cavell 12-A
1900 Lisbon
+351 218 149435

Aqua Protect Portugal
Centro Empresarial Sintra
Estroril VI
2710 Sintra
+351 219 239 200
aqua.protect@mail.telepac.pt

Canalex
Tv. Prazeres 2/4
1300 Lisbon
+351 213 968444

Efcis
Rua Henrique Paiva Couceiro 1517
2700-451 Amadora
+351 214 999000

Help
Edificio Rivieira R/C
Viveiro
2765 Estoril
+351 214 687838

Lucano
Norte Camoes 75
1200 Lisbon
+351 213 421736

Pinto and Cruz Lda
Rua Eng Ferreiras Dias 469
4100 Porto
+351 226 100901

Termomat
Zona Industrial Sul de Cortegaca
Rua da Gandara
Apartado 17
3886-908 Cotegaca Ovr
+351 256 798036
termomat@mail.telepac.pt

Property Management

Canterbury's Overseas
8 Kempsford Gardens
London
SW5 9LH
0207 5654256

HolidayLets.net
Cranfield Innovation Centre
Cranfield
Beds.
MK43 0RT
01234 756166

Rent a Villa Abroad
208 London Road
East Grimstead
W. Sussex
RH19 1EY
01342 312626

Sunny Homes
+351 282359062/3
sunnyhomes@clix.pt

Removals

A.1. Worldwide Movers
Unit 17
Highfield Industrial Estate
Willingdon Drive
Eastbourne
BN23 6PT
01323 508000

Bishops Move Group
Overseas House
102 - 104 Stewarts Road
London
SW8 4UG
0207 5014990

Bradshaw International
Units 2 and 3
Tilson Road
Manchester
M23 9GF
0800 3892233

David Dale Removals
Unit 3
Langby Industrial Estate
Millby Road
Boroughbridge
YO51 9BW
01423 324948

Guardian Movers
173 Haydon Road
London
SW19 8TB
0800 393904

International Movers
Eurolink Way
Sittingbourne
Kent
ME10 3HH
01795 427151

Overs International loted
Unit 9
Spring Lakes Industrial estate
Dead Brooke Lane
Aldershot
GU12 4HU
0800 243433

ENNIS PROPERTY MANAGEMENT

Taking care of YOUR property in the COSTA DE PRATA and PRAIA D'EL REY - GOLF

We are a long-established, family-owned property management company offering clients complete peace of mind with regard to their properties. To enjoy your property to the full you need to know that it is in good hands when you are not there.

Check our website at:
www.villa-management.com
Tel: 00351 262 979419
email: ennis.admin@mail.telepac.pt

PROPERTY SEARCH AND ASSISTANCE WITH BUYING YOUR VILLA

Directory

TRANS-PORTUGAL EUROPEAN LTD

Specialists in international removals of household effects
& fine art to • **Spain** • **Portugal** • **Worldwide**

Tel: **0044 208 340 8434/37** Fax: **0044 208 340 8409**
Mob: **0044 7836 644510** (Luis Correia)

www.trans-portugal.co.uk

Richman - Ring
Eurolink Way
Sittingbourne
Kent
ME10 3HH
01795 427151

Trans Portugal European
Unit 1-5 Cransford Way
Industrial estate
Tottenham Way
London
N8 9DG
0207 4031440

Supervisory Bodies

APEMI- Associacao Portuguese Das Empresas Med. Imobiliaria
Rua Prof. Correia Araujo 593
Ent. 8 - Sala 2, Porto
+351 2250 89163/4

FOPDAC
Lacey House
St Clare Business Park
Holly Road
Hampton Hill
Middlesex
TW12 1QQ
0208 941 5588

The International Real Estate Federation
Gran Via, 66, 9°, Oficina 10
28013 Madrid
+34 915 474069

Swimming Pools

Antonio Bacalhau Lda
Urb. Da Passagem lote 3
Parchal
8400 Lagos
+351 282 417144/5

Bakewell Pools loted
38 Bagley Wood Road
Kennington
Oxford
OX1 5LY
01865 735205/07885 847150
bob@bakewellpools.co.uk

CarvoRega
Rua dos Pescadores 114B
Carvoeiro
+351 282 356769

Equipiscina
Rua de Pescadoroas 114 B
Darcoaio
+351 214 690674
equipiscina@clix.pt

Piscirega-piscinas rega Lda
Rua de Angola 525
3700-036 Sao Joao Da Madeira
+351 256 833066
piscirega@mail.telepac.pt

Revipool Lda
Rua 46- Quimpiparque Armz 12
2830 Barreiro
+351 212 061179
revipool@revipoool.com

Sintalgarve
Rua Angola lote 10-cv
8500-605 Portimão
+351 282 411248
sintalgarve@mail.telepac.pt

SulPools
sulpools@clix.pt

Unihidrica
Urb. Qta da Amoreira
Edf. Amoreira Mar, loja 2
Alvor
8500 Portimão
+351 282 457803
unihidrica@clix.pt

Vertagua
Rua Sao Miguel 61
4050-560 Porto
+351 222 001220
vertagua@oninet.pt

Tax Specialists

Henley and Partners AG
Haus zum Engel
Kirchgasse 24
8001 Zurich
+41 126 76090
zurich@henleyglobal.com

Directory

KPMG - Tax and Accounting
Edificio Monumental
Avenida Praia da Vitoria
71A-11
1069-006 Lisbon
+351 210 110073

Telephone Services

Alcatel
Rua do Moinho da
Barrunchada 2
2795 Carnaxide
+351 214 169500

Portugal Telcom
Avenida Fontes Pereira de Melo 40
4050 Lisbon
+351 213 540020

Travel – Coach

Eurolines
52 Grosvenor Gardens
Victoria
London
SW1W 0AU
0870 5143219

Travel – Ferries

Brittany Ferries
The Brittany Centre
Wharf Road
Portsmouth
Hampshire
PO2 8RU
02392 892239

P&O Ferries
P&O Portsmouth
Peninsular House
Wharf Road
Portsmouth
PO2 8TA
0870 5202020

Travel – Flights

Airline Network
Airline Reservations
The Trident Centre
Port Way
Ribble Docklands
Preston
Lancashire
PR2 2QA
0870 2410011

Air Luxor
Luxor Plaza
Avenida da Republica, 101
1050-190 Lisbon
Portugal
+351 210 026890

Air Portugal
22 Chapter House
London
SW1 4NP
0870 6070535

BMI Baby
PO Box 737 Castle
Donnington
Derby
E Midlands
DE74 2XP
0870 2642229

easyjet.com
Easy Land
Luton Airport
Luton
London
LU2 9L6
0870 6000000

Flight Centre
10a Camden Road
Tunbridge Wells
TN1 2PT
01892 530030

Jet 2
Leeds Bradford International
Leeds
LS19 7TU
0870 7378282

Just Flights
Airline House
56 Newport Street
Boloteon
BL1 1PB
01204 364747

Monarch Airlines
Prospect House
Prospect Way
LutonAirport
Luton, Bedfordshire
London
LU2 9NU
08700 405040

Portugal Airlines
1st floor Room 1011
Olympic House
Manchester Airport
Manchester
M90 1QX
0161 4895040

Portugália Airlines
Aeroporto de Lisbon
Rua C. Edf. 70
1749-078 Lisbon
+351 218 425559

Ryan Air
Dublin Airport
Co. Dublin
+353 181 21212

Thomas Cook Flights
Unit 1-3
Conigsby Road
Thomas Cook Business Park
Coingsby Road
North Bretton
Peterborough
PE3 8BL
0870 7500316

Virgin Express
Brussels Airport
Virgin Express
Building 116
1820 Melzbrook
Belgium
0207 7440004

Travel-Rail

Eurostar
Waterloo Station
12 Lower Road
London
SE1 8SE
0870 5186186

Rail Europe
34 Tower View
Kings Hill
West Malling
Kent
TN23 1AP
0870 5848848

TV and Satillite

Luz e Som
Rua .Roberto Ivens 1351
4450 Matosinhos
+351 229 385560

Directory

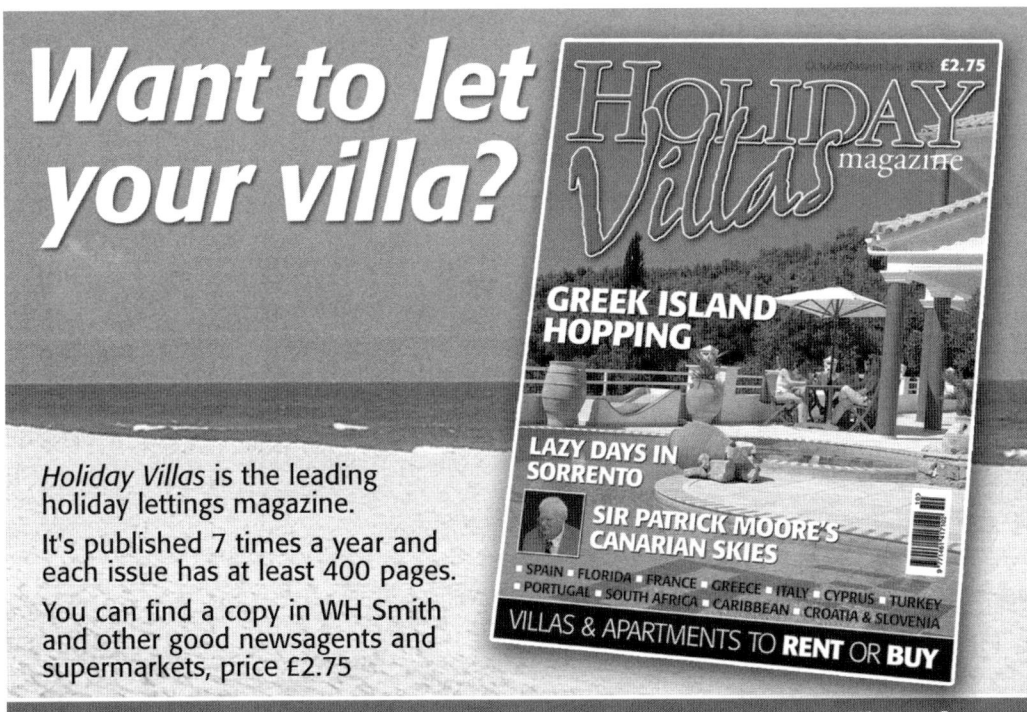

Marc Electronica
+351 282 410400
info@TV2029.com

Mundo Logico
Rua Dr Manuel Pacheco
Nobre 33 A-B
2830 Barreiro
+351 212 026469

Silva and Sintra
Parque Empresonel do
Algarve CN125
lote NC 1c
8400-431 Lagos
Portugal
+351 282 342641

Utilities

Cenel
Rua do Brasil 1
3030 175 Coimbra
+351 239 400800

Cppe
Avenida Defensores de
Chaves 4
1000 Lisbon
+351 213 525353

Lucano
Norte Camoes 75
1200 Lisbon
+351 213 421736

Lusagua
Avenida5 de Outubro
N293-7
1600-035 Lisbon
+351 217 928670

Ren
Avenida Estados Unidos da
America 55-120
1749-061 Lisbon
+351 218 470180

Vitterra Energy Services S.A
Rodriguez San Pedro,
10-oficina B
28015 Madrid
+34 144 44630
consuloteor@viterra-es.es

Vets

Clinica Veterinaria do Carmo
largo Carmo, 7
1200 Lisbon
+351 213 428 842

Clinica Veterinaria do Restelo
Rua Jeronimos 40 R/C
1300 Lisbon
+351 213 648959

Clinica Veterinaria Meerypets
Avenida Dos Maristas lote 5 - R/C loja
2775 Parede
+351 214 530864
equisport@mail.telepac.pt

Dr Gomez
Rua do Coudel, loja 9 D
2725-276 Men Martins
+351 219 216478

Hospital Veterinario
Rua da Alagoa 26
2815-168 Charneca Caparica
hospital.veterinario.
principal@mail.teleweb.pt
+351 212 974997

Instituto Vetenario do Parque
Rua Catilho 61 c/v E
1000 Lisbon
+351 213 860663

Vetalverca
Rua Domingos Jose Ferreira 4
2615 Alverca
+351 219 575752

Vet-America
Avenida Estados Unidos da
America 7-A
1700 Lisbon
+351 218 482313
rdc3657@mail.telepac.pt

INDEX TO ADVERTISERS

Algavida	227	Sociedade Imobiliária Balancal S.A.	285
Aquarius	227	Michelin Travel Publications	Inside back cover
Barclays	9	Morgan Price International Healthcare	19
Banco Totta	233	Nonplusultra	231
Bennett & Co Solicitors	307	Novus Med	221
Caldeira and Stevenson	289	Numero Urbano	227
Central Portugal Property Finders	271	Parque de Floresta	221
Classic & Antique	233	Paula Aco Real Estate	219
David Headland Associates	10	Portugal Airlines	14
Ennis Property Management	311	Praia del Rey	253
Filneto Grupo	211	Premier Property International	243
Finespo	207	Premier Real Estate	203
French Magazine	271	Properties of Portugal	265
George Knight	255	SC Med	233
Halewood International	4	Silver Holidays	221
HolidayLets.net	310	Silva & Sintra	313
Holiday Villas Magazine	314	Spanish Magazine	293
Imoalgarve	227	Sulgar Lda	231
Imolacco	231	Sunseaker	231
John Howell & Co	6	Trans Portugal European	312
John Wallis	309	Vilamarque	209
KG Villas	215	Vila Castelo	221
Landmark	233	Vilasol	201
Mackenzie Real Estate	199		

Notes

Notes

Notes

Notes

Notes

Notes

Notes